MW01686844

Been There Done That

A treasury of 101 light-hearted true tales and 71 serious travel tips harvested by an intrepid Canadian travel journalist during his off-beat bumblings around the world.

David E. Scott

Copyright 2004 by David E. Scott and DESPUB
© Typefaces by Corel

Printed and bound in Canada

All Rights Reserved. No part of this work may be reproduced in any form or by any means without the prior written permission of the publisher, except for reviewers who may quote brief passages.
All DESPUB titles are available at special quantity discounts for bulk purchases for sale, sales promotion, premiums, fund raising, educational or institutional use.

The Publisher: DESPUB
2340B Clifton Street
Allanburg ON L0S 1A0

National Library of Canada Cataloguing in Publication Data

Scott, David, 1939-
Been There Done That / David E. Scott.

Includes index.
ISBN 0-9735205-0-7

1. Voyages and travels--Humour. 2. Travel
1. Title.

PN6231.T7S38 2004 910.4'02'07 C2004-901717-9

Design and Layout: Pat Dracup
Printing: AGMV Marquis
Cover Art & Design: Melani Pyke

A DESPUB publication

By David E. Scott

Non-Fiction

On The Road

The Ontario Getaway Guidebook

A Taste of Ontario Country Inns

Ontario For Free

Ontario Place Names 1E, 2E, 3E, 4E

Quick Escapes Toronto 1E, 2E

Days of Wine and Rascals

One Man's Meat is Another Man's *Poisson*

Been There Done That

Anthology

Great Canadian Fishing Stories That Didn't Get Away

MORE Great Canadian Fishing Stories That Didn't Get Away

Fiction

Azteca

Contents

Contents

Contents

Contents

Contents

NOTE: There are also 71 tips about travel scattered through this book. Some could save your life; most, if observed, will save you time, money and frustration.

Introduction

For better than a decade I was one of the hosts of Canada's largest travel show, sponsored by the newspaper where I worked as their travel editor. I was front and centre at the show in the first booth people saw when they entered and it was my job to answer their questions about travel. Travel anywhere. Any destination. Any type of travel. Anything about travel.

Half-page newspaper advertisements leading up to the bi-annual three-day shows touted me as a "travel expert" and urged the 20,000 or so visitors to let me solve their travel problems.

At some shows I'd do packing demonstrations up on the main stage, or a presentation on how to improve vacation photographs or just field questions about countries or cities people hoped to visit, cruise ships or resorts.

It was a tough act because the questions were spontaneous and because human nature being as it is, there were always those who researched the world's most remote or little-known destinations in the hopes of tripping up someone who had so blatantly been shoved in their faces as an "expert." The irony, of course, was that I usually learned more from the audience than they did from me . . .

By far the most frequently-asked question was one to which I still have no answer: "What's your favourite country, region, city?"

Travel is people. People experiences make or break any trip. And I've had the privilege of meeting so many wonderful ones all over the world that there's no way to provide the sort of answer people really want when they ask that question.

I'd be happy living in most of the countries I've visited -- even some where the poverty is all-pervasive and grinding. In fact those are the countries where you're most likely to find human nature at its finest. Close to home, consider the history of Newfoundland and see what super people have resulted from that historical back-ground of hardship, deprivation and isolation.

There was another breed of person who came to those travel shows and I'd cringe each time one of them marched up to my booth.

These people brought axes with them that they wanted me to help them grind. Something had gone wrong on their vacation trip and they wanted somebody's blood, and money . . . and I couldn't tell most of them that they should never have left home in the first place. That they didn't deserve the opportunity to travel. That they would never enjoy travelling no matter where they went and that the best thing they could do for everybody's sake was to stay at home.

Overly judgmental? I don't think so. How do you pacify a lady who's enraged because she took a vacation to Venezuela "and I couldn't talk to anybody because they all spoke Spanish"?

Or the man who felt cheated because he had gone to Scotland and "I couldn't get a decent hamburger anywhere. I bought a 'hamburger' in one place and it was bits of chopped up ham on a bun!"

Or, "I was paying top dollar at this Caribbean resort and they didn't have cable TV. I couldn't watch any of my favourite programs for two whole weeks."

"Our flight was delayed and we missed an afternoon at the beach. We should get our money back" (for all of a seven-day trip).

"There wasn't enough hot water at the hotel; it rained for five days out of seven; we want our money back."

You get the idea.

If any of the shoes I've mentioned happen to fit you, read no further and put this book back on the shelf. You won't enjoy it! You won't understand or appreciate any humour in this collection of travel stories. And you'll never understand why I kept on travelling to 97 countries (last time I bothered to count) and am ready now to take off to any of them again, or some new ones, at the drop of a hat. My suitcase is already packed. It has never been unpacked for decades.

I've been swindled, robbed, conned, and severely injured in car crashes caused by idiotic or drunk drivers. I've suffered food poisoning on a five-star cruise ship and in a Third World village. I've survived three hotel fires and a flash-flood that wiped out my motel. I've been mugged, insulted, gypped, short-changed and victimized by over-booking and lost airline, hotel and rental car bookings. I've lived through tornados, hurricanes and typhoons; survived earthquakes and blizzards.

But I have met wonderful people in every place I have ever visited and been the fortunate recipient of inestimable kindness and largesse world-wide. It is people and people experiences that make places memorable and this probably explains why my list of favourite places stretches for volumes and the list of never–go-back places doesn't fill a quarter of a page of a small notebook.

Your doctor will assure you that it takes less effort to smile than to frown. And smiling is better for your face. When you hit the wrinkle years, the smiler's face will be far more appealing than the frowner's face. The smiler will also get a much better ride through life -- particularly if he or she decides to travel.

-DES

The Captain and the connoisseurs

Aboard the M. V. *Neptune* in the Aegean Sea

When the ship's First Mate rapped sharply on the open door to Claude's cabin, I wondered if we'd gone too far this time.

We were trying to find places in the tiny cabin to stow the 18 gallons of wine we had just brought aboard from the Greek island of Santorini. The six-litre plastic-wrapped glass containers were roughly the size of industrial fire extinguishers and stacked like cordwood on the lower bunk.

We were having a hell of a time finding places where the round containers wouldn't roll into one another and possibly break, as the ship heaved through heavy waters in the Aegean Sea. The one container we'd opened was braced upright in the toilet bowl since we hadn't been able to devise a way to plug the ragged hole Claude had punched in the plaster seal at one end.

"Excusing me sirs." The First Mate's command of English was limited. "The Captain he is send me to asking who it is who is bringing from the island so many wine. He is thinking it is you mens." As he now was goggling at our hoard of wine casks -- what lawyers would call *prima facie* evidence -- it seemed pointless to concoct even a token denial.

"Yes," I said. "It is so good. We cannot buy wine like this in Canada where we live. I hope we have done nothing wrong . . . " Claude explosively belched his approval of the ghastly wine.

The First Mate recoiled from Claude's eruption and stood more stiffly at attention in the doorway. "The Captain, he say he must to see you. He say you go to main salon bar in ten minute. You be there. Yes?" It didn't sound like an invitation.

Claude and I were aboard a 300-foot ship on a seven-day cruise out of Piraeus, calling at Santorini, Crete, Port Said in Egypt and Ashdod in Israel. Twenty-odd nationalities were represented on the passenger list and the gimmick of this voyage was that we would be the first cruise ship to call at Port Said since the Suez Canal had reopened to civilian shipping after umpteen years.

Couples were paying thousands of dollars for this cruise and our newspapers were paying our way at a special, vastly-lower press rate. But neither of us wanted to be there. Claude had flown to Greece direct from a tour of Spain and Portugal and I had been home only a few days from a 17-country blitz through the Caribbean and Central and South America, crammed into 18 days.

The Canadian travel-writing fraternity is a small one, but I hadn't met Claude until this trip, though his reputation as "that wild and crazy Frenchman" had preceded him far and wide. Claude had heard about me, too, and figured we were birds of a feather. The organizer of this trip who worked for the Greek National Tourist Office got us both on board by assuring each of us that the other had signed on for the trip.

I met Claude in Athens two days before we sailed and the party began -- in earnest. Our first stop was a mom-and-pop store near the hotel from which we provisioned our rooms. By afternoon we were back for more supplies. And the next morning we began getting concerned about bar stock on the ship. By our fourth visit to the store, Mom and Pop had hired a pretty, young assistant.

Friends helped Claude get his cases of beer and my boxes of Metaxa brandy on board. And they helped us aboard, too. The party roared on. The crew was tolerant about the procession of drinks we brought from our cabins to the small swimming pool on the aft deck. We had explained we weren't trying to beat the ship out of bar sales -- just save the crew a lot of work. Besides, the plastic drinking glasses we'd brought on board were triple the size of those available on the ship and saved us a lot of steps.

On the afternoon of the second day at sea the organizer of the press trip tracked us down at our usual stations by the pool and commanded us to join her at a nearby bar for a brief meeting.

"Tomorrow morning we'll be anchored off the island of Santorini," she said. "Passengers will start going ashore by tender at 6:30. You both will be ready to leave the ship at 6:30. You *will* be there. We will then ride donkeys up to Thera, the village at the top of the cliffs. You will both ride donkeys to the top of the cliffs."

"Chrise," whined Claude, "I've done dat stuff before. I'm not gonna go!"

I recalled a long day spent in the rain on a bad-tempered donkey riding down a cliff to a leper colony on the Hawaiian island of Molokai. "If it's okay with you, Marie," I said, "I'd prefer to photograph *others* riding donkeys -- and whatever else is on the island. I've done donkeys."

Marie took a deep breath and tried to glare at both of us simultaneously. "Look," she hissed between clenched teeth, "in Athens I couldn't get you guys out of the hotel to see the Metropolis or take the city tour. Neither of you probably remembers meeting the Minister of Tourism and his staff at a special dinner he threw for you on top of Mount Lycabettus. He didn't appreciate your rendition of Frère Jacques, either! And I'll bet . . . I'll bet neither one of you even knows the name of this Goddam boat, or even how you got . . . "

"Ship." Claude smiled at Marie. "Dis h'is a ship. Not a boat." Marie's complexion edged from red into the mauve spectrum.

"Look, guys," she cajoled. "You're costing the Greek Tourist Board a lot of money. They're expecting some kind of return on that investment . . . you know how the system works. Tomorrow is the last day you can see or do anything Greek. We don't care what you do in Egypt or Israel . . . or if you even get off the boat . . ."

"Ship." Claude smiled engagingly at Marie. "Dis h'is a ship. Not a boat. You see, when a boat get to become a certain size . . ." he started. I could hear Marie's molars grinding over the thumping of the old engine down in the bowels of the ship.

Marie struggled for a smile that more closely resembled a grimace. "So guys, have we got a deal? Will you do that? Will you be ready to go ashore at 6:30?"

"Dat mean we gotta get h'up h'at aboud six," Claude sulked.

"Yeah," I agreed, "no way! It's impossible." I waited a beat. "We'll have to stay up all night to be there on time."

"Hokay," Claude agreed, signalling the bartender for a refill.

Marie looked like she had won the lottery but discovered her dog had eaten the ticket.

So we were hanging off the deck railing at 6:15 the next morning, cameras around our necks, oversized drinking glasses topped up and firmly in hand. We were the happiest folks on board.

"Look at deese fool," Claude hissed in my ear as we watched the other passengers shoving and pushing so they could be aboard the first tender to shore. "Dey alla dem pay a fortune to be on dis Goddam ship h'an dey gonna pay a whole bunch more tuh ride a Goddam stinkin' ass up a cliff! Not me! But we're 'ere, huh? Jus' like we promise Marie. I 'ope she will be 'appy!"

Most of what Claude had just said was actually in French. His English was good, but deteriorated in a direct proportion to his alcohol intake. His fuel gauge now was reading full. It had been a long night. Fortunately I'm fluent in French.

Since we didn't give a damn whether or not we went ashore, Claude and I graciously stood aside to permit the more enthusiastic -- or pushy -- tourists to cross on the tender's first trip. The wait for the second trip permitted us each to have three more drinks we didn't need but thought we should have, since we anticipated an alcohol drought on shore at that hour.

By the time we landed on Santorini, Claude was monolingual -- and intransigent. He flatly refused to get on a donkey and ride up the cliffside, selected a bench near the dock, curled up and passed out. Having experienced Marie's wrath on a previous tour of Greece, and being a sucker for any damsel in distress, I tried to appear enthusiastic about joining her and the other members of the press group on what is considered a touristic "must" in Greece.

However I took the precaution of buying a Greek fisherman's hat from a vendor, noting that its crown was padded and deciding it could double as a crash helmet. (To this day I pull out that same hat when revelries reach a certain level, probably baffling friends by referring to it as my "Greek crash helmet.")

So we rode to the top of the cliff -- all 900 feet -- and I didn't fall off my donkey, God alone knows how. By virtue of my size, I was given one of the largest donkeys and the creature immediately resented its assignment. No sooner was I on its back than it whipped its mangy head around and snapped yellowed teeth at my ankles. That got it a yank on the reins and as soon as we were out of sight around the first corner from its owner, a smart kick in the chops the next time it snapped. Two good kicks and the donkey and I reached an understanding: neither of us wanted to be labouring up this steep, rocky pathway in rapidly escalating heat, but it was going to be a lot more comfortable for the donkey if it stopped trying to bite me.

The view from the top of the cliffs was spectacular -- according to film I shot. The cruise ship was away down there on the bluest of waters, about the size of an acorn shell. The whitewashed buildings of Thera sparkled like new-fallen snow. And the sky was blue; a spectacular shade of blue peculiar to the Greek islands. If you've been there you know what I mean. My photographs told me later I was glad I had made the trip. Besides, I now had a few brownie points in den-mother Maria's ledger which I hoped would get me through the rest of the trip.

No serious injuries had been incurred by any of our group by the time we hiked back down the hundreds of cobblestoned steps.

Claude was exactly where we had left him four hours earlier, but vertical.

"Ay, Dave," he hollered across the dock. "Viens içi!" He was beaming as I limped across the cobblestones towards him.

Claude was clutching a brick-coloured cylinder about two and a half feet long and eight or nine inches in diameter. "Try some of dis!" he ordered, indicating a jagged hole poked through one end. "H'its wine! Not bad!"

He helped me lift the container so I could pour some into my mouth . . . and down my neck. It was almost five hours since my last drink of anything. During that time the sun had been climbing relentlessly into a cloudless sky and now was blazing almost directly overhead. During that time I had spent more than two hours hanging onto a rank-smelling donkey going up what felt like 45% grades.

The wine from the clay container was cool and delicious.

"Where did you get this?"

"Dat guy over dere. Four bucks a tank. Not bad, eh?" (This was all in French; Claude had been nipping on the wine for at least three hours.)

"We'd better get some more."

"Hokay. I go wit' you. De guy's my buddy." I wondered whether the six-litre container might be Claude's second.

So I bought one. Then Claude bought another. And I bought a second. The wine merchant was ecstatic. Then we worried whether 3½ tanks would get us through the rest of the voyage. Pro-bably not. By now some of our colleagues had wandered over and they kindly agreed to solve our logistical problem. Sure, they'd each haul a tank on board for us. So we bought the merchant's last two tanks of Santorini wine. Canadian-Santorini relations have likely never soared higher before or since.

And then we were back on board the ship where Claude promptly reverted to his beer and I luxuriated with a flagon of Five-Star Metaxa and a dozen ice cubes topped up with bottled water. Secure on our alcoholic terra-firma we decided to try some of the Santorini wine from a bathroom (sorry, head) tumbler. It was putrid. With an ice cube added and swirled it was just as bad.

And now the captain, who had been staring down from the bridge at our pile of wine canisters in the tender, had ordered us to the main bar just outside the dining salon.

"No big deal," I said to Claude after the First Mate was out of earshot. “If we’ve broken some sort of law we can just dump this crap overboard. Or if he thinks we’re doing the ship out of liquor sales we can get the steward to show him our bar tabs.” Despite the supply of booze we had hauled aboard, we both had hefty bar tabs. We spent most of our time at the ship’s several bars and used our personal supplies after they closed and before they opened or out at the pool when the weather was decent.

“H’okay,” agreed Claude, topping up his beer container, “fill h’up dat ting of yours an’ let’s go see dat guy.”

When we staggered into the bar on the ill-timed tilt of a big wave, the captain was holding court with a few of his senior crew members at a huge round table in the main bar. They all had polite-sized glasses in front of them. We held firm to our industrial-sized drink containers. The Captain was not a big man and his black hair was lightening around the edges. Late fifties, probably, with eyes like black olives sunk into deep sockets in a swarthy clean-shaven face that appeared to be scowling at us. The glittering gold braid and buttons scattered across his sparkling white tunic gave him an extra eight inches of stature and another hundred pounds of bulk; an intimidating authority figure.

The First Mate leaped to his feet to introduce us and we shook hands with the captain . . . and then the Purser and the Ship’s Doctor and several other officers. The captain didn’t get up, but his initial glower seemed to warm as he asked in a surprisingly deep voice and quite good English: “You appear to enjoy the wine of my island. Elio,” he indicated the First Mate, “tells me you have bought so much wine to take home to your Canada. Few who are not from this country know of the wines of Santorini.”

There was a little click in the back of my sodden mind. Previous visits had taught me that Greeks are extremely proud of their magnificent country; they are ferociously proud of the particular region of their country where they were born and raised.

“Oh, no,” I assured the Captain, lying through my teeth. “The reputation of Santorini wines is widely known. I heard about it in Canada -- as did Claude, here -- and that is why we bought so much. Perhaps we will be unable to take much of this home, but at least we can enjoy it during our cruise. You do not serve it on your ship, I have noticed.” (That was a wild guess, but turned out to be correct.)

The captain beamed proudly. “You have heard of the wines of my island in Canada,” he purred. “Surely Canada is a land of wine connoisseurs. We do not serve the wines of Santorini on this ship,” he scowled, "because the provisioning is all done by the company that owns the ship. What do they know of fine wines," he sneered. "But you, you have heard of Santorini's wines in Canada," he marvelled. He seemed unaware that Claude was busily swilling Olympia beer and I was pulling on a flagon of dark liquid loaded with ice cubes that clinked treacherously as Claude and I swayed back and forth thanks to the waves and our refreshments.

"Please join us here," the Captain invited, ordering several of his officers out of their chairs and sending them to find new ones for themselves. "Will you join us for a drink . . . " he started. And then stopped, noticing our large glasses, apparently for the first time. "Well, when you would like another, please just ask. And I will be honoured if you will join me at my table for lunch."

When, a few minutes later, I asked the attending steward to top up my huge cup with Five-Star Metaxa, lots of ice and some water, the captain was positively radiant. I could probably have been granted his daughter's hand in marriage. If he had one. And if I hadn't been married. And if I'd bothered to ask. A Canadian drinking Greek brandy? And by choice!

And then the First Mate was rapping on Claude's door later that afternoon with a request from the Captain that we join his table for dinner. And then it was lunch the next day . . . and dinner again that night. It was downright embarrassing. Some folks gloat over being invited to a meal at the Captain's table. They dine out on the experience for months after they return home from their cruise. To get to the Captain's table in the first place you usually have to be somebody. Billionaires go to the top of the invitation list. On a ship with a casino it's the highest roller (loser) and his companion.

Claude and I were just plain folks drinking our way through another boring week on the road away from home and loved ones. We'd have preferred being at the other end of the dining salon with our equally impecunious colleagues, swapping travel tales. We would even more have preferred being at home. But there we were, up at the captain's table on the raised dias (which both of us fell off several times during the trip) occupying chairs for which many others on the ship would have happily paid small fortunes.

The Captain and his officers all spoke fairly good English, but the ship's doctor knew only a few words of English. We chatted with him in French and when others were interested in our conversations he translated them into Greek and passed them along to the table. I turned out to be just what the doctor might have ordered because I then smoked unfiltered Gauloises cigarettes to which he rapidly became addicted. He claimed they were unavailable in Greece and during the rest of the cruise made serious inroads into the large supply I had bought in Athens. By the third meal he had arranged to be seated next to me so he no longer had to reach across the table each time he wanted to liberate another cigarette from my pack.

The wines served at the Captain's table were French. And they flowed, rather than poured. As soon as the level in a glass got anywhere near the mid-point, a glistening white sleeve would appear beside your shoulder with a hand at the end tilting the neck of a bottle into your glass. But champagne also came with some dishes, beer flowed for Claude and Metaxa for me and liqueurs for everyone. Claude and I were grateful for the typhoon through which the ship now heaved because others were also falling down on their way to and from the dining salon.

At our first lunch with him, the Captain was called from his table before dessert was served. Several minutes later the ship altered course and half a minute later it pitched over on its port side. It remained there for a frighteningly long time while plates and glasses crashed to the floor and diners and their chairs tipped over and crashed to the port side. The noise from the adjacent galley was horrific as stacks of crockery and glassware slid from their shelves and exploded on the tiled floor.

After what seemed like eternity the ship finally righted itself but then immediately heeled over again to port as the course was changed about ninety degrees to starboard. And then the motion was away up and away down instead of the terrifying rolls.

Two days later the captain told us what had happened. The bridge watch had called him from lunch because they had received warning of an approaching hurricane. As he started to change course the ship was hit on the starboard bow by a massive rogue wave running ahead of the storm centre. Had the ship rolled over one more degree, he admitted, it would have capsized. The old Poseidon thing.

Half of the kitchen's supply of glassware and crockery had smashed. For the rest of the cruise, passengers had to make do with one bowl and one plate through the four or five courses of each meal. At the Captain's table, however, each course was served on fresh, clean dishes and glasses were changed for servings of each new wine.

The doctor told us the injuries had been few -- a lot of bruises, some lacerations, a broken leg and several broken arms. One of the cooks had been badly scalded by simmering dishes that toppled on him from the stove top. Several of the geriatric crowd had suffered heart attacks, but the doctor had them stabilized and was confident they'd survive until we reached the next port. Evacuation by helicopter was impossible because of the weather which continued to be Force 10 on the Beaufort Scale.

Claude and I had no problem moving about on the wildly-pitching ship. In calm weather we might stumble about like the drunks we were, but the opposite was often the case when we were navigating the rolling decks. Most days during the hurricane we'd be the only ones walking straight and upright in and out of the bars and dining salon without having to stagger from handhold to handhold.

The after-hours drinking sessions were now being held in my cabin because Claude's small compartment had been shrunken by the six large canisters of wine and his few remaining cases of beer. Despite elaborate sales pitches to our colleagues -- most of whom gamely tried a sip and refused more -- five of the wine containers remained unopened. And the sixth that Claude had cracked open was still at least half full. Claude had to balance it somewhere every time he wanted to use his head (toilet).

The wine casks were becoming our albatrosses and despite conniving all sorts of schemes to get rid of them, they remained stacked in Claude's room, held in place by suitcases and padded with towels and laundry so they wouldn't knock together and smash in the violent seas.

Our most favoured scenario was to smuggle the canisters up onto the aft deck one at a time in the wee hours of the morning and heave them overboard. But how to do that without being noticed by the watch? And what if the watch caught a glimpse of something hurtling overboard or noticed the splash? We had visions of the ship running a grid search through the night for a man overboard. And how to explain to any crew member we might encounter en route to the aft deck what we were doing carrying a tank of wine around at that hour of the morning? While making six trips we were bound to run into somebody, and even the lowliest member of the crew by now knew we were very special passengers. Anything we did with that damn wine would be immediately reported to the captain.

And if we did get rid of the stuff, how could we explain to our buddy the captain as we went ashore in Piraeus, why we didn't have any of that fantastic Santorini vissanto wine left to take home to Canada?

It was on the long bus trip back to the ship from Giza that the inspiration struck. Claude and I had both sobered up during the hot, dusty, jolting trip because the driver hadn't allowed us to bring drinks on the bus and refused to stop at the few bars we passed on the seemingly-endless pothole-riddled highway through the desert. We were sulking in the back of the bus and I was wondering how many more hours of this hell I'd have to endure before getting back to my cozy little cabin just down the companionway from the ice machine.

That reminded me of the wine casks . . . and suddenly the solution was crystal clear!

Exultantly I laid out the plan for Claude. His face split in the first smile I'd seen all day. "Chrise, Dave, you're a genius-guy!"

We launched the idea at lunch at the captain's table the next day. One of our colleagues, I told the captain, had advised us we could only legally take one small bottle of wine each through Canada Customs on our return to Canada. We had done some checking through our documents and found this appalling situation to be fact. The wonderful Santorini vissanto wine we had acquired would have to be left behind in Greece.

We were desolated, Claude assured the captain with a wonderfully straight face, but as journalists we couldn't even consider trying to break the law of our country, however stupid it might be.

That left us only two choices, I picked up the narrative. We could make a gift of this very special wine to the captain as a microscopic token of our appreciation for his outstanding hospitality, or . . . we could share the magnificent bounty of Santorini with the other passengers.

"No, no, no, no," the captain waved off the offer with both hands. He couldn't possibly consider accepting such a gift, he assured us.

Well, perhaps after dinner that evening the captain would permit Claude and me to host a gathering of fine wine aficionados in the aft bar room for just an hour, or two? Perhaps the captain could make the announcement at dinner and also attend the event . . . a great opportunity to mix informally with many of the passengers he had perhaps not yet personally met and spoken with . . .

Yes! He bought it!

That afternoon we slipped quite a few drachmas into the palms of the staff of the aft bar on the upper deck. We were already well acquainted, of course, and the barmen seemed to get a kick out of the special preparations we requested. They assured us of their cooperation and more importantly, their discretion.

The Captain extended the invitation during dinner and made Claude and me stand up to accept a smattering of applause from bewildered shipmates. The applause was limited, because many who had been invited didn't understand English or Greek and therefore didn't know why the ship's two best-known drunks were being singled out for even more attention.

But a lot of people showed up at 9 p.m. in the aft bar: the free-loaders en masse, some who never missed any special event offered on their very expensive cruise and a lot of fellow travellers we'd never seen at any of the ship's bars. All eagerly grabbed wine glasses and thanked the stewards who topped them up with vissanto from large glass pitchers. On the small tables between the chairs were bowls of nuts and snacks. It was a class act.

The Captain and his senior crew members were there in all their dazzlingly-white-jacketed splendour, thc Captain bcaming as he chatted with passengers and noted approvingly how quickly so many glasses were being refilled -- including those of some of the senior crew members. Of course, quite a few of the guests stayed for only a couple of sips before quietly slipping away, leaving their almost-full glasses wherever they hoped they wouldn't be noticed. The lounge's potted plants took quite a beating that night . . .

They drank all of that ghastly wine by about 11 p.m. All 16 gallons of it! Probably, in most cases. just because it was free. The captain had made his exit after about an hour -- and, we noticed, only one glass of wine.

Claude and I had a wonderful time. We watched a few of the more greedy freeloaders fall down and saw a few others carried out of the lounge and down to their cabins. There was one classic husband-wife confrontation, but unfortunately in a language neither of us understood. The high point was when she wound up to slap him. He dodged the slap but fell down; she missed his face, did a 360° spin and also fell down.

At all times we circulated with our wine glasses, chatting with those whose languages we could handle, smilingly clinking our glasses against those with whom there was a total language barrier.

And of course, Claude and I got just as loaded as anybody else. Little wonder. My bar tab for that date included five bottles of a very pleasant French wine we'd discovered the ship stocked . . . and with which the very-well-tipped Antonio had been keeping only *our* glasses topped up throughout that memorable evening.

A day at the leper colony

Kalaupapa
Island of Molokai, Hawaii, U.S.A.

In the many countries through which I've wandered over the years, I've seen tourists do a lot of strange things. And in the usually sun-drenched tropical islands of Hawaii, I didn't expect to find what can probably qualify as the world's weirdest tourist attraction.

But there we were in a corral on a damp, chilly day, coaxing -- and in some cases cussing at -- our $55 per day rental mules aboard which we would descend a 520-metre (1,664-foot) cliff to tour a leper colony. That's right . . . a leper colony.

The 20 or so people aboard the mules all looked pretty much normal, except for the foolish grins most of us wore as we rapidly learned the mules were masters of their mounts and would go where they darn well wanted -- and when.

The mule I was assigned, mis-named Friendly, bore me towards a pleasant-looking grey-haired lady from Minnesota whose mule had found some long grass Friendly coveted -- and got. "The weather here is a lot better than back home in Minnesota," the lady said, sidestepping neatly when asked what she was doing on top of a mule about to descend a cliff to a leper colony. She arranged her high collar against the slanting rain as her mule grumpily stumbled away to find more grass.

Then we followed our "skinner" on the Molokai Mule Ride, a unique experience which has brought tourists to this tiny island since someone decided in 1973 that some tourists will pay good money for just about anything, no matter how off-the-wall it might sound, and in this case, was.

"The mule knows the trail. You don't," the skinner told us as we started off on the trail to the village of Kalaupapa, a five-kilometre zig-zag with 26 switchbacks across a steep flank of the volcano that formed the island of Molokai.

Kalaupapa is on the Makanalua Peninsula, a flat ancient lava flow jutting into the Pacific from the north side of the island and surrounded on the land side by almost sheer cliffs, some more than

1,000 metres high. Since the leper colony was started in 1845 by King Kamehameha, the corkscrewing path followed by the mules has been the colony's only land route.

Until modern medicine found sulfone drugs which arrest the leprosy infection, a round-the-clock guard post was maintained at the top of the trail and armed guards had orders to shoot to kill anyone attempting to leave Kaluapapa.

Mule rides leave the Kalae Stables around 9:30 a.m. and from then until arrival at the bottom of the cliff around noon, smoking is forbidden and dismounting is unthinkable. It's possible to hike the trail on foot. In fact if you weigh more than 225 pounds, the weight limit allowed on the mules, that's the only way to get there short of chartering a boat or aircraft. A pass to enter Kalaupapa on foot costs $22, but includes a picnic lunch and guided van tour of Kalaupapa and the old settlement of Kalawao.

The 2½-hour mule ride down the side of the volcano is pleasant once you're able to accept that your mule is better suited for the trail than you are. The sort of person who would elect to take such a trip should experience no fear, mainly because trees, vines and other heavy rain forest vegetation obscure the near-perpendicular drops between the slope's traverses along 70 per cent of the route.

At the foot of the trail the mules are turned loose in a fenced field. The riders shake, stretch or jog out their cramped muscles and the smokers desperately light up before boarding the tour vans.

There are no children here because the children of lepers do not develop the disorder if separated from their parents at birth. Nor are children under 16 allowed into the settlement because they are carriers of diseases to which lepers who have been treated with sulfone drugs, have little resistance.

The homes are modest frame structures on streets where only the occasional pet dog may be seen moving when a tour comes through. Leprosy can cause hideous deformities, from body extremities which have become deformed or which have dropped off, to lesions and sores or acute skin discolouration. Lepers are as sensitive to their disfigurations as any human and when the tourist vans roll through the colony, no lepers are around for visitors to gawk at, be distressed by, or try to photograph.

The peninsula held 3,500 residents at one time but since 1942 when there were 600 residents, there have been no new arrivals and the average age is 55-65. Jimmy Brede, guide and driver of one of the vans, is an exception to the average age. He came here as a child about 35 years ago and his leprosy was arrested before it caused much physical damage. Brede's skin is the colour of a newly-minted penny, but the only other sign of the disorder which can be seen is his fingers which appear to have the stiffened joints of an arthritic.

Kalaupapa has a fire hall, meeting hall, tiny airport building for the twice-weekly light aircraft which brings in fresh provisions, and a dock for the twice-yearly shipment of large items such as refrigerators, automobiles or television sets.

There's also a general store where we stopped for drinks. I bought a can of cold beer and wondered why it was taking the shopkeeper so long to make change from the bill I had given him.

It was too late to tell him to keep the change by the time I noticed he had no fingers or thumbs and was trying to slide coins out of the change box with his hand stumps.

The key attraction on the tour of the 36-square-kilometre (14 square miles) colony is the little church of St. Philomena built by Father Damien (Joseph de Veuster) a Belgian priest who devoted his life to working here and who died in 1889 at the age of 49, from leprosy. Father Damien refused cure because that would have necessitated leaving the lepers. For his selfless dedication, he has been nominated for sainthood.

When Father Damien arrived here in 1873 and began holding church services, he was disappointed to find his church nearly always empty. It was eventually explained to him that the hideously deformed lepers would like to attend services, but didn't want to frighten the priest with their appearance. And they had another problem: some forms of leprosy cause the afflicted to drool continuously and none wanted to despoil the church. Father Damien promptly had small holes made in the floor of the church so the lepers who wished to attend could drool into palm fronds rolled up like funnels, with the small end projecting through the floor.

The box lunches provided by Molokai Mule Rides are put up by the island's Hilton Hotel and are eaten at picnic tables on a meadow overlooking one of Hawaii's more spectacular seascapes. Then it's back to the mules and up the cliff to the stables.

For the same reason, perhaps, that everything else about mules is unpredictable, the trip up the steep trail takes less time than it takes to go down. You're back at the stables only two hours after leaving Kaluapapa.

Strolls with the Bucerias beach bum

Bucerias
Mexico

It doesn't take long to get back into the lifestyle of a hot country and only a few days after setting up house in a villa here we were keeping the same hours as the natives. That means you rise early and before the sun gets too high in the cloudless sky, do whatever chores have to be done.

Lunch is a leisurely affair from perhaps 1 to 2 p.m. and then you snooze until 4 or 5 p.m. It's still bright and sunny then but cooler from 5 to 8 p.m. and that's when you do whatever didn't get done earlier in the day. Dinner is late; usually around 9 p.m. and then you entertain, or are entertained, until 1 or 2 a.m. Then it's up early again, usually just as the sun is starting to colour the sky.

Five or 6 a.m. is a hideous hour to even contemplate getting out of bed in Canada -- especially when you know the best part of the day is going to be spent in a factory or answering the insistent commands of an office telephone.

But if you're vacationing in a warm country, you'll find yourself leaping out of bed at those hours with a bounce in your step and a smile across your face . . . even if the previous night's party wrapped up only a few hours before. The air is warm, you know it's going to be another great day and there's also the thought of that afternoon *siesta* to keep you going.

Most mornings I was out on the beach before 6 a.m. I don't like getting out of bed early and I'm not crazy about walking. But most mornings I'd log seven or eight kilometres before breakfast.

Bucerias is a hamlet on the coastal highway linking Tepic, Puerto Vallarta and Manzanillo, about 25 kilometres north of Puerto Vallarta. There are no high-rises here and no resort hotel complexes. Apart from a few clusters of villas like the fully-equipped two-bedroom one we had rented, the only other rental accommodation was a very "rustic" motel used only by those south-bound travellers who ran out of daylight, or gas, en route to Puerto Vallarta.

Our villa was roughly at the mid-point of the eight-kilometre-long crescent beach which ringed Bucerias Bay on the Pacific Ocean and it wasn't unusual to wander to either end of the beach and back at that hour without encountering another human being.

Those strolls were seldom made alone. Every Mexican town or village abounds in dogs in varying states of physical disrepair. Many are gaunt and mangy; many limp from encounters with automobiles or heavy boots and most are scarred from battles over scraps of food. They roam at night when it's cooler and they snooze in the shade during the long, hot days.

Our villa complex was about a kilometre north of the village centre and dogs weren't allowed on the grounds. But one mutt had managed to pull it off. He did this by endearing himself to the *gringos* on the beach, who then brought him up to their villas for snacks. The dog's friends then protested whenever the manager or his wife or assistants tried to run the dog off.

After several weeks of unsuccessfully trying to run the dog off the property -- and incurring each time the indignation of the dog's mentors who were also the manager's customers -- Barnaby, the manager, gave up and instructed his staff to leave the dog alone. If the *loco Ingleses* (crazy English) insisted on sharing their food with the stray dog they had called José, then it was easier to let them have their way, he apparently rationalized.

José was quick to take advantage of his new situation. He made friends with all in the complex who were prepared to make friends with a rather scruffy stray dog and established his headquarters on our tiled and shaded porch. This was either because we always cooked too much food and saved the leftovers for him, or because our patio faced Barnaby's office and José could laze in the shade and keep tabs on the one person in the compound who surely didn't like him.

It was comical watching José sneer at Barnaby from the assured safety of our patio every time that hapless individual went in or out of his office.

José was so popular with the tenants -- for many of whom he was a surrogate for a pet left at home -- that every new arrival was introduced to him. And as each set of tenants left for home, they'd check with their neighbours to be sure José's safe future was assured. Some even offered money for his food.

José stuck close to our villa complex, but he would make an exception for those morning walks. He'd ascertain whether I was going north or south and then lead me down the beach, prancing along with his head and tail held high. He'd stay 20-30 metres ahead all the way, except while passing two or three properties with whose resident dogs I guessed he must earlier have had painful encounters. As we'd pass those properties I'd feel a furry body pressing against my seaward leg and José would use me as his foil for the 100 or so metres across which another dog growled and glowered from a distance and over which it clearly held sway.

José was a playful and inquisitive companion, but for all his curiosity he never solved either the mystery of the waves or the crabs . . . though it wasn't for lack of trying.

As each wave curled up the beach, José would tilt his head and study it carefully. When it got too close to him he'd bark at it and he seemed both puzzled and frustrated when the wave just rolled towards him, forcing him to scamper to higher ground to avoid getting wet. When he'd turn to check, there would be no wave . . . just the frothy whiteness of the wave receding. Sometime José would follow that out, only to get smacked by the next wave that rolled in over the receding wave. That would make him angry and he'd shake off the water, glare at the wave and bark at it until it disappeared.

The crabs were fascinating -- for both of us. They'd skate across the wet sand and disappear into the froth of a wave only to reappear seconds later and then vanish instantly down a hole in the sand scarcely visible to the human eye. If José particularly wanted to catch a certain crab, he'd dig frantically at the place where it had disappeared, only to have his efforts wiped out by the next wave that rolled in.

José chased those crabs every morning, but he never caught one. Even when one would overshoot its hole, or fail to find it, José just never caught up. The crab would just change direction and hurl itself into the next wave which would bring Jose to a skidding stop.

Those were magic times, those wanders up and down the beach at Bucerias with José. They're warm, treasured memories which can be called up when it's cold and sleeting back home in Ontario or when there's a moment to daydream in an office full of jangling telephones and raucous voices.

José is probably still scampering up and down the beach with another *gringo* he captivated with his ale-coloured eyes, floppy ears, irrepressible exuberance, unquenchable curiosity and bottomless repertoire of comical expressions. And he's probably still trying to catch one of those crabs.

Birders put off by Arctic puff-in

Pangnirtung
Baffin Island, Canadian Arctic

The cockpit of the small boat was cramped, the board benches along the sides were uncomfortable and the air reeked of gasoline fumes. We were part of a flotilla bound for Kekerten from Pangnirtung, a Baffin Island community of 1,050 people in the Northwest Territories, about 2,600 kilometres north of Montreal.

The occasion was the opening of an historic park on Kekerten Island, site of the first permanent whaling station in Canada's eastern Arctic. Officials from the territorial government, assorted politicians and every local person who could find space on a boat, was going along on this July day that was making local history.

There were 23 boats in the ragged procession which began forming up at 7 a.m. The 32-mile voyage didn't start until about 9 a.m., after scouts reported the mouth of the fiord was clear of drift ice pushed in by the previous night's incoming tide.

I was a guest in the 25-foot fishing boat of Jay Karpak, one of the first boats to leave shore and maintain a holding pattern in the fiord while passengers were assigned and loaded into other boats and freighter canoes. Grey clouds lay just above pewter-coloured water between the steep grey sides of the fiord. The air was damp and chill.

I was grateful for the meagre warmth of a camping stove in the cockpit at the bow of the boat which Karpak used to boil tea. Some children were aboard, plus two ladies of uncertain age who said they had come to Pangnirtung from Connecticut to birdwatch.

They had been invited to make the trip to Kekerten by the locals who believed the women were either government officials, specially invited guests, or members of the media. The women were dressed in thermal foul-weather gear and spent the entire voyage on the exposed rear deck scanning the fog banks and passing ice floes with expensive binoculars.

I huddled miserably in wet shoes and a too-thin jacket on the hard bench thinking about the heat wave back home in Ontario and wondering what had driven me to spend a week in a place where, among other hardships, possession of alcohol was illegal.

Mid-morning, somebody in another boat shot a seal. About half the flotilla immediately tied up to a large, flat iceberg in order to eat the seal -- raw -- and get fresh water to fill the tea kettles which apparently were kept boiling non-stop.

Karpak hadn't smoked up to this point, and as a guest on his boat I felt it best not to smoke, either. Besides, there was that constant reek of raw gasoline.

So the moment our boat scrunched up to the iceberg, I bounded onto it with delight, cigarettes and lighter in hand. While the Inuit scurried about securing their boats with grappling hooks and getting their share of the grisly hunks of bloody, raw seal meat, I revelled in the soul-satisfying pleasure of my first unfiltered Gauloises cigarette in about four hours.

On the second or third puff I became aware of somebody standing behind me, sniffing theatrically. I turned a few degrees and saw the Connecticut bird watchers.

"I'm sorry," I said, intending to be amusing in view of our surroundings and a vicious, cold gale, "do you ladies mind if I smoke?"

"If you must," one huffed peevishly, trudging off through the slush to windward.

I could not prevent myself from breaking into an enormous smirk as my imagination painted the wonderful and vivid image of the lady stomping to the other side of the iceberg -- and falling into the Arctic Ocean as the rotten ice gave way beneath the indignant pounding of her designer Arctic bird-watching boots.

Travel tip: *All in the way you ask*

To some extent, the price of a hotel or motel room is up to you, particularly during off- or shoulder seasons.

Try asking "What is your rate for two (or however many you need) people," rather than "Do you have a vacancy?" -- when the sign outside has already assured you there is a vacancy.

This puts the ball in the owner's court. He's aware you may just walk out if he quotes a high rate. And a bird in the hand . . . is better than an empty unit.

Mixed smoke signals

Hobart
Tasmania, Australia

There weren't enough rental cars for everyone who had opted to participate in what turned out to be a rally around the Australian state of Tasmania. You can organize a group of your friends for car-sharing, but my wife and I enjoyed leaving our chances of companions to the luck of the draw. It's a great way to meet interesting new people and we have yet to get lumbered with unpleasant jerks.

This time we drew a couple from California. He writes for a senior citizens magazine and we had met a few years before in Thailand, when he was a bachelor.

On the flight to Tasmania, Ken asked if I'd mind doing the driving. My wife and I smoked, but had decided that since we would be sharing a small car we would refrain from doing so in the car. Since I was driving, we'd be able to make frequent "photo" stops during which we could light up.

As we were loading the car at the airport, I thought I'd allay Ken's possible concerns that he and his bride, Polly, would have to spend three days in a cloud of second-hand tobacco smoke.

"We won't smoke in the car, Ken," I assured him.

"Okay," he said after a pause.

We drove about 300 kilometres that afternoon to a delightful lodge overlooking the harbor of Strahan, but we stuck to our resolve to be considerate non-smoking companions.

Before dinner that evening the four of us settled in comfortable chairs in the lounge for a drink. After a bit Ken leaned forward, "Do you mind if I smoke here?" he asked, with more than slight emphasis on the word "here."

"I enjoy a pipe," he explained, "and I missed it all day in the car."

José can you ski?

Soldeu
Co-Principality of Andorra

Jaime "*El Doctore*" Ramirez said he had treated 29 fractures at the first aid station atop Andorra's *Soldeu* Mountain on that blustery Sunday, but there were only two skiers waiting when I sheepishly slouched into the waiting room with what turned out to be a shattered shoulder.

There was only enough warmth in that room above the bar to melt the snow from ski boots and condensation trickling down the bilious-green cement walls created an inch of slush and the aura of a medieval dungeon.

I sat beside a diminutive Spaniard who was staring woodenly at his smashed finger. Even I could tell it was broken; fingers just don't bend that way.

A boy with a broken leg was carried in barely sustaining a tear-stained smile. While El Doctore built the boy's cast I chatted with the Spaniard who told me he was from Barcelona and on his first ski weekend. He didn't look like a man accustomed to vacationing; his brow was lined with worry creases.

The boy was helped out, sneaking admiring glances at his huge cast and smiling more gamely than before.

José -- for that was the skier's name -- gingerly carried his finger into the doctor's room. "Aha!" El Doctore exclaimed in the best detective movie manner, "you've broken your finger! Does it hurt?" José conceded it did hurt and I heard pills being shaken from a bottle and José being instructed to swallow them.

El Doctore sent his assistant, a young boy, to mix plaster while he set the skier's bones. Presumably to minimize José's injuries, the doctor maintained a running commentary in ghastly detail about grisly accident cases he had recently treated.

"There you go," El Doctore announced and I slunk to the doorway in time to see him slap José good-naturedly on the arm above the splinted finger. José screamed. The doctor grabbed for his arm. "My God," he said after a swift examination, "you've broken your wrist, too!"

The boy was sent for more plaster; I retreated to shiver on my bench and El Doctore joked about his oversight. "You should have told me it hurt," he chided José. "Does anything else hurt?"

After a pause José admitted his left leg hurt a great deal. I heard the rustle of nylon, gasps from José and then El Doctore in amazement: "Sacred Holy Family, man, your leg is broken, too!"

I settled in for a long, miserable wait. The kid rushed up and down with tubs of plaster. José's male friend arrived to pace the hallway. El Doctore was mercifully silent. I guessed he was rehearsing the vignette with which he would regale skiers later at an après-ski bar. José's pain killers and the casts seemed to lessen his pain. There were fewer gasps and moans.

"There now, that should fix you up," El Doctore said. "Have you got someone to help you?" José's friend darted into the room.

"Are you sure nothing else hurts," the doctor said, probably hoping to terminate the visit on a light note.

"Well," José choked, "I hate to mention it, but I don't feel well -- in the stomach. I'm having treatment for ulcers . . . "

"Sacred Mother of Our Lord!" El Doctore cried out. "Why didn't you tell me that when I gave you those pills? Get to the *clinica* (hospital) as fast as you can. I will telephone ahead to them."

José's friend tried to rush him out, but with his right arm in plaster from finger tips to shoulder and his entire left leg in plaster, it was slow going. When they reached the concrete steps, the friend decided to carry José down on his back; a good idea, perhaps, but the friend was even shorter than little José.

All went well until the friend slipped on some slush. He didn't fall, but he lost his balance. To avoid falling he ran down the remaining eight or ten steps. On his third step, José's bare toes projecting from the cast hit the first step from the top . . . then the second, third, fourth, -- slapping on each with the sound of a freshly-landed cod.

José's screams reverberated through the building and trailed off into the gelling afternoon.

We never learned whether José got to the *clinica* in time to have his stomach pumped -- or whatever life-saving treatment he required. And though I kept an eye out for him throughout the rest of that ski season, I never saw him again on the *pistes* or in any of the après-ski lounges.

Even seasoned travellers sometimes lose their hotels

London
England

Most people develop habits to prevent themselves from getting into difficulty. You don't slam a locking car door, for example, unless you are holding the keys in your hand.

People who have to travel a lot develop even more protective habits -- most having been learned the hard way.

You don't drive away from a car rental lot, for example, until you've walked around the car to check for damage which might not have been noted on the rental agreement, and looked in the trunk to be sure there's a spare tire and jack.

So my hand was on the hotel key in my pocket as I closed the locking door to the room. Another business trip was almost over: a week of meetings in New York, five days crossing the Atlantic by ship in a Force 10 gale and a week trying to photograph rural England in the incessant rain and sleet of late November.

The rental car was turned in, my bag was re-packed, cameras broken down and film stowed in lead foil pouches. My morning flight was reconfirmed and all travel documents handy in their usual places. Time for a good pub supper in Chelsea which I'd chosen for a reasonably-priced hotel and because it was on the Heathrow Airport side of London.

After sampling the food and having a few pints in a number of pubs, it was time for bed. I had wandered a dozen or so blocks from my hotel not bothering to keep track of directions; a heavy fog would have precluded doing that anyway.

Before hailing a cab I pulled out my hotel key so I could tell the driver where to take me. In the dim light of a street lamp I read from the plastic key fob: "In the event you unintentionally carried away this key, kindly deposit it in any mail box and postage will be paid: P.O. Box 461, London, etc."

The reverse side of the fob was blank. No hotel name. I had been so happy to find a parking place after such a long search for one that I hadn't noticed either the name of the hotel, what its facade looked like, or the name of the street on which it was located. There was no need to trouble with that information when leaving the hotel because the key was in my pocket and all hotel key fobs bear the name, address and telephone number of the hotel.

Except that damned bit of plastic I was now holding in a clammy hand.

I started walking in ever-widening squares, recognizing less each time I went a block wider. The drizzle continued and the fog got heavier.

The more I tried to recall what the hotel entrance had looked like, the more my mind painted detailed pictures of other hotels where I have stayed.

In desperation I entered the lobby of a small hotel where lights were still burning in the reception area.

I ended my explanation to the turbaned reception clerk by producing the very anonymous key fob for his inspection. This man obviously knew his hotels because he led me through the sort of ident-a-kit examination police artists use on TV when they're trying to sketch a suspect's face from the scant description of an addled eyewitness.

He used the yellow pages and gradually narrowed the field by eliminating hotels which were on street corners, or of red brick, with street level entrances, parking lots out front, or the few other salient features I was able to recall.

He then began patiently telephoning the short list of hotels, enquiring politely at each whether a Mr. Scott from Canada was registered. On about the ninth call my benefactor's face brightened and he scribbled something on a note pad.

I was surprised when he started dialling the telephone again instead of sharing his triumph with me. He gave precise instructions over the telephone to a dispatcher, disconnected and told me: "It's only four blocks from here but I thought I had better send you there in a taxi."

There are some times when you just can't get huffy . . . even when you feel getting huffy might seem to be justified.

Been There Done That

A bottle a day keeps the (Chinese) doctor away

Kowloon
Hong Kong

"You know that smell that hangs around after a house fire? Well, that's what this wine tastes like," Betty said, gingerly taking another tiny taste.

"I think with the right kind of food it could be quite pleasant," Eric said, rolling some of the *Tzepao Sanpien Jiu* around his mouth.

"It's like *LePage's* glue," was Wendy's contribution.

My palate sided with Betty's. The dark, oily wine smelled like *slivovich* but its bouquet was decidedly that of burned paint.

There were eight people at this wine tasting in my Hong Kong hotel suite, but only four were taking the exercise seriously and we were not to be hurried. Not when we were sampling a wine which cost about $4 for a 20-ounce bottle and which promised to cure: "untimely senility, kidney trouble, neurasthenia, sores in waists and backs, overburdens of the brain, anaemia, dizziness, poor memory, involuntary perspiration, insomnia, pale faces and poor appetite."

It was one of six different bottles I had bought in a Kowloon department store. Eric, a Hong Kong-based Canadian friend, had told me about the Chinese wines. "Just look at the claims they make," he suggested. "They promise to cure everything from headaches to bunions." Betty, a friend visiting Hong Kong from Honolulu, was another willing volunteer as was my long-suffering wife, Wendy. She'll try almost anything -- at least once.

We moved on to the *Zhenzhu Hungchien* wine which was the color of muddy varnish. It should be noted this was a serious tasting. Each wine was introduced to a fresh glass and tasters had glasses of bottled water to rinse their mouths. (The hotel's room service had been perplexed by my order for 48 wine glasses, eight water glasses and several litres of bottled water.)

The molasses-colored *China Nutritious Liquor* at $8 a bottle made the wildest claims: "enables the blood in good circulation, has special effect towards the diseases as sexual impotence, pre-age weakness, pains in loin and vertebra, faint in kidney and spleen, no birth, etc. It can refresh your spirit, increase blood supply, reblacken the hair, restore high complexion so you will be constantly healthy and can prolong your life to the maximus."

"It's just like that cough medicine they took off the market in the States because it had too much codeine in it," said Betty.

Eric, whose palate had weathered many years in Hong Kong, was more charitable. "Pleasant," he said. "It grows on you." But he didn't drink nearly enough for it to even start blackening his light brown hair.

The *Cordyceps Tonic Wine* from Shanghai had been distilled from "the rare, valuable Chinese drug *cordyceps sinensis* in combination with high quality wine of sorghum." Frequent drinking of it, the label said, "has a marked nutrient effect on senility and general debility during convalescence."

The vintners apparently concentrated all their skills on medicinal properties, leaving bouquet and taste to chance. "Like white lightning overlaid with dandelion bitter," Betty ventured.

It was perhaps presumptuous of us to expect the *Boat Brand Special Tiger Bone Tincture* to fondly recall a vintage *Bordeau* or *Médoc*. Manufactured by the National Changsha Pharmaceutical Works, some of its many ingredients include: "tiger bone, 5.6 percent; *Rhizoma ligustici wallichii*, 5.6 percent and *Fructus chaenomelts lagenariae*, 11 percent." It was described as "mellow, a roborant and anti-rheumatic of remarkable potency."

"It has a woody taste . . . but not the burned-down house taste," proclaimed Betty, now at ease with oenological terms. "It's the worst yet."

"It has hundred-year-old-egg smell," Eric said, "but it tastes like varnish."

"Yech!" contributed Wendy, heading for the bathroom.

The most interesting wine was saved for last. This was the chartreuse-coloured *Snake Bile Wine*. It tasted just as one might have imagined snake bile would taste . . . and snake bile, for the benefit of those with unsophisticated palates, tastes just like rubbing alcohol.

Wendy, after carefully scrutinizing the fine print on all the labels, noted that the six wines I had selected claimed to cure or improve every spiritual malady known to man, and every bodily organ she had ever heard about. Except the liver.

Colonial's palate bamboozled the sommelier

Le Mont St. Michel
France

Dinner that night was to be special. We were finally off on our Great European Adventure which had been delayed several weeks because the Halifax shipping agent had sent our car to England while we waited for it in France.

We had received the car that afternoon in Le Havre, and headed south. It was mid-May and sunny and a delight to put the fast Italian sports car through its paces with the top down on the narrow, winding roads through Normandy to the medieval town of Le Mont St. Michel.

We had strolled the worn cobblestones of the town as the sun sank and the evening grew chilly. And then we found a three-star hotel whose rooms contained all the modern comforts within centuries-old stone walls.

When we entered the grand dining room the maître d' placed us at a conspicuous table where others could admire my strikingly-lovely blonde companion. Silver utensils on the white linen cloth reflected the candelabra's flickering flames by which we scanned the exciting menu. My companion mentioned her choices and I translated them for the waiter. I was ready for the sommelier too, when he swept up to the table.

A half bottle of a regional white wine was ordered to complement the appetizer: a heap of steaming mussels for my lady, a cocktail of fresh shrimp for me. The offerings were superb.

A half bottle of a different white wine was ordered to accompany the soup, a specialty of the house, we were told. The wine steward seemed impressed with my choice. "Monsieur is familiar with our great wines," he murmured, reverently easing the cork from the bottle and presenting it to me with the aplomb of a high priest offering a sacrifice.

But it was the selection of the litre bottle of wine to accompany the entrée which undid him.

It was to accompany my companion's platter of local seafood and my saddle of spring lamb. "Monsieur's palate has great sophistication," exulted the sommelier, slicing the lead foil from the bottle's neck with a flourish. "Only a true connoisseur would select this wine which flatters both dishes."

I acknowledged his fawning compliment with what I hoped would pass for an insouciant shrug. I had decided there was nothing to be gained from admitting my three choices had been made the same way I pick race horses -- on a hunch about the name.

And although the wine steward was enraptured to be serving someone he had decided was an epicurean -- perhaps some renowned travel guide book writer or wine columnist -- the taste of the wines I chose was on a par with my usual race track selections: two losers and a show.

After I'd chosen the second wine, the maître d' began sliding past our table more frequently, clucking over a knife out of alignment in the table setting and ordering the bread basket topped up.

But when the sommelier reported to him on my third wine selection, he became a veritable nuisance by pulling rank on the wine steward for the privilege of topping up our glasses. And where, during the first two bottles he had pointedly enquired only of "madame's" enjoyment of various dishes, he now solicited only my opinion and affected to treasure my appraisals.

The cuisine was exquisite. But with all the traffic to the altar of the cognoscente we had little opportunity for our own conversation. My companion neither spoke nor understood French, but we had shared some snickers as I reported to her in English what was happening with the wine selections.

During one of the maître d's rare absences I asked my companion, with a wink, how she was enjoying the third wine.

She squinted around to be certain nobody was hovering over her shoulder, leaned across the glittering silver, and slurred: "It's bloody awful and every time I have a sip that creep refills my glass."

The bottle was almost empty and we were picking desultorily at the remnants of our entrées. "I'm sorry about the wine," I said, chuckling, "just trying to maintain the image. I'll order something with dessert I know you'll like. I'm tired of whites, too."

The wine steward hovered at my elbow like a proud parent waiting for the prodigy he had sired to start the valedictory address.

"We'll have a litre of the Mommesin," I said, having finally located a familiar name away down in the listing of also-rans.

"Beaujolais?" he gasped -- as a waiter had done the previous week in Paris when my companion ordered a steak tartare medium-rare. And then he recovered. "White, of course," he smiled, flicking a polished fingernail down an adjoining column.

I fixed him with what was likely a slightly glassy stare. "Certainly not. The red."

He appeared to teeter on the brink of mutiny and then got control of himself. "Certainly monsieur. I shall send for new glasses." He seemed deep in thought as he left the table and headed directly for the maître d'.

The rich, robust dry red wine didn't go at all well with the sweet pastries. But we didn't have appetite for them anyway.

We spent the next hour in a warm glow of delicious beaujolais, coffee, candle light . . . and privacy.

And it was very clear from their strained deference as we swept out of the dining room many francs lighter, that the staff had still not decided whether they had served another pair of gauche North American tourists . . . or whether they had yet to learn of the "in" people's latest wine-drinking trend which had just crashed on the rocky shores of Normandy.

Travel tip: *Do it now before you forget*

The next time you're going to have access to a photocopy machine bring along your passport. Lay out your passport open to the page with your photo on it along with all your credit cards, club memberships, Canada Customs green cards, driver's licence etc.

Make as many copies as you have flight bags and suitcases and additional copies for your office, home and whoever looks after your affairs when you're travelling. Should you lose your wallet or purse you will have at least one list with you to help police identify your documents, if recovered.

If you're in a country from which it's difficult or prohibitively expensive to make a lot of telephone calls, you can contact that person who has another list and have them cancel the appropriate credit cards. *Do this soon -- before you forget about it.*

Stuntman's motoring panache even beat the airline schedule

Soufrière
St. Lucia

Stuntman was a very good driver. No doubt about that.

But I kept wondering what would happen if something suddenly appeared in our lane around one of the hairpin turns. It's hard to stop a car that's already in a four-wheel slide.

And for the first half of our 60-kilometre trip to the world's only drive-in volcano there were lots of heart-in-mouth situations as Stuntman hurled his compact Ford around the narrow, pot-holed highway which had more curves per kilometre than most voyeurs see in a lifetime.

Stuntman wasn't playing Mario Andretti just to get his kicks or to impress me. I had paid the hotel taxi dispatcher the night before to line up a good driver with a reliable car to get me here and back to Castries Airport before my flight left for Barbados at 2:10 p.m.

My driver/guide the previous day just laughed when I told him I wanted to make the trip in 5½ hours in order to get to a Castries bank before it closed at 5 p.m. I soon found out why. He was a good guide, but his car -- which sported a huge For Sale sign taped across the passenger's windscreen -- was a wreck. With the gas pedal mashed to the floorboards he couldn't coax more than jogging speed out of it on most of the many hills.

The hotel dispatcher got me what I had asked for and got only one detail wrong: he told Stuntman my flight left at noon. So Stuntman was determined to do the six-hour trip in four and was unaware of the time cushion until I wanted to stop for a photo.

"We can't stop," he protested as we shot past another car on a blind hairpin. "If we stop once you'll never catch your noon flight."

"But I'm not leaving until 2:10. I don't have to be at the airport until just before 2 -- maybe not even then because the flights never leave on time."

Stuntman said the dispatcher told him he had to make the return trip in four hours. He seemed prepared to lay down his life --

and that of his passenger -- to meet the deadline. Now he condescended to follow the car ahead over a narrow bridge, before passing it.

We drove into the volcano precisely two hours after leaving the hotel, perhaps some kind of island record for the trip and one I'm not anxious to ever have to defend.

The return journey allowed photo stops in several places and a chance to get acquainted with Stuntman whose real name is Andrew Solomon. "No, not Solomon the wise," he chuckled. "What's to be wise about? I'm Solomon the hopeful; I have been hoping for years I will have a chance to live in Canada. I want that more than anything and I will do anything I have to to get to Canada." The 30-year-old single ex-cop said he'd take any job but I couldn't help thinking how much I'd like to have him as my taxi driver back home on those occasions when I left it a bit close to get to the airport in time.

Stuntman -- who earned his nickname by performing a variety of gymnastic feats as a boy -- delivered me to Veegie Airport in Castries at 1 p.m. in lots of time for the 2:10 flight.

Arriving at that time saved the day because there is no such thing as a 2:10 flight from St. Lucia to Barbados.

But I was just in time to catch the noon flight . . . which took off sharp at 1:15 p.m.

Travel tip: *Stay with the crowd*

Don't leave populated areas with a "tour guide" who has just picked you up. He may be offering to show you a great restaurant or superb view from some nearby (isolated) vantage point. And the view might be wonderful when you get there . . .

But often at that vantage point are friends of the "guide" who assert that he is indeed a licensed guide and his deserved fee is X number of dollars. They just happen to be there to make sure your "guide" is paid -- now.

A common variation of this theme is to demand payment for "guiding services" in an area from which the tourist would have difficulty finding his way back to the hotel. The "guide" is often accompanied by large companions whose presence isn't calculated to reassure the visitor of his well-being if he doesn't pay up.

Norwegians had a boot for tourist's trophy fish

Stjordalshalsen
Norway

We'd heard so many stories of the fabulous sport fishing in Scandinavia that we bought a lot of new and expensive equipment before going Rain wear would have been a wiser investment; it rained every day. But that doesn't deter any angler, so I was ready when The Right Moment arrived.

Just north of Stjordalshalsen I swerved the car into a rutted layby, waking my companion. Wendy is not a dedicated tourist or fisherperson. In Holland she stayed awake long enough to see a windmill; in Norway she stayed awake long enough to see a reindeer.

"Do we have a flat tire?" she asked.

"No. We're here."

"Where . . . all I can see is fog and rain?"

"We just passed a fantastic fishing spot."

"Good luck," she murmured, snuggling into the blanket.

The fishing spot belonged on the cover of an angler's magazine -- except editors don't use cover photos that show fog and horizontal rain. A small river leaped from the mountains into a deep pool which in turn emptied into the Atlantic. The tide was coming in. There were no overhanging branches to trap a wind-tossed lure.

Two men were working nearby on fish nets spread across a small boat. I returned their friendly waves and they came over as I was rummagine in my tackle box. One of them pointed to a Red Devil lure, bobbing his head eagerly to indicate it was my best bet.

I waited until they left before clipping on a two-inch silver *Williams Wobbler*. There isn't a fish anywhere in the world of the size I wanted that can't be suckered by one of those.

I snagged some seaweed on the first cast . . . and a heather bush on the second. The two fishermen watched my every move from down by their boat.

The fifth cast dropped the *Wobbler* precisely where I knew a monster waited with its mouth open and I was rewarded by a snap.

Not a strike. The fish simply hooked itself and headed for deep water. My new reel screamed and I cranked the drag. It didn't slow that fish. Its first run was 30 metres. I ran down the bank regaining line in case it ran again, but it sulked at the bottom away downstream.

I decided to play a waiting game. With two-kilo test (4.4 pound) line you don't get impatient with a 20 pound fish -- not if you want to see its eyeballs.

The two men ran up as I kept steady pressure on my fish. One grabbed my line and began pulling it in hand over hand, jabbering excitedly. How can you convey to a commercial fisherman -- in a language he doesn't understand -- that the reason you're not just winding in the fish is because you want to play it until it is tired, which is what the sport of fishing is all about?

My fish was 10 metres from shore when it broke water -- a beauty, easily 20 pounds. It made another run but my "helper" gave it line, paying it out by hand. When the fish ended its run the man eased it back to shore.

I was on the verge of hysterics and probably foaming at the mouth. Both of the men were now working my line.

Well, they did land "my" fish. Very skilfully. As one drew it close to shore the other stepped into the water and got a finger deep into a gill. "My" prize, a lovely salmon, lay gasping on the bank. My colleagues pressed friendly handshakes on me and indicated the fish would make good eating. I imagined Wendy changing her tune about my lust for expensive fishing equipment when we had thick salmon steaks on the grill that night instead of pork chops at $6 each.

"My" fish dinner flipped just then -- a great heave that turned it over. My companions grabbed at the fish uttering cries of dismay. Its entire other side was a mass of open, bloody sores and growths of vivid white fungus.

One of the men tore my lure from the fish's jaw, shouting what sounded like oaths, and booted my trophy fish into the river where it disappeared like a raindrop. The fishermen explained -- I think -- that the fish wouldn't have been good to eat.

That was the only fish I saw anywhere during our two-week fishing tour of Scandinavia.

Wendy -- who saw neither the fishermen nor "my" catch -- has an irritating habit of occasionally referring to our $5,000 Scandinavian fishing trip and "Dave's fish that got away."

One man's meat is another man's *poisson*

Panama City
Panama

Merlyn said she'd love to join me for dinner and suggested a club just outside Panama City. She was from a wealthy Panamanian family and had been my driver/guide that day.

As she weaved her compact car through heavy traffic, Merlyn touted the dinner prospects. The club specialized in sea food and surely I had heard of Panama's bounty from both oceans? I recalled a political reception in Canada where Panamanian shrimp were served. They were the size of small bananas and the caterer confided each had cost $7. "All the fresh seafood is available," Merlyn promised. I patted my credit card pocket and began fantasizing.

Anyone who has tasted properly prepared swordfish can appreciate my drooling anticipation. Gently broiled on the dying embers of olive roots, dribbled with the juice of fresh lemons is one way, but if the club's cuisine was as Merlyn boasted, the chef would likely know the Andalusian method: tenderly sautéed with vegetables, awash in butter, roast almonds, oregano and parsley. Swordfish bones are as big as axe handles so you can't choke on them.

The maître d' ushered us to Merlyn's "usual" patio table. Violinists were doing Strauss things while I located a French friend on the wine list. If this place didn't honour plastic the Canadian consul was going to get a panic call.

Merlyn didn't bother with the menu; I didn't open mine either because I knew what I wanted and saw no point in spoiling the meal by looking at prices. There was no mere waiter for such a valued patron as Merlyn; the maître d' materialized after a decorous interval, Cross pen poised over a tiny order pad.

"How is André's salmon tonight?" Merlyn asked after ordering escargots, whose culinary demise would likely cost me more than a local funeral.

"At its finest," he purred, and then it was my turn.

"Can your chef sautée swordfish?"

The maître d' gasped and I assumed he'd been insulted by the intimation there could be a technique unknown in his kitchen. He didn't reply and gave all his attention to the violinists.

"Do you have swordfish today?" I pursued.

Merlyn grabbed my arm then and pulled me close to hear her hiss: "Don't embarrass me; of course they don't have swordfish." To the maître d' she explained, "Maxwell, Mr. Scott is from Canada; he'd like more time with the menu."

Maxwell disappeared and Merlyn, making no effort to conceal her annoyance, harrumphed: "Really! Well, I suppose I should have told you; that was so embarrassing."

Equally irritated, I demanded an explanation.

"Only labourers eat swordfish," she huffed.

"I can't help that; in most parts of the world it's considered a delicacy. In Canada," I continued, galvanised by my second glass of wine, "farmers spend millions of dollars on pesticides to kill snails like the ones you just ordered."

"That may be so, but please don't humiliate me by mentioning swordfish to Maxwell again."

I didn't apologize and when Maxwell returned I tried to score a point by eulogizing Panamanian shrimp and ordering some as an appetizer. I must have made them sound exotic, or perhaps it was those Canadian farmers, because Merlyn cancelled the escargots and also ordered shrimp.

The violinists switched to peppy stuff; Merlyn either decided to make the best of dining with a social slug, or the wine was having an effect, because she chattered gaily.

Maxwell must have been attending the presidential entourage because a mere waiter brought our shrimp. They were on ice chips in crystal bowls and averaged an inch in length. They had come out of a can; you could tell just by looking.

Merlyn seemed not to notice. I waited until she had a mouthful before observing, "I seem to recall the Panamanian shrimp I've had in Canada were much larger . . . "

She was flustered -- but not for long. She flagged Maxwell down and fumed about the shrimp. He looked aggrieved and took them away after apologies which included threats of dark things to happen in the kitchen to "that new sous-chef."

He returned with some superb shrimp. It was so good I had a second serving as my entrée. The bill for dinner wasn't criminal and the place did accept credit cards.

But the long day had given Merlyn a headache, she said. She didn't feel up to the nightcap I proposed. In fact she dropped me off unceremoniously at my hotel so early I was able to find a downtown restaurant still open -- one that had a great ice cold local beer on tap and that also served a passable swordfish steak.

Earning their hosts' contempt

San Miguel
Cozumel Island, Mexico

The shoeshine boy was about eight years old and undeniably cute. Coal-black hair and huge, black, soulful eyes. He wandered into the open-air restaurant in downtown San Miguel, eyes cast down, looking for leather shoes in a sea of rubber flip flops and plastic thongs. The woman off the cruise ship spotted him and rushed over to hug him.

"You're so cute," she gushed, pressing something into the kid's hand. I want my husband to meet you," and she hustled the boy over to a portly man with a tomato-red face, quietly perspiring in the little patch of shade he had located.

"Oh, aren't you just so cute," said the husband fishing in his pocket. "Here's five pesos (about 25 cents) for you."

He patted the boy on the head and the couple moved off to a table that had just become vacant.

The boy shuffled slowly past my table gazing incredulously at what was in his hand. It was a $100 U.S. bill.

A man at a nearby table called the boy over to shine his shoes. When the job was done the man asked how much. The lad held up five fingers indicating five pesos. The man handed the boy a $5 U.S. bill.

The shoeshine boy had picked up in ten minutes what it would take his father at least a week of very hard work to earn.

Hapless guest euchred in new card game

Kansas City
Kansas, U.S.A.

Because they apparently don't credit their guests with enough intelligence to look after a numbered room key, an increasing number of major hotels are issuing cards to guests with which to open their room doors -- if they're lucky.

Each new guest gets a new card perforated with a series of holes to activate an electronic door lock. The number on the key-card does not correspond with the number of your room; that number is on the envelope containing the card. The guest is expected to memorize the room number and then destroy the envelope.

Security is supposedly the name of the game. The system prevents a thief from renting a room, having a key cut and returning after he has checked out to rob the new occupant. Or, should a guest be robbed off the hotel premises, his key-card won't give the robbers any clue which door in what hotel it fits.

Perhaps there are other equally compelling reasons for hotels to install these costly security systems, but that doesn't mean this frequent hotel user has to like them.

So there I was in my socks in a 10th floor hallway of Kansas City's Allis Plaza Hotel, watching that expensive lock chew pieces off my cardboard key-card and spit them on the carpet.

I had been changing for dinner and stepped out to get some ice. My door was cleverly weighted so it couldn't be left ajar while I skipped down the hall. It meant using that card again and this time, after six days of use, it had won.

The maids were nowhere to be found. But then, maids only knock on your door when you're taking a shower or have finally reached some elusive and very important customer by long-distance telephone.

So, clutching my ice bucket, I padded down the hall to the elevator, grateful I hadn't nipped out wearing only a bath towel. As it was, the marble lobby of the Allis Plaza isn't the sort of place to loiter in a sweat shirt, cutoffs and socks.

I parked my ice bucket on the reception counter. A young lady offered to help. "The door lock ate my card," I explained, tendering the ragged bit of cardboard. "I'm Scott from 1069."

"Do you have any identification, sir?"

"Certainly."

She drummed crimson fibreglass fingernails on the marble, waiting, giving no quarter.

"The identification is in my room." A dinner jacket and a Brooks Brothers suit were now waiting behind me. The receptionist continued to drum her nails, apparently expecting me to extract a Dun and Bradstreet profile from my ice bucket.

"If someone will be so kind as to let me into my room," I said, "I will then show some identification to that person." It is hard to be forceful when you're standing in your socks in the lobby of a posh hotel, but my ice bucket and I stood our ground.

The clerk excused herself and returned with a senior who gave me the once-over with gimlet eyes but appeared to conclude she would be at minimal mortal risk sharing an elevator with me.

She made the trip in silence, although I offered several witty conversation openers about the weather and the nuisance of newfangled locks.

The "Do Not Disturb" sign on my door threw her, even though I explained it is my protection against maids who knock when I'm showering. (I also hang out that sign when I'm leaving the room. That's a better security precaution than any of those stupid door locks because if a thief is around, the last door he's going to try is one wearing a Do Not Disturb sign).

My escort's crisp, new key-card opened the lock on the first try and I bounded happily back into my smoky lair. Who wouldn't believe such a messy room was mine?

The lady with the key-card, that's who. "I'll need some ID," she said coldly, moving towards the telephone.

"This suitcase is locked, you'll notice," I said, hefting my battered Haliburton onto the bed. "If this wasn't my room, how would I know the combination?"

I showed her the case was locked, deftly spun the tumblers and yanked open the suitcase. A week's accumulation of dirty laundry cascaded to the floor.

"I'll need some ID," she said, very coolly.

She was polite, but insistent. I whipped my passport from its hidey-hole with a flourish, opened it to the picture page -- and realized it was a photo taken when I didn't have a moustache.

"Do you have anything else?" she asked in a voice so cold it threatened the peach crop. It was a driver's licence with a recent photograph that got me my room back.

My benefactor managed a tiny smile as she turned to leave after bestowing the new key-card upon me. "We are only being so careful for your own security, Mr. Scott."

Wanna see your luggage again?

Luggage goes astray as inevitably as night falls, but there are some things you can do to lower the odds on it happening to you. And even if you've read this sort of advice before, take a moment to brush up on the pointers; they could save exasperation and untold inconvenience.

- Put identification tags on the outside *and* inside of your luggage. It's wise to have two tags on the outside in case one is torn off in handling.
- If you have a business card with office address use that instead of your home address.
- Remove all tags (other than those with your name and address) from your baggage before check-in at the luggage counter.
- The airline puts a baggage destination tag on your luggage at check-in and gives you a stub as a claim check.
- Before your luggage starts down the conveyor belt, double check the code and flight number on the tags to make sure your bags are going where you are.
- Hang onto that claim check! It's your only proof that you did check your luggage. When you have picked up your luggage at your destination keep that claim check.
- Some airports have alert security people who won't let you out of the airport if you don't have the claim checks matching those on the baggage you're carrying.

Deac's very own fishing story

Puerto Vallarta
Mexico

When Deacon said he was game I decided to hell with the budget. We'd go deep-sea fishing in the Sea of Cortez, as some maps call that huge bay between the west coast of Mexico and the east coast of Mexico's Baja Peninsula.

The sea is surrounded by Mexico, yet when you take the car ferry from La Paz to Mazatlan, as we had done some weeks earlier, you have to pass through Mexican customs and immigration on both sides. Kind of like running the gamut of customs and immigration between Québec and Ontario or Québec and New Brunswick -- which we may have to one day if some Québec politicians get their way.

We made arrangements in Puerta Vallarta with Ramirez who proudly captained the *Angelena*, a 25-foot wood-hulled cabin cruiser he chartered to sport fishermen. Ramirez said his not inconsiderable rate for a day included use of fishing tackle, bait, a *muy bueno* (edible) sandwich lunch and all the cold *Corona* (beer) we might care to drink. He guaranteed we would not return to port without catching something because he was a *capitano éstupendo por los piscadores* (fantastic fishing captain.)

Is there a fishing charter captain anywhere who does not make that boast long and loud when setting out his price schedule for the charter fishing trip of a lifetime?

Deacon is my brother-in-law, older brother of my wife, Wendy, and was so nicknamed because when he was born some fawning relative observed, "he looks just like a little deacon." His receding hairline now complements the nickname; his lifestyle is often at odds with it.

Deac agreed with me that Ramirez's concept of enough cold beer for his three passengers could prove drastically inadequate as we tossed about all day on the briny deep under a scalding sun miles from shore and *Corona* reinforcements.

Ramirez muttered something we couldn't understand the next morning when we loaded two backup cases of iced beer on board along with our sun screen and my camera equipment.

Been There Done That

It was early and still cool, but it was going to be another in a long procession of scorching hot days we'd enjoyed since moving to the little fishing village of Bucerias, about 30 kilometres north of Puerta Vallarta.

Ramirez ordered his first (and only) mate to bait up two lines while he ran up the engine, checked his fuel supply and loudly boasted to his neighbouring charter colleagues about the trophy fish his discerning *gringo* passengers would be weighing in that evening.

All of which buoyed our expectations for the day because that's how we'd chosen Ramirez in the first place. When fishing charters return at the end of each day, the captains make a big production of displaying what their customers have caught. Huge shark, marlin, sailfish and other creatures of the deep are impaled on spikes at dockside beside the boat that caught them, certainly the most convincing form of advertising.

The crew and fisher folk pose proudly for photographs in front of the dead fish and the boat with the biggest catch is usually chartered on the spot for the following day by other eager anglers. Deac and I had cased the marina for several nights and noted that the *Angelena* consistently brought in the most and biggest fish -- and the happiest, laughingest fisher folk.

Ramirez planed his boat across twenty kilometres of mirror-like water before throttling back off Punta Mita and instructing his mate to settle us in the chairs and stirrups. We'd agreed to take turns with the two rods; Deac and I didn't reckon Wendy would want to hog a rod because she'd already found a comfy place up on the bow to offer most of her skin surface to the now-blazing sun.

The mate slung a bucket of gory offerings overboard and we trolled back and forth through the chum for several hours with no results, save for Deac's normally-sallow complexion turning eggplant-coloured despite slatherings of sun screen and shade from a long-billed ball cap.

From time to time Ramirez screamed instructions from the flying bridge down to his first mate. To one who didn't understand Spanish it would have sounded as though the hapless fellow was being excoriated because we hadn't had a strike. But Ramirez was actually shouting encouragement that he'd seen a shark off the port bow or a sailfish dead ahead or that right about here we ought to hit something *muy grande* (a keeper).

Perhaps the fish overheard him, because none troubled our bait.

In early afternoon a dozen kilometres south of Punta Mita there was great excitement and yelling between the first mate and Ramirez and Deac and I were instructed to reel in. When our grisly bait was aboard, Ramirez opened up the engine and we roared further out to sea. Within a few miles we could see what he had spotted from the flying bridge: a cluster of at least a dozen smaller boats.

It was a really big fish, Ramirez said he had learned from radio contact with one of his colleagues on the scene.

And a really big fish it was. About forty or fifty feet big. And it wasn't a fish, either.

It was a massive whale shark. It floated like a small grey island mottled with pale yellowish spots, oblivious to the small boats that floated around it, the sun glittering off tourists' camera lenses.

The whale shark is a peaceful creature, but a careless flick of its huge tail could have reduced the *Angelena* to splinters; a couple of gulps could have provided its ubiquitous cruising cousins with some tasty, beer-basted *tapas* (snacks).

Ramirez, no doubt inspired by the three Nikon cameras I'd brought aboard -- the sort of photographic arsenal seldom sported by tourists -- apparently decided he might score some badly-needed points by stirring the shark to action I could photograph. Perhaps he envisioned a photo spread in *National Geographic*, or *Life*, with prominent mention of Ramirez and the *Angelena*.

When the boat's engine suddenly roared, I guessed he'd realized the potential danger and was backing rapidly to safety. Let the other fools hang around until the shark tired of the nuisance boats and flicked them and their passengers to kingdom come.

Judge of my horror when the *Angelena's* bow suddenly lifted under the torque and crashed down on the shark's back with all the impact of hitting wharf pilings. Bottles and plates crashed down in the galley, one of the beer coolers upset and the first mate scurried to right overturned bait buckets.

The dappled grey island didn't even quiver.

Ramirez threw the boat into reverse, then, and like déja vu I knew he was planning another run at the shark to jolt it into action. I was on the flying bridge long before he could reverse the boat's direction for another run. In my panic, my hands were around the poor man's scrawny neck. My screams of "No-no-no-no *muy pelligroso* (very dangerous!) -- SHARK," could probably have been heard on the mainland. Startled, Ramirez dropped the engine to idle; my hands left his neck and I apologized, explaining again that he had not been thumping his boat into a big fish, but a potentially very dangerous shark.

Ramirez looked sheepish, explained he had never seen one before and offered, "okay, let's go fishing, okay?"

He gave the shark an exaggeratedly wide berth as we headed north again to try our luck off Punta Mita which he still insisted was one of the most productive sailfish locales on the entire west coast of North America.

That claim may be well founded, but you can't prove it by me or Deac. Ramirez drove us up and down and back and forth, maintaining his raucous flow of invective-laced instructions to the mate whose eventual reaction was to clandestinely join Deac and me in decimating both stocks of iced *Corona.*

The alacrity with which we had earlier monitored the tips of the fishing rods, tensed for the inevitable strike, waned during the sultry afternoon, in a direct ratio to the stock of *Corona.*

The tip of my rod may have been bobbing for some time before I noticed it and finally reacted by striking. Something was on the line and a yell to Ramirez got the engine shut down. Deac clambered into his chair and began reeling in his line as we both speculated wildly about the length and weight of the trophy fish that had finally seized my bait.

The *Angelena* bobbed quietly on a gentle swell, slowly skewing at right angles to the distant smudge of shoreline under a travel poster sky whose merciless sun had turned Deac's face the colour of strawberry jam. The only sound within miles for a few moments was a tiny hiss as the mate surreptitiously eased the cap off another *Corona*, out of Ramirez' line of sight, tight against the cabin wall.

My trophy fish didn't make that fantastic, frantic lunge after I set the hook. The reel didn't scream that wonderful shriek as brute force ripped yards of monofilament off the spool, hard, enraged muscle overriding the drag. There was no heart-stopping display of tail-walking by a massive sailfish that would steal the show that night back at the marina.

The initial strike, in fact, had become more of a flutter. There was definitely something attached to the hook in addition to the bait, but it wasn't fighting back.

And then Deac and I spotted it simultaneously.

"Jesus Christ!" he yelled in mixed parts of astonishment, disgust and amusement. "You've hooked a Goddam pelican!"

Far off the port bow in smooth waters which had been astern

before Ramirez shut down the engine, we watched a continuing explosion of white spattering against the burnished brass surface of the gentle ocean swells.

The mate had seen it, too. He grudgingly stowed his sweaty *Corona* bottle out of Ramirez' sight and reached for my fishing rod. As he did so, the pelican rose a few metres in the air, but quickly dropped again to the water and resumed its thrashing. The mate hollered a string of words up to Ramirez. Moments later the boat's engine burst into life, the gears clashed and the *Angelena* began slowly backing towards the commotion staining the placid waters.

The mate reeled in the line and I was relieved to see how gently he did so because I adore pelicans and would never wish to see one harmed. It was obvious the mate shared my respect for these huge, comical, ungainly scavengers. I hoped the bird hadn't swallowed the bait; imagined horrible things about what might have to be done if it had.

The boat eased backwards, the mate carefully reeling in the slack. Perhaps fifty metres from the bird we could see it snapping its enormous bill up and down and from side to side. Again it tried to fly and this time rose half a dozen metres. We could see no trail of glistening monofilament hanging from its beak.

Thank God! The big bird was free and apparently unharmed.

The mate let out a triumphant cry and began reeling in the bait as quickly as his hand could crank the handle. We could see the bait skimming across the water's surface.

So could the pelican. It wheeled like a doomed helicopter in a war movie, crashing down onto the bait in a shower of spray. The mate's mouth opened wide, but he was too stunned to voice whatever exclamation had frozen on his tongue.

His hand froze on the reel. Ramirez slapped the boat's engine out of gear. Time froze, too. In complete silence.

Then we saw the pelican shake its mighty bill again. A moment later its huge wings hauled it aloft into its trademark clumsy flight. Mercifully the bird was again not trailing the fishing line.

The mate waited until the bird was a good distance away before he resumed slowly cranking the reel.

I cracked another *Corona* and carried it up to Ramirez on the flying bridge.

"Let's call it a day," I told him. "Let's go back to PV."

"But you must catch something," he insisted. "I promised you would catch something." There was pleading in his voice that suggested he'd been stiffed by other *gringos* who had held him to his guarantee of catching something, after he brought them back to port empty handed.

"We did catch something," I smiled at him, "and we'll pay you the full fare. It wasn't your fault we didn't catch a fish."

Back at the dock, Deac cheerfully ponied up his share of the charter fee.

"It's worth it," he managed after unsuccessfully attempting to stifle a 20-*Corona* belch. "It's worth it just to have my version next time you start telling one of your fish stories."

When you're certain, stay certain

Aswan
Egypt

An Egyptian vendor tried to sell me a lovely necklace of alexandrite. (That's the beryllium and aluminum oxide gem more properly known as chrysoberyl. It's always cloudy or opalescent and changes colour under different lights.)

The vendor claimed the necklace was a bargain at only $10 U.S., a claim I didn't dispute since an alexandrite necklace like the one he was waving in my face would easily fetch $150-$500 in any Cairo jewellery store.

I held his necklace up to the light. "This isn't alexandrite," I told him. "It isn't changing colour in the light."

"No, no, you've got that all wrong," the man protested. "If it *doesn't* change colour in the light it's real alexandrite. If it changes color, it's glass.

I didn't buy his "alexandrite" necklace and also passed on a beautiful amber necklace he offered with nuggets the size of acorns for which he only wanted $30 U.S. It, too, was a bargain. Real amber the size of those plastic replicas would have been worth $400-$500 or more.

Long, long road to Chibougamou

Chibougamou
Quebec, Canada

The young girl in the tourist information booth said most of it in her one-word answer to my question, "what is there to see and do in Chibougamou?"

"Fish?" she asked hopefully.

That wasn't quite the answer I had hoped for after driving 1,300 kilometres to get here. This town of 12,500 people is the most northerly point you can reach by road in Quebec without having to retrace your steps.

Had I asked the girl the same question a couple of months later her answer, I was told, would have been "hunt?"

Fortunately she was wrong. There are some things to do here. But there are more interesting things to see and do en route through northern Ontario and on your way home -- if you opt to make the circle tour from here to Chicoutimi, Tadoussac, Quebec City and Montreal.

While here you can stroll around a well laid-out town site with a wide main street. Almost every shop connects with its neighbour so you go into one to browse and keep on browsing until you're a long block away from where you started. This probably has something to do with winter when the average high and low temperatures in January are -12° and -24° Centigrade.

During your wanderings you'll come across St. Marcel Roman Catholic Church a block south of the town's main intersection. The architecture is unique, to say the least, but no explanation for it is available. "We call it the mother hen," two residents explained. "It looks like she's sitting on her eggs."

To get an overview of the town site and surrounding area you can hike to the top of a nearby mountain and climb a tower . . . but to get to the base of the tower you first have to hike 1.5 km through the woods . . . and the blackflies here are like winged piranha.

There's *Centre Indien cri* where you can buy Indian handicrafts. And that does it for Chibougamou unless you enjoy drinking beer out of quart bottles, playing pool or staying in your hotel room reading novels -- novels you brought with you, that is, because it isn't easy to find English-language novels here.

Yet that's another curious thing about this almost totally Francophone community. Every single person of the several dozen I addressed in French, responded in English though their first language obviously was French. And most conversations overheard around town were in English between people whose mother tongue was clearly French.

The loop from the Ontario border just west of Noranda-Rouyn through Chibougamou and down to Chicoutimi is paved and in fairly good shape except for some broken frost heaves. It's kilometre after kilometre through forests, mostly fir but with scatterings of poplar and birch. Occasionally you'll cross a river or brook of dark brown water, lakes and beaver ponds. But otherwise that highway just goes on and on and on, straight as a yardstick.

This is not a must-see excursion and it isn't a trip you're likely to repeat. But it's different enough that you'll remember it for a lifetime.

And after all, Chibougamou as a name to drop at a cocktail party has just the right sort of ring. It's right up there with Come-by-Chance, Kicking Horse Pass, Upper Musquodoboit, Dildo and St. Louis-de-Ha!-Ha! And, what are the odds that any of your friends have either heard of the place, or made the trip?

Travel tip: *The simpler things are . . .*

A plain, old safety pin used to keep your pocket closed will defy even the best of pickpockets. In some areas, the bit of nuisance it will cause you are moments well spent.

Husbands/wives whose spouses are compulsive shoppers could cajole their mates into safety-pinning their pockets while wandering shopping plazas and flea markets. The safety pin on the money pocket could serve the same sort of function as those humourous magnets that some weight-challenged people put on their refrigerator doors. If nothing else, the safety pin would slow down the number of monetary transactions!

Give some cabbies an inch . . . and they'll take you

Gambles
Antigua

Never, never, never leave your hotel selection to a taxi driver -- not anywhere, and particularly not in the Caribbean, South or Central America. If you wind up in a country or city without a reservation or the name of a recommended hotel, fake it! Ask for the Holiday Inn, the Hilton, the Marriott, the Best Western, or some other chain you know or have heard about. But don't ask the driver to take you to a good, or even the best, hotel in the city.

That's like giving a binge drinker the key to your liquor cabinet and leaving town for the weekend. The driver will pocket not only your fare and tip but also a hefty kickback from the Ma and Pa joint where he takes you . . . and you'll pay for that kickback, too.

Like most other travel tips I've learned this one the hard way. On one Caribbean trip I was "had" for three nights running. That's three nights with no bath, no air conditioning, no choice of dinner menu, no light bright enough to read under, the list goes on . . .

So I'm wary of all cab drivers everywhere . . . but the one who met my flight in Antigua got me and got me good! I was happy to find a cab because I was the only passenger disembarking from the long-delayed, inter-island flight that Sunday evening.

The airport is a few miles from St. John's, the capital, and just outside the airport the driver stopped at a gas station which was closed and pointed at the fuel gauge of his car which showed empty. The best he could do, he said, was to get me to St. John's best hotel . . . which turned out to be a motel at the end of an unlighted and unpaved side street in a suburb of the town.

There was no way he could get me the 20 or 25 kilometres to the posh resort hotels on the far side of the island I had requested. The motel owner said he couldn't raise another taxi by phone. He offered me an air conditioned room, a bar and dining room. It was late, the edge of a passing hurricane was drenching the island and I was exhausted. I paid the driver and he left.

The motel owner then told me he didn't accept credit cards and I had to fork over most of my remaining U.S. cash. There was no hot water for the bath I had lusted for all through that busy, sweaty day. There was no bath tub either -- just a cold shower.

I opted for the bar, which opened on my arrival. The bar stock consisted of a dozen dusty liquor and liqueur bottles and when I declined a drink the bar tender became the waitress and told me dinner was served -- immediately. She led me to the dining room where only one place was set in the entire room. Dinner, she said, would be chicken and rice, preceded by chicken soup.

There was no other choice . . . and that's when I dug my heels in. Antigua is known for its excellent West Indian cuisine and I was determined to salvage something from the evening. The motel owner couldn't -- or wouldn't -- call a taxi and it was still pouring rain, but my drip-dry suit needed cleaning anyway, so I walked.

The passing hurricane presented a bonus during the several miles I had to walk en route to the only restaurant I could find open in St. John's. The pleasantly warm downpour washed my suit, socks and underwear, and even laundered my few remaining dollars. Dinner was delightful -- spiny lobster and a salad washed down by some questionable brandy which had been on the shelf for so long the label was illegible.

Another bonus of the hurricane -- or tropical depression as they're called by Caribbean tourist boards -- was that all I had to move during dinner was my plate. I had chosen a fairly dry spot, but the handful of other diners kept changing tables to dodge new leaks.

* * * * * * *

A really heavy downpour woke me at 5 a.m. and being unable to get back to sleep I got up to do some writing. All went well until 5:30 when the lights and air conditioner went out, turning the tiny room into a sauna.

But I got that taxi driver! He drove out to that motel at 3 p.m. to take me to the airport for the 4:20 flight to Martinique. I had checked out at 8 a.m. and the driver who took me on a tour of the island, left me at the airport with a hefty tip in his pocket.

I just hope the taxi driver who went out to the motel to get me . . . ran out of gas on his way home.

Honouring the Thai water spirits

Khanchanaburi
Thailand

On the full moon of the 12th lunar month, every surface of water near the inhabited areas of Thailand twinkles with the reflection of burning candles floating on thousands of tiny rafts made of leaves.

The occasion is Loy Krathong and the explanations of the tradition's origins are as diverse as the event is popular. Loy means "to float" and krathong means "leaf cup." And not to float a krathong on full moon night here is like not hanging up a Christmas decoration in Canada in December or not having treats for the wee ghouls and goblins who make the rounds on Halloween Eve.

The traditional krathong is round, about the diameter of a pie tin and people make their own, or buy them from market stalls. Nowadays some are simply leaves attached to a thick, round styrofoam wafer. Others are huge and elaborate and fashioned from sturdier materials into the shapes of ships, pagodas, temples and palaces.

Whatever the size or shape, each krathong carries a lighted candle, a lighted stick of incense and a small coin as it is pushed gently from shore. If it floats out of sight from its launching place while candle and incense are still burning, the owner will have good fortune during the next year.

The most consistent explanation of the tradition is that the krathongs honour the water spirits and float away the sins of the year. Usually in November all the rivers and canals in Thailand's lowlands are flooded. The rainy season has ended and it is a time for rejoicing because the weather is fine after the rains.

Three months of dawn-to-dusk ploughing and planting rice is over and the farmers have only to wait a month or more for the reaping of the harvest. During this unpressured time most of the country's major feasts and festivals are held.

There didn't seem to be anyone here last month who was not involved in Loy Krathong. At the big tourist hotel in town the swimming pool was awash with krathongs and a pall of candle and incense smoke swirled on the still night air through the hundreds who had gathered to participate in the ceremony and watch a fashion show.

Old and young by the thousands walked to the banks of the Kwae-noi river after dusk, mostly in family groups. Each member of the family carried a krathong.

At the sandy riverbank some paused to kneel and pray before lighting the candle and incense stick. Others waded into the shallow, warm water to their knees to gently push their offering to the water spirits well away from shore, ensuring it would float away and take their sins with it.

There were larger krathongs, too. About a dozen of them, some the size of an old Cadillac and built to resemble ships and temples. It was explained that a prize would be awarded for the krathong judged to be the most beautiful.

As the evening wore on the river became an avenue of flickering candles as wave after wave of Thais came to the river to perpetuate one of their treasured traditions.

Vendors set up food and drink stalls and carts along the riverbank and gangs of youths tossed firecrackers . . . and empty beer bottles into the gutters.

The life of the krathong isn't very long. As it floats near shore away downstream, its candle burned out and incense stick burned away, small boys wade out to recover the coins. But any krathong which drifted back to shore with either candle or incense still burning, was gently pushed out into the river by the boys who did not touch the coin.

In the middle of the river, almost completely hidden by darkness and the clouds of candle and incense smoke, an ancient man in a black cape lurked in the shadows in a tiny dugout canoe. Every now and then a stray krathong would come his way.

He'd retrieve the coin from the tiny raft with a deftness that didn't appear to cause a ripple on the water.

Travel tip: ***Heaviest at the bottom . . .***

When packing a suitcase, place heavy items next to the suitcase hinges so they won't crush clothes when the case is turned upright.

Czech-mate

Ceske Velenice
Czechoslovakia

The kid pointing the machine gun at my left temple held his weapon with the steadiness of a surgeon's scalpel.

He couldn't have been a day over 17 and suffered badly from acne but his vividly-blue eyes were as unblinking as those of a fish. They held the same degree of warmth and compassion. Behind the black canyon of the gun barrel I could see his finger on the trigger. It had been chewed clean of most of the nail and cuticle.

Warm sun streamed from between greyish clouds and something that sounded like a cicada was doing a solo number with a repertoire of only three notes high in a nearby pine tree.

What was intense personal drama for me was likely routine for the Czechoslovakian border guard. It lasted perhaps a minute, but it was long enough for me to compose the first two paragraphs of a hometown newspaper obituary. And it was long enough to ascertain that my every sweat gland was in perfect working order.

During that minute everything froze but the cicada. My outstretched fingers – four inches from the convertible's ignition key – were the steadiest they've ever been before or since.

The guard didn't have to explain further that he didn't want me to start the car. When his gun was finally lowered I sank back in the bucket seat – soggily.

It was a lovely September afternoon and we were meandering the secondary roads of southern Czechoslovakia hoping to eventually reach Innsbruck, Austria, having learned from a friendly policeman in Prague that our visas allowed us to wander off main routes.

We knew the border was close, but hadn't expected it to be around a sharp bend and unannounced by warning signs. The Italian sports car with heavy house trailer in tow only just stopped short of the wooden barricade at the clearing in the forest.

The barricade was a long city block away from the actual customs checkpoint, a low modern building between the north- and southbound lanes. Between the barricade and the customs building was the no-man's-land so familiar to Iron Curtain country residents:

the snarls of barbed wire, the jumbled anti-tank devices and the mine fields neatly raked like sand traps at a posh golf club.

We'd waited at the barricade for about ten minutes. At the customs building the occupants of an Austria-bound bus were being cleared one by one. Half a dozen border guards materialized individually from the surrounding forest. The cicada and the scrunch of their heavy boots on the gravelled pathway were the only sounds.

As a deliberate gesture of pride in the capitalistic system I'd waxed the Kodak-yellow sports car two days earlier in Berlin. It glittered now like an expensive toy and I regretted that arrogance as we fidgeted in the sun under the baleful glare of the young guards.

The baby blue and white house trailer -- tiny even by European standards -- was larger than any we saw behind the Iron Curtain and it was being stared at, too. Not with interest, envy or awe, but with unmitigated disgust, loathing and contempt which the guards made no attempt to disguise.

None was even interested or amused by our caricature of a dog, Tarzan, who had been awakened by the sudden stop and was peering myopically and quizzically over the side of the car from his rat's nest in the back seat.

The guards were all young and lean and looked very bored. Most had bad postures and worse complexions. They were as handy with their ungainly machine guns as majorettes with batons and several were able to twirl them as dextrously, always catching them with the finger in striking distance of the trigger.

Their drab olive uniforms were unpressed but clean and their black boots glistened even through the patina of dust raised by incessant patrols along the narrow, gravelled paths.

A guard near the small sentry box raised his arm in a signal I believed was directed at us and it was then that I reached for the ignition key. The kid nearest the car had been twirling his machine gun but he had it aimed at my head before my hand reached the key.

The customs officer we drew was a pretty young lady who seemed to enjoy her work and brought to it a sense of humour. We managed to joke with her as she peremptorily shuffled through the car's trunk and the house trailer.

The lady's search appeared directed at books, magazines, newspapers and Czechoslovakian currency which is not permitted to be taken out of the country. We could never figure out who would want to smuggle Czech currency out of the country. You can buy it in some Berlin banks for a fraction of its face value.

The search took less than ten minutes and ended with smiles and handshakes all round and a pat on the head for Tarzan who had won the lady's heart.

It was several more miles to the Austrian frontier and no country's border had ever seemed more welcome. Perhaps it was reaction from the machine gun incident -- though we'd had plenty of those pointed at us in East Germany, too -- but the Austrian border guard seemed to be the most friendly, considerate and helpful official we'd ever encountered. He was tall, rugged, bronzed by the sun and as handsome as a dinner jacket model.

He understood German and some French and found an itch under one of Tarzan's floppy ears which made them fast friends.

The Austrian border guard apologized for the inconvenience, but asked us both to get out of the car and follow him to a foam rubber mat about two feet square which had been soaked with some sort of disinfectant.

We were to stand on this, he explained, in order to disinfect our feet before entering Austria. And there was a section of roadway in front of the car across which disinfectant-soaked sawdust was neatly raked, to clean the tires.

No, we needn't bother disinfecting other shoes we had worn in Czechoslovakia and Tarzan didn't have to stand on the disinfectant.

We could only conclude the entire operation was a tacit political comment by the Austrian government about its Communist neighbours. Whether it was, or not, nothing ever felt more welcome beneath our feet than Austria's foam rubber "welcome mat."

Travel tip: *A reminder - just to remind you*

When you check into a hotel room where you have been advised the water isn't safe for drinking, or even brushing your teeth, wrap a bit of masking tape or a Band-aid around the sink faucets.

We're creatures of habit and no matter how good your initial intentions to remember not to use the water you're likely to have a memory lapse or just use the water without thinking. The tape or Band-aid will instantly remind you.

When they get a cuppla drinks Glasgow *does* belong to them

Glasgow
Scotland

There was last fall's Western University Homecoming football game and post-game revelry; there was the Munich Beerfest; the Running of the Bulls at Pamplona and the Great Casa No No Beer Drinking Competition in Andorra.

But those paled to the level of the kind of sobriety experienced at the annual church choir picnic when contrasted with that Saturday night in Glasgow. It wasn't any special occasion. Just an ordinary Saturday night in Glasgow and, according to Glaswegians, the level of activity was "just normal."

I was transcribing notes of an interview from hieroglyphics to legibility in a second-floor room of the Royal Hotel when it started shortly after 11 p.m.

" . . . But when I have a cuppla drinks on a saddidy, Glasgae belongs to me . . ." The singing was raucous and slurred but the familiar refrain was unmistakable.

I parted the window drapes and looked across the intersection of Sauchiehall (pronounced Suckey-hall) and Hope streets. The male quintet had arms linked around each others' shoulders and was making slow progress. A few lurching steps forward, a joint stagger to the left until the end of the line bumped against a storefront and sometimes a couple of lurches backwards, before another to the right.

But they never lost the beat of one of the drinking mans' favourite songs. They ran through the verse half a dozen times -- and paused for a brief scuffle between two of their number -- before they passed out of earshot up Hope Street.

Long before they were out of sight four girls came stumbling down Sauchiehall Street arguing loudly over ownership of a "bloke" at the disco where they had been drinking.

Opposite my window one of them shoved another into the doorway of a store where she sat on the pavement and stared glassily up at my window. I waved. But she apparently couldn't focus that far. She remained there for half an hour before wobbling off in the direction from which she had come.

By 11:30 torrents of men and women flowed north on Hope Street and east on Sauchiehall. They came in pairs, threes and fours, in all-male, mixed and all-female groups. I stared in vain for one pedestrian who walked without weaving, hiccoughing, staggering or occasionally tumbling to the street or sidewalk.

I was an island of sobriety in a sea of celebratory intemperance.

Despite the damp cold, I opened the double window full and sat on the windowsill, marvelling at the exodus from the nightclubs, discotheques and pubs of the district.

It was like watching ants escape from a hill flooded with moonshine.

Without exception the men were dressed in their finest; the girls and women were carefully coiffed and their faces reflected painstaking make-up preparations for the big evening.

But they all looked as though they were coming from a big wedding reception where somebody had spiked the punch.

Another group of four lurched past under my window arguing about the punch line of a joke that had amused them. Without warning one of the lads suddenly took a wild swing at the jaw of another, missed and sat down heavily on the sidewalk overturning a dustbin into Sauchiehall Street.

His companions didn't seem to notice he was no longer with them and carried their argument around the corner.

The would-be pugilist picked himself up and weaved across the street to a group of girls who were chattering busily and dribbling an empty beer tin down the sidewalk.

At times the pedestrians surged in waves along Sauchiehall, spilling off both sidewalks and blocking the roadway. The occasional car or lorry honked its horn for clearance but inevitably had to squeal to a stop and wait, engine roaring and horn hooting, for an opening through the crowd.

There were four-way traffic lights at the intersection but only motorists seemed to notice them. Pedestrians who escaped death or injury at the expense of motorists' tires jeered the drivers and laughed uproariously at their close shaves.

One purple-faced motorist whose companion bumped her head on the windscreen yelled an obscenity at the youth who had stumbled in front of his car. The lad's friends circled the heavy Jaguar and began rocking it from side to side.

The motorist clashed gears and spun his tires on the pavement making good his escape.

Some of the revellers had apparently smuggled bottles of liquor and tins of beer into the nightspots and the contents had been drained en route home. The chorus of hoots, songs and yells was accompanied by the clatter and tinkle of empty cans and bottles kicked along the sidewalks and roadways. Every so often somebody would throw an empty bottle against a stone or brick wall and the smash would be loudly cheered.

The first police didn't show until just after midnight by which time the pedestrian flood had slowed to a trickle. The two officers cruised their Land Rover at walking pace along the street.

Two men were sharing a tin of beer in front of a lighted window. The Land Rover purred past, its occupants ignoring the man who teetered on his heels as he drained the can. The empty can flung down the street just missed its target – the police vehicle.

The next day while discussing his hotel's security system with the manager, he explained the role police play in Glasgow on Saturday nights. "They more or less hide from the time the bars close until about midnight," he said. "They only come out if a lot of windows are being broken, or something like that. They give everybody a chance to get home and then they round up the stragglers. It's everybody's big night out and they make the most of it. The police don't want to arrest anybody just because he's had a bit too much to drink."

At 12:15 two more officers came down the street in a Rover car. They drove slowly past two girls who were walking down the street with the deliberate and exaggerated concentration of drunks climbing a steep stairway.

The Land Rover came past again at 12:45 by which time only a dozen people were in the areas of the streets I could overlook from my perch.

Three of them were pretty girls passing 'round a large bottle of what appeared to be gin. They had established themselves at the hotel's front door and were quietly singing old-favourite songs, slightly off-key.

One of them had looked up and noticed the appreciative audience of one.

"Will you no come down and have a nip . . . and bring some orange juice?" she invited. The coffee in the room hadn't been that good and the idea of a nightcap had appeal; after all, it seemed *de rigeur* in Glasgow on a Saturday night.

I said I'd be down, bought some orange drinks from the dispenser in the hallway and went to the front door. The girls cheered when they saw the bottles in my hand.

But the front door was locked and my room key wouldn't fit the lock. The manager either didn't hear the bell I pounded on the reception desk, or didn't want to respond to it.

The girls soon tired of waiting and sang their way off down the street.

I retired to my room, thought about the super-cute girl outside the locked door with the gamine face, blonde bangs and unbelievable figure . . . and miserably choked down a nightcap of orange juice – straight.

Travel tips: *If you really have to take it with you . . .*

If you must travel with expensive, or expensive-looking jewellery there are some precautions you can take in addition to discussing floater insurance with your agent.

- Never pack jewellery in luggage that's going to be checked. Carry it in your hand luggage. If your jewellery won't fit into your purse because its already overloaded put the contents of your purse and your jewellery in a tote, or flight bag. That way you'll only have one item to carry -- which is all that most airlines allow -- and there should still be room in that tote for those last-minute items you acquire en route to and from your destination.
- If you're wearing an expensive necklace to or from some special function, hide it under a scarf until you reach the place where you want to show it off.
- With flashy rings, keep the eye-catching setting turned to the inside of your hand until you're where you want people to notice it.
- When you're checking in at your hotel or cruise ship take advantage of the facilities both have for jewellery, extra cash or travellers cheques.
- Whatever cash you carry with you should be spread around -- small amounts in a number of pockets.

Pride goeth before a fall

Soldeu
Co-Principality of Andorra

People can make the damnedest offers in the dying hours of a cocktail party that has gone on for too long; the damnedest people can remember and take advantage of those offers.

So it was that three bright-eyed young ladies pounded unkindly loud on my door at 8 a.m. that Saturday announcing they were ready for their ski lesson.

They were quite right . . . it was a beautiful day and a fresh fall of snow overnight would have provided a day of powder thrills on the little-used mountain pistes.

Helen, Alice and Ruth were not to be denied their ski lessons. “I wouldnae ha’ kum but yae insisted,” Helen gurgled in a brogue that would baffle most Glaswegians.

Ruth, a South African, was more to the point. “I won’t hold you up long. I don’t want lessons, just want a photo of me on skiis.”

Alice, a soft-spoken Scot more easily understood than Helen, was the last to explain her participation, but had a more ominous message. “If you can have me skiing as well as the best of them in a week I reckon I’d be daft to no take you up on the free lessons,” she said. “The instructors told me it would take them two or three weeks,” she added, a cheeky challenge twinkling in her brown eyes. I recalled she had been the last party attendee offered lessons.

We drove to the ski equipment rental shop at the foot of the mountain that towered 3,000 feet above. “Ach, I’m no gonna ski doon thot,” Helen stated flatly, settling deeper into the back seat of the car with every indication that only wild horses might move her.

“D’you think I’ll be able to handle that by the end of next week?” Alice asked impishly.

We were outfitted and near the Poma lift by 11:30 waiting for Helen who had left the shop with us but was having difficulty walking in ski boots. “The damn soles dinnae baind,” she lamented, collapsing into the snow with a clatter of poles and skiis.

Alice had her skiis on -- correctly -- before any of us. I could see I was going to have trouble with her.

Ruth insisted she didn't want her bindings adjusted. She just wanted to stand on the skis to be photographed. We decided to complete her program first. Each time the photographer was ready and told her to smile, she fell down and had to be hauled upright again and dusted off. At last we got the photograph. "Thank you," Ruth said. "I'll be in that bar over there whenever you finish your lessons."

Alice supported Helen while I got Helen's boots clamped into the downhill bindings. When she found her heels were held to the skis she panicked and fell again with shrill screeches.

The ski lesson progressed to step two, walking on skis. Alice managed that handily. Helen remained in the same spot. Standing up was a full time job for the time being, she said. Why didn't I take Alice up the hill for a wee run and then come back for her?

Alice herringboned with ease up the slope to the bottom of the beginner's Poma lift. I explained how it worked and went behind her. She was a bit wobbly, but made it to the top. We snow-plowed slowly down without mishap, Alice learning rapidly how a shift of weight altered direction. She had total control by the end of the run and slithered gracefully to a stop at the end of the lift queue.

She announced she wanted to make a solo run while I looked after Helen who was exactly where we had left her. She had mastered the balance problem and was working on walking. She'd obviously been at it for some time. The snow under her skis had turned to ice as the skis slipped forward and back. One step forward . . . the same step back as the other ski moved forward.

"Ach," she raged in disgust, "some blighter has put slippy stuff on these skis. I cannae move ahaid." Skiers know there's a weight shift that allows one to walk straight ahead on skis, even uphill over ice -- or you can just skate with them. But Helen just couldn't get the feel of that. Any attempt at herringbone resulted in crossed skis and another tumble.

She promised to be at the lift by the time I made another run with Alice who was there when I hiked back up. She'd fallen once, she said, but knew what she had done wrong. She now wanted to get into stem turns on a steeper hill. We took the next Poma lift higher up.

Damned if she didn't fall into a natural, easy rhythm after only a few tries. Not a polished style, but her legs were strong and picked up that essential timing and swing.

Helen was where I had left her, muttering that she'd rent some "less slippy" skis next time.

After lunch we put Helen back where she had spent the morning. She couldn't go downhill until she was able to get uphill, I explained.

Alice wanted to make a run from the top. Slowly and in stages, she said, but she felt confident and in control.

I'd ski down a couple of hundred feet, stop and watch her follow my trail. She could thus be given pointers all the way down. For an alleged beginner, Alice was astonishingly good. A natural. She needed only practice and polish. I'd run out of pointers for her halfway down and decided to have at least one good run for the day.

I learned to ski in Quebec and used to race in downhill competition. My idea of fun skiing is to spend as much time in the air as possible. To hell with style or staying in tight control by making a lot of check turns.

It was exhilarating to be free for the last half of the run. I got about eight metres out of the first mogul, turned left and hit another for 10 metres. I cut to the right and there was a super one, good for about 15 metres . . . but the area I'd picked to land came up bad, a field of short, sharp moguls. When you're in the air you can't speed up, slow down or turn more than a few degrees. Every now and then when you ski the way I do you don't plan far enough ahead -- like right now. The old look-before-you-leap thing. That's why most ski centres usually have doctors on staff.

My right ski shattered a foot back from the tip when it slammed into the sharp, icy edge of the mogul and the jagged end was imbedded in the next mogul before I could raise it. The somersaults were too fast to count.

"Are you OK?" It was Alice, trying hard not to laugh in case there were a lot of broken bones. She looked down at the tangle of equipment and the blood running into one eye from a scalp nicked by a steel edge.

I finally made it to the bottom on one good leg and ski. Helen, Ruth and Alice helped me into the car and to the *clinica* for x-rays.

"Don't worry about us," Alice said considerately as she helped me organize the crutches to leave the apartment elevator. "I can get ski lessons from Norrie until your leg is better, and Helen has decided she doesn't like skiing anyway."

Feliz Navidad is a way of life

Taxco
Mexico

We were all feeling a little homesick that Christmas Eve in Taxco, Mexico; delighted to be there, but missing the traditional trappings most North Americans associate with that greatest of celebrations.

We'd dined lavishly at the hotel, danced to a peppy band on the outside terrace and, reluctant to leave the balmy night air, the two sisters and I were strolling a dimly-lighted cobblestone street down in the old village.

Taxco (pronounced Tass-co) is in south-central Mexico, almost 6,000 feet above sea level in the Sierra de Taxco mountains. It's an ancient silver-mining centre, founded in the 1500s, and a popular stop for tourists motoring between Mexico City and Acapulco.

The twin spires of the baroque Santa Prisca church loomed above us, silhouetted by a part moon. At midnight, we had been told, its bells and those of all the churches would peal in tribute to the anniversary of the birthday of Jesus Christ.

And in homes throughout the country the oldest child would break open the piñata, a star-shaped papier-mâché decoration filled with fruit, nuts and candy.

The buzz of the drinks from the dance floor bar wore off on the hike to the village. Each of us was lost in private thoughts; Christmas-type thoughts in my case, of relatives and loved ones back home in Canada. None of us had spoken a word for several blocks. The street was dimly lighted, if at all, and a cloud had obscured the moon.

We heard footsteps coming up behind us, fast. The sister's hand I was holding, tensed.

I turned, uncertain, to see who was overtaking us.

Panting up the cobblestone street was a boy, perhaps ten years old, and a younger girl. They slowed as I turned, unsettled by finding strangers on their street. The boy examined us carefully and then his face broke into a bold smile.

"Feliz navidad," he said, and his companion, prompted by a yank on her arm, shyly murmured the same words. I recalled the words meant Happy Christmas in Spanish, and returned the greeting. Interrupting my thoughts as it had, the youngster's greeting was particularly poignant.

I'd been jingling some unfamiliar Mexican coins in my pocket as we strolled, and quickly calculated their worth: perhaps fifty cents.

It couldn't be an ugly tourist gesture, I reasoned, to offer these coins -- which would otherwise be left as a bartender's tip -- to the youngsters.

"Amigo," I called as the pair began leaving, "Feliz Navidad." I held out my hand and clinked the coins.

The youngsters hesitated but wouldn't come any closer. I moved slowly to them and gave each a few coins.

Both were wide-eyed as they examined their bonanza which -- so far as they could tell -- had no strings attached. Each said something along the lines of "graçias, señor."

Then the girl cupped her hands to the boy's ear and whispered something. He replied, nodding his head in excited agreement, walked over and took my hand. He started to lead me down the street.

The sisters, clearly ill at ease, tagged along. The boy, who conveyed that his name was Carlos, and his sister, Maria, led us several blocks through the maze of the old village.

Outside a doorway in a communal wall, Carlos indicated we should wait. Maria was given instructions which seemed to be that she make us stay put.

Carlos disappeared through the doorway and we heard him speaking rapidly. He ducked back outside and grabbed my hand again. I followed him inside.

Carlos' home consisted of one room about 20 feet square. When Maria and the two sisters also crowded in, it shrank alarmingly.

The room was lighted by a single flickering electric bulb in the far corner which might have provided 20 watts. Even coming from the darkened street it took a few moments for my eyes to adjust and take in the details and occupants of the room.

Carlos rattled off a speech of introduction during which he displayed the coins I had given him and concluded it by solemnly introducing each member of his family.

There was mother, father, grandmother, grandfather and what could have been -- by virtue of her wizened features -- great-grandmother. Several younger brothers or sisters were asleep on a mattress of sorts in the far corner.

Carlos' parents and grandparents sat on wooden stools. They were admiring what Carlos and Maria had brought us to see.

The nativity scene occupied about one third of the room. The figures of the wise men, Mary, Joseph and the Holy Child had been crudely but painstakingly fashioned from papier-mâché and painted with water colours.

The animals in the manger were ingeniously crafted of straw tied with string. Brown-eyed Baby Jesus lay in a nest of cotton batting in the straw.

I thought of the mass-produced nativity scenes with china figurines sold in North American stores for more money than this family would see in a whole year . . . and of the time and care taken by Carlos' family to set up this display.

Carlos pointed proudly to a lamb made of straw and cotton wool, and not to be outdone, Maria hesitantly pointed to another. These must have been the children's contribution for they weren't as skilfully crafted as the other animals. But that didn't diminish the glow of pride on the children's faces. Each had assisted in the presentation.

We admired the display and complimented the children with a verbal patchwork of hastily-recalled Spanish words and many gesticulations.

After a few minutes we shook hands all around again, wished each other yet another Feliz Navidad and exchanged thanks -- Carlos' family for the coins; we for a never-to-be-forgotten experience.

And then we walked silently back to our North American-style hotel where the lobby reverberated with recorded Christmas music and the sound of ice cubes against crystal, and glittered with coloured lights and garish tinsel.

Travel Tip: *The fake stuff is just as dangerous*

Using paste imitations of expensive jewellery while travelling isn't very smart. Any person desperate enough to kill, maim or just risk a jail term for robbery, isn't likely to know at a glance the difference between the real thing and an imitation.

The ladies lusted for local culture

Bridgetown
Barbados

Loneliness is probably the biggest bugbear of the professional travel writer on assignment. You're constantly surrounded by happy holidaying groups or business people talking shop, but your conversations are usually limited to terse exchanges with airline clerks, taxi drivers and bartenders.

And though the job often involves sampling the fare of some of the world's most exotic or interesting restaurants, conversational opportunities are frequently restricted to shamelessly eavesdropping on the nearest -- or loudest -- table, unless you care to chat with yourself. It can reduce some of the finest cuisine to just another boring evening.

So when the ebullient manager of a Caribbean resort hotel asked me with a wide grin just before dinner on my second night there how I was enjoying my stay, I decided to tell her:

"The place is great; my room is super . . . but I haven't found anyone to talk to. Everybody here is in couples and they all seem to be honeymooning."

"Nonsense, honey!" the jolly lady cried, leaping from her chair. "We gots lotsa singles here. You come with me . . ." and I was marched into the dining room and propelled across it to a corner table shared by two young ladies who appeared to be in their late twenties.

"D'is han'some man (her precise words) all alone from Canada say we got no singles peoples here," my mentor boomed so none of the other diners would have to strain to hear. "Where you girls been hidin' on him?" Without pausing for a reply she intro-duced Helga from Norway and Inge from Germany.

"See, honey," the manager trumpeted, "we gots lotsa singles." She paraded out of the room leaving me in her wake, standing by the girls' table with the pleased-to-meet-you grin frozen on my reddening face.

Helga, bless her, headed off what probably would have been a very long silence by inviting me to join them for dinner, and pouring me a glass of wine.

Neither girl could ever be accused of being gorgeous, but both were pleasant and spoke quite good English. And conversation was what it was all about anyway. The advertised special that night was roast beef, so I looked forward to a pleasant hour or so with the girls before making my solitary inspection rounds of nearby hotels and night spots.

The maître d' bustled up with silverware and set the third place. "Yes, sir?" he asked, pencil poised over an order pad.

"The roast beef, please, as rare as possible."

"I'm sorry sir; there isn't any."

Dinner was served from 7 p.m. to 10 p.m. It was now 8 p.m.

"Ok, a steak please, very rare."

"No steak sir."

In desperation: "A sandwich . . . a hot dog . . . hamburger?"

"Sorry sir. We have no food at all."

"A basket of bread? . . . an omelette?"

"Sorry." I wondered why he had bothered with the cutlery, pencil and order pad.

"You can share our bread," Inge offered, glaring at the maître d'.

I ordered more wine to repay the girls' kindness and munched on a bread crust as we chatted about Norway and Germany and the Caribbean. We were serenaded by the hotel's three-piece reggae band and every so often bombarded by the amplified shrieks of a female vocalist who will never be a singer.

Helga had been here four weeks and was going home the next day; Inge had been here two weeks and would stay for two more. It was Helga's fourth trip and the girls had met two years before on Inge's first visit.

"Why come all the way here for a summer vacation when your own country or others in Scandinavia are so beautiful at this time of year?" I asked Helga. "Or if you want sun and sand, why not Spain or Greece . . . so much closer and less expensive?"

"Yes, it's expensive to come here," Helga said thoughtfully, "but I live all year for my month here. It was about five years ago when I first heard reggae music. Now I play it all the time at home and I save all year for my month here."

Helga's face came alive as she spoke of the island's culture, history, golden beaches, warm evenings cooled by the trade winds, but above all the culture and reggae music. Almost drowning out her rhapsody was the vocalist who sounded as though she and her microphone had been hurled into a cactus hedge.

Inge's dark eyes flashed as she sailed into a pitch for the island which would have done any encyclopaedia salesperson proud. She was hooked on the reggae music in the discotheques, the total freedom of the country, the genuine warmth of the people and the superb West Indian cuisine, available nowhere else, she said.

I reached for the last crust of bread. "Yes," I agreed, "the local cuisine is superb." The vocalist was still bleeding to a noisy death in the cactus.

Inge was still chattering about island culture when Helga's face suddenly became illuminated. She leaned towards me slightly and said in the most sultry voice I've ever heard off the silver screen: "David, darling. I was afraid you weren't going to come, lover . . . and it's my last night here . . ." Her lips parted, inviting a kiss.

I was still choking on that damn bread crust minutes after the man who had walked soundlessly up behind me had accepted Helga's kiss and sat in the fourth chair at the table.

"David -- isn't it fun having two Davids at the same table?" Inge observed, was one of the biggest men I had seen in some time. He was built like a water buffalo; muscles rippled like conger eels under his skin-tight T-shirt.

His smile was the keyboard of a black baby grand piano and the gentle hand he offered me could have hidden and then crushed a football.

"Where were you lover?" Helga asked.

"Roun'," David said.

Helga reached across the table for David's hand and her eyes glazed over when it disappeared in his fist.

I began to feel like an older brother tagging along on his sister's wedding night.

Inge and I tried to nurse along a conversation but it was heavy going through the electric field between us created by Helga and David. The girls had finished their meal. The wine bottle and the bread basket were empty. I felt quite unnecessary and suspected Inge might be uncomfortable, too. I asked her if she'd like a liqueur at the nearby bar.

Helga laughed gaily. "She's got a guy, too," she told me. "The four of us are going to a disco. Why don't you join us?"

"Huh?" David grunted as Helga mentioned the disco.

"Well, darling, I don't want to go to bed right this minute," Helga explained to David. "Maybe around 10?"

"You de boss," David said sulkily.

Inge's guy came along then. He wasn't quite as massive as David, but looked as though he could hoist the front end of a Buick off the ground with one arm. Only his teeth and the whites of his eyes showed in the gloom of our corner of the dining room. It was Inge's turn to stare with the kind of gaze lottery winners must lavish on their million-dollar cheques.

"Right on, man," David said as I excused myself. "Cool, baby," added Andrew.

Helga and Inge didn't see me leave.

They were too entranced with the culture of the Caribbean island which had drawn them here from their distant homelands.

Travel tips: *Before leaving home*...

- Let a neighbour know the dates you'll be away so he can keep an eye on things for you. If he's a good neighbour he'll also water the plants and feed the goldfish.
- Make certain that neighbour, or somebody else, will gather up all your junk mail from porch, driveway and in between your doors. Junk mail lying around an otherwise well-kept property is an invitation to cruising thieves.
- Notify your newspaper carrier (and the post office if it's a long trip). You'll save paying for a paper you aren't going to read and Canada Post will hold your mail for you for your return.
- Check the expiration dates of insurance policies. While you're at it make sure your householder's insurance policy covers lost luggage and theft or loss of specific valuable items you will be taking with you. Some insurance companies may refuse claims for things like damage from leaking water pipes if someone has not checked on your premises at least once every 48 hours during your absence.
- If you'll be away in winter, make arrangements for someone to shovel your walkway and driveway. That clean, white blanket with no footprints 24 hours after a snowfall is a dead giveaway to the enterprising house-breaker.
- If you'll be away in summer, make arrangements for someone to keep your lawn cut, for the same reasons as above.

Mudder-in-law doors reflect lifestyle

Dildo
Newfoundland, Canada

It doesn't take long for the visitor to Newfoundland to discover that there's little artificiality in the makeup of Newfound-landers or their province. Things are pretty basic and usually exactly what they seem to be since the way of life here traditionally has been a struggle for survival with little time or energy left over for frills.

One of the more obvious examples of practicality taking precedence over convention or nicety, is Newfoundland's mother-in-law doors (usually pronounced mudder-in-law). In some parts of the province it seems that every second house has one. Mother-in-law doors are usually the front door of a house and there are no steps leading from the door sill to the ground. Since many homes are built on steep hillsides it's not unusual to see drops of three metres or more from door sill to the ground.

The doors get their name at the expense of mothers-in-law who are often not in favour with their sons- or daughters-in-law. The implication is that unpopular mothers-in-law are invited out the front door where -- in Newfoundland -- they'd fall a few metres onto the driveway, if there is one.

The reason so many homes have mother-in-law doors is that in Newfoundland everybody enters houses by the back door. Since nobody uses the front doors, there's no need for steps from the ground to the front door and the detail of building the steps is one of those things many Newfoundlanders never seem to get around to.

The dedicated mother-in-law door spotter can find examples even on homes a century old. What nobody is able to explain, however, is why Newfoundlanders go to the expense and inconvenience of incorporating front doors into their building plans in the first place since most accept that it's a feature of the house that will never be used.

Frequent travellers don't have to watch soap operas

Miami
Florida, U.S.A.

Part of being an effective travel writer is being an effective eavesdropper in public places. When you're eating alone at a restaurant in or near a major amusement theme park, for example, you try to get seated near the couple with the two children aged 6-10, whether or not you enjoy the proximity of children.

Chances are good those kids have taken at least some of the rides offered and who can best handicap those rides but the age group for whom they were designed?

So it was probably a reflex reaction that turned on one ear in the airport cafeteria here.

It was a table with three places on each side and the waiter seated me at one end of the table. In the middle place on the opposite side, a tired-looking blonde lady in her very late 30s was busy with a hamburger.

A younger blonde dragged herself to the table and slouched in another chair at about the time my sandwich and iced tea was served.

I ignored both blondes and attacked the sandwich which at 2 p.m. was breakfast.

Suddenly there was a conversation explosion.

The blondes didn't even know each others' names, but seconds after one of them had broken the ice by asking the other to please pass the salt, they were swapping deeply personal experiences.

They were the sort of intimate things one confides to a friend of long standing, or after many sessions during which trust has been established, with a marriage counsellor or psychiatrist.

Perhaps because the circumstances of their lives were so similar, the case histories poured out unchecked. Both blondes had just given their common law partners of some years' standing their walking papers.

The older blonde could no longer put up with her companion's infidelities and the transparent lies he told to cover his whereabouts when he should have been with her. She was going to stay with a lady friend in the Los Angeles area and perhaps make a new start somewhere in California.

The younger blonde's former companion used to hit her when he had been drinking and in recent months he had apparently been drinking quite often. "I put up with it for a long time because I thought I loved him," she confided to all within earshot, "but he put me in the hospital twice. The last time I was in there for three days. He's always sorry -- afterwards -- but that didn't stop him from doing it a couple of weeks later when he had another skinful."

I had another five hours to kill and the public waiting rooms were wall-to-wall shrieking children, so I ordered another iced tea.

The exchange of deeply personal experiences flowed on.

How strange is the human being, I mused. Neither blonde had likely ever been as frank with the lover she had just left as she now was being with a total stranger. Each was ridding herself of the painful memories, justifying getting on the aircraft that would take her to a new beginning far from Florida where she had experienced despair, disappointment, anger, frustration, humiliation . . .

"Well, gotta get my flight!" the younger blonde announced while the older blonde was still in mid-sentence. "See ya around." She strode to the cashier's station with her head held high, a bounce in her step. A few minutes later the older blonde left to catch her flight to California.

I was left to ponder: if more people travelled and experienced random encounters as had the two blondes, would our society have any need of psychiatrists? Would suicide statistics wane? Would battered wives continue to allow themselves to be battered?

Would anyone ever again feel the need to watch a soap opera?

Travel tip: *Please pass the vinegar*

If you enjoy vinegar on your French fries and will be travelling outside Canada, make sure you have a handful of those little packets of vinegar from one of the fast-food restaurants stashed in your flight bag. Many other countries offer great French fries, but even in the U.S. it's often impossible to find white vinegar in a restaurant.

Malta's laws were made to be broken

Valetta
Malta

The authorities had set up a small counter at Malta's only airport just ahead of the immigration and customs counter where a tired old man checked passports to locate the incoming travellers' ports of origin.

Wendy and I were the only passengers on the flight from Rome whose journey had originated in Spain where the annual cholera outbreak was being parleyed by news-starved European newspaper editors into a full-scale re-run of the Bubonic Plague.

The health inspector was polite, but firm. Nobody arriving from Spain or nearby North Africa was allowed into Malta because he might bring with him the dreaded cholera. The inspector didn't know why nobody had told us this in Barcelona or Rome. They should have known, he said, because there were the instructions right on his desk!

He paged the people meeting us and our English friend flew into one of his predictable tantrums, loudly damning each member of Malta's parliament by name.

It wasn't long before the head of immigration was involved and explaining the rules to the man at the health inspection desk. The rules, it seemed, stated persons arriving at Malta would be permitted entry provided they passed a daily inspection by a local doctor. There was no charge for this government-financed inspection.

The inspector admitted he hadn't read the rules, assuming they'd be the same as they had been several years before when some other epidemic was sweeping North Africa.

The immigration chief handed us a printed list of every doctor within the 122-square-mile archipelago. There were about 50 names and for some reason no doctor held office hours later than 8:30 a.m.

We protested that visiting a doctor before 8:30 a.m. each morning was no way to enjoy a vacation. The immigration officer reminded us an alternative existed: a stiff fine should we fail to comply with the law.

Malta is an independent parliamentary state at the east end of the Mediterranean Sea, 58 miles south of Sicily, 220 miles north of Libya and 180 miles east of Tunisia. The 322,000 Maltese gained their independence from Britain in 1964 and in some quarters hard feelings remain from the years of British rule.

We'd heard some not-too-nice stories (which may have been merely anti-Malta propaganda) about Brits who had been held on the island against their wishes. One concerned a woman whose name was identical to another who owed money to a Maltese and refused to pay. The innocent woman was held until her name-sake eventually paid.

Another was a tourist who rented a fully-insured automobile that was wrecked in a crash caused by a drunk Maltese who ran a stop sign. Nevertheless, an "impedimenta" kept the tourist on the island for months until traffic court convened, by which time he had lost his job in England and owed hundreds of pounds for hotel bills.

Our friends were staying at Mellieha Bay on the north end of the main island about 15 miles from Valetta, the capital. A combination of time zone changes and a reunion featuring some ghastly, green Maltese wine, caused us to sleep late the next morning.

And when we called at the office of the Mellieha Bay doctor around 11 a.m., his door was locked. A gardener advised the doctor held office hours until 8 a.m. and thereafter was available only for extreme emergencies. The gardener diagnosed our green complexions as not constituting an emergency.

Back at the apartment-restaurant-swimming pool complex our host recalled that a "house doctor" made daily calls for the convenience of guests.

The following day we met the doctor and explained our problem. He enquired whether we felt well, examined our faces, pronounced us fit and signed the health department documents.

After chatting for a time he offered to fill in the blanks for the remaining days of our visit on assurances we wouldn't leave the island earlier than stated and that we'd notify him if any illness developed.

With that hazard apparently safely dealt with, our week in Malta flew. It was full of sunshine, sightseeing and gourmet dining. There were frequent references to the doctor whose trust and kindness had spared us both inconvenience and running afoul of the law.

The Italian-registered ferry boat from Malta to Sicily on which our friend had made reservations for us and his car departed Malta each morning at some horrible hour. But it was the only way to get a car off the island and we'd offered to deliver his to France for him.

On departure day we arose in the dark and sped to the wharf. Our friend had spent weeks collecting the necessary papers for the export of his automobile. We had double-checked drivers licenses, passports and -- what we considered most important -- the Maltese medical certificate which stated that we had been checked by a doctor each day of our stay and had been found cholera-free.

The activity at dockside might have been a Monty Python scenario. It was a blend of linguistic chaos further tangled by a web of petty and apparently incompetent officialdom.

Orders screamed by the Italian ferry crew were countermanded by Maltese officials who waved their arms and displayed as authority varying amounts of braid on their uniform sleeves. A car cleared by one Maltese official might be halted by another, or temporarily refused on board by an Italian ship's officer.

Our friend's car which he had bought in Malta was one of those sent ahead, called back, sidelined and then sent on again. The dealer had transposed the engine and body numbers on the registration form. At times there were up to six uniformed officials peering into the tiny engine compartment and arguing loudly with each other.

During their commotion I was trying to find somebody to accept the medical certificates.

The customs man didn't want them. The ferry boat purser didn't want them and neither did the civil police. An official whose concern was the importation to Sicily of diseased agricultural products examined one of the documents and decided it wasn't his problem.

Meantime it was decided the car could be shipped and a deck hand roared it up the gang plank with tires shrieking and the gearbox crashing expensively.

The ferry whistle sounded a warning and at that moment I spotted a Maltese immigration officer. Surely he'd accept the papers and grant us government clearance.

"Passports, please," he said as we hurried up and he shuffled through their pages like a card shark.

"What is this?" he demanded as the health certificates were offered. "This is not my concern."

In a rush I told him of the delicate conditions under which we'd been admitted to Malta and the threat of being fined for not complying with the emergency regulations.

"That may be so," he roared over the ferryboat's final whistle, "but I don't want these. Maybe the Italians will want them . . . and if they don't, why don't you keep them as a souvenir of your holiday here?"

The ferry's bow was swinging away from the wharf as we scampered up the gang plank.

Nobody on the boat wanted the documents. Nobody in Sicily wanted them, either. Not even the customs and immigration inspector on the Italian mainland wanted them.

I've still got those Maltese health inspection certificates in a safe place where I keep important government documents . . . like my rejections for a Canada Council grant and assorted rejected Revenue Canada tax deduction claims.

Gender distracting - - *mais oui!*

Murray Bay
Quebec, Canada

After the inevitable conversational triumvirate of language, politics and separatism had been exhausted, I suggested to my new-found French-speaking acquaintance that bilingualism might be assisted to some degree by changes in the French language.

"Yours is a very difficult language to speak perfectly," I complained. "Each of your nouns has a gender. A tree is masculine but a crowbar is female; a dog is male but a hose is female. There's no rhyme, reason or logic for most of the choices.

"Look at the parts of the body, for example. Finger is le (male) doigt; hand is la (female) main, but the wrist is le poignet. The arm is le bras, the elbow is le coude, but the shoulder, l'epaule, is female.

"Then there's la poitrine, the chest, or breast. It's also female . . ."

"Ah, yes," he sighed deeply, glancing at the passing cocktail waitress. "Thank God for la poitrine . . ."

My theory for simplification of the bilingualism process was not resumed.

Bahamian bartering can be costly

Nassau
Bahamas

A beautiful black girl from Los Angeles told me how to do it. Her name was Virginia and she said it was really very easy; in fact she had just stumbled on the successful formula.

Virginia had returned to the resort carrying some lovely, hand-woven grass handbags from the straw market of Rawson Square. Most of the tourist literature for the Bahamas touts the straw market and it was on my mental list for a visit the next day.

The trophies Virginia showed me were a reminder that loved ones usually expect consolation awards when I return to chilly Ontario from some exotic southern destination. Straw handbags would be just the ticket; typical of the country, not too expensive or heavy and easy to pack.

Rawson Square was in full swing the next day because a cruise ship was in port. The ships tie up almost daily just a stroll away from the market and few of the passengers miss the opportunity to come ashore and pick up souvenirs.

A Bahamian I chatted with one day told me Nassau has two prices -- one set when the cruise boats are in port and another on days when no cruise ships are in port, or expected. The trick is to find one of those rare days when some ocean giant isn't snugged up to the pier disgorging hundreds of souvenir hunters.

Gord, an Edmonton lawyer, was beside me on the little ferry to Nassau from Paradise Island. He said he was buying souvenirs for two nieces back home and didn't have a clue what they'd like. I told him of the straw handbags, and moreover, my "inside track" on how to barter with the natives.

We wandered twice through the market before I found the handbags I wanted. They'd fit in my suitcase and the bold colours were attractive.

A squat black woman who introduced herself as Maggie attached herself to us when she noted my interest in her wares. She told me each handbag took a whole evening to make. She squinted dramatically while explaining the difficulty of doing such fine needle work by a kerosene lamp in her hut.

The bags were $5 each, but only $4 for me, she explained. She had only two at her stall but could find another in a moment. The bags were identical to the three Virginia had bought for $10.

"How about the three of them for $10?" I asked Maggie.

She spun to face me with the speed of a scorpion. "Lissen honey! I tole you for you dese five-dollah bags you pay oney four. Doan go gimme none a dis t'ree-fifty jazz! You wannem or not?" Her vast bulk quivered with indignation as she spat out the words in an apparent rage, as though her morals had been publicly questioned.

"Yes, thanks. Sorry I suggested that. Somebody told me you should try to bargain here."

"We already did. For you $4."

Maggie bustled off indignantly to a nearby stall where Gord had just happened to wander. The heated exchange broke out moments later and Gord was explaining again when I got there:

"Look, you're selling that to my friend for $4. You're buying it from this man for $3. I just think to be fair you should either sell them to my friend for $3 or pay this man $4."

Maggie's massive bulk quivered with indignation. "And I think you should maybe mind your own business. We knows what we's doin'. If you don't think dat's fair to dis mon you pay him de dollar; he's happy with my $3.

The big man heaved himself up from behind his stall, lumb-ered over to Gord and towered over him, hand outstretched, palm up.

"Maggie's right," he boomed. "Pay me de dollar."

Gord started to say something, thought better of it, pulled a dollar from his pocket and handed it to the man.

Gord couldn't refrain from laughing out loud. Maggie and the other vendor laughed too. "I tole you, honey, we knows what we doin'," Maggie told him. I paid Maggie $12 for the three bags and we left, still chuckling.

"Aren't you going to get something for your nieces?" I asked Gord as we side-stepped through the heaped stalls of the market.

"Yes," he said, pausing by a display of straw purses as though undecided. Then, apparently throwing his habitual tact to the wind, he said, "Look, there's a bar across the square. How be you go grab a table and order a couple of beers? I'll join you there when I've bought the stuff I want."

The fruits of communism

Gruningen
East Germany

They take their socialism seriously in the Iron Curtain countries – just as seriously as we Westerners guard the remnants of our democratic processes.

My companion and I had entered East Germany around noon and planned to lunch in a restaurant en route to Berlin. We didn't know then that our visa permitted only transit along the heavily-patrolled "corridor" from the border to Berlin.

As soon as we had cleared East German customs and crossed the no-man's-land of mine fields, we started looking for a town or village that might have a restaurant -- or at least a food store.

Each time we turned off the highway armed police materialized like leprechauns and waved us back to the highway at gunpoint.

By the third time police caught up with us on a side road outside a small village the word must have been out. Armed officers on motorcycles escorted us 20 miles down the highway before turning off. They left no doubt in our minds that we should remain on that highway. We got the message and reconciled ourselves to making do for lunch with whatever supplies were in our house trailer.

The Berlin "corridor" doesn't let a visitor see much of the countryside through which it passes. You can see some trees, some fields, some telephone poles and some clouds.

There might be other attractions but the road is a narrow two lanes and heavily travelled by huge trucks and kamikaze-inclined West German Mercedes drivers. There's little opportunity for rubber-necking.

Gruningen is a town about 40 miles west of Berlin and just about the only one the corridor planners haven't bypassed. The permitted route went straight through the heart of the town and right past the front door of a food store.

Compared with other East German food stores in which we later browsed, the one at Gruningen was large. That made it one quarter the size of a small Loblaws or A & P store.

There was no vestige of merchandising as we know it. Goods

were stacked in wooden bins or on wooden shelves. Labels on canned goods rarely illustrated the contents and about half the foodstuffs were in glass mason jars or bottles with no labels at all.

Perhaps -- like the mould cultures on some exotic cheeses -- the layers of mould in most of the mason jars had been carefully introduced to enhance the flavour. But that certainly didn't inspire us to buy any.

In fact, hungry as we were by then, none of the food held any appeal. Even the cookies were pitted with mould. We decided to buy half a dozen bottles of local beer and two tomatoes. We had found a lettuce and a tinned ham in the trailer that would make a salad.

To get the tomatoes we had to line up behind half a dozen customers. A young lady stood behind the tomato crate filling orders. Customers were not permitted to choose which tomatoes they wanted.

"Trie tomaten bitte," I told her in my best German when it was my turn. Without batting an eyelash she picked up one acceptable tomato and one which had been partially crushed. Rot had started around the edges of the split.

"Nein – nicht," I told the girl, wagging a forefinger from side to side.

She ignored my protestations and began filling the next order.

To get two edible tomatoes I had to line up again and buy two more. The old woman outside the store to whom I offered the two rotten ones was jubilant and pathetically grateful.

Fortunately we poured the beer into glasses that night at the trailer park in Berlin. All six bottles were rotten. Not skunky. Rotten, with stringy mould skeins floating in them. We'd wondered why other shoppers were holding bottles up to the light.

By contrast, West Berlin shops offered everything from fresh lobster to Canada Dry ginger ale and American peanut butter. In ultra-modern Western-style supermarkets counters were laden with fresh corn on the cob, turnips, beets and asparagus, vegetables seldom offered fresh in most European grocery stores.

We crammed our tiny refrigerator with these treats but by the time we'd been in Czechoslovakia two days the fresh produce was gone. The only "fresh" vegetables available in stores there were potatoes and carrots, and they were far from fresh.

The explanation offered by somebody we found who spoke some English was that international sports competitions were then taking place in another part of the country. All fresh produce was being shipped there for the duration of the games.

It must have been the day after the competitions when we were strolling one of the main streets of Prague. There were few pedestrians on the street so the lineup of 30 or more people outside one store attracted our attention and we joined it.

When we got inside the store we learned the queue was for lettuce. One head to a customer. Half the crate had badly damaged heads and every second customer got one of these. There were no apologies and no complaints. The recipients of the damaged heads accepted them as a matter of course, paid their money -- the same price as for good lettuces -- and went on their way.

I didn't see how we could lose out this time. If I got a damaged head then Wendy, behind me, would get a good one. Or vice versa.

The lady ahead of me got a good head. I was handed one that appeared to have been run over by a truck. I turned to wink at Wendy who was next in line and whose turn it would be to get a good lettuce. But the system didn't work that way. The clerk handed a good lettuce to the woman waiting behind her. Wendy and I were obviously together and the policy seemed to be one head per family, not per customer.

We tried to push the point but the clerk just ignored us and continued handing out good and bad lettuces to others in the lineup.

We gave our squashed offering to the first "loser" to follow us out of the store and headed, hungrily, for Hungary.

Travel tip: ***A tan can save hassles***

If you're visiting a sun destination resort, particularly on a Caribbean island, try to acquire at least a bit of tan before you leave the resort property to go sightseeing, or shopping.

The pale-faced visitor in a sunny country is the easiest "mark" for the higgler. Higglers are "street vendors" who will offer you merchandise, unsought advice or exploit you for whatever personal gain they can devise.

If you have a bit of a tan and indicate you don't want whatever merchandise or service is being offered, chances are there's someone behind you with a more pale complexion and the higgler will quickly abandon you in favour of a more likely prospect.

What am I doing here?

Ocho Rios
Jamaica

In Funchal, Madeira, men in straw boaters drag you at high speed down the steep, cobbled streets in a toboggan with seats. On the Greek island of Santorini you ride a surly mule up a steep path-way on the side of a cliff to reach the picturesque village at the top.

And at Giza, Egypt, you ride a mean-tempered camel up a hill to where the Sphinx and pyramids await your camera lens. (The camel owner is often nastier then the camel: if you don't tip him frequently enough he'll whack your camel in a very tender part of his anatomy, making the beast rear up and then sprint).

In Jamaica, you hike up a series of small waterfalls . . . whether you want to, or not.

These are the things travellers must do. You may not want to do them, but they are the price you pay for having gone to the place which is world-renowned for that unique activity. If you wind up on the north coast of Jamaica you simply have to climb Dunn's River Falls just east of Ocho Rios. You have to do it as surely as you have to go to the top of the Eiffel Tower on your first visit to Paris.

So there you are knee-deep in the refreshing flow of Dunn's River following the exhortations of the local guide to hoist your fish-belly-white and overweight body up this seemingly never-ending cataract through the jungle. You never had a choice about that since the falls trip showed up on the agenda for Tuesday.

Feeling foolish?

Look around. Sunlight slants down through the palm fronds and the jungle foliage is refreshing shades of green. It's relaxing. There are no jangling telephones demanding your instant attention.

In the party coming up the falls behind you there's someone you ought to climb beside – if you're self-conscious about your weight or shape. This chap would go 300 pounds easily.

He's having a ball. You can brighten your day by occasion-ally checking on his progress.

The guides here rely on tips they get from people they have jollied up the falls. They'll carry your camera so you don't fall into the river with it and they'll shoot your photo with your own camera whenever you want to stop and smile into your own lens.

They also help you over the tricky spots. If you watch the guide hoisting the jolly, overweight fellow up the tricky spots, you're treated to a rare spectacle. But everybody's laughing because we're all in this together. When we're finished we won't ever have to do it again. When you've climbed Mount Vesuvius once nobody expects you to do it a second time.

On the way up the falls there are several pools in which you can have a dip. At one point there's a comfortable seat in the rock where you can sit while a small waterfall cascades over your head and face. A lot of people have their photos taken here.

A bit higher up there's a smooth trough in the rock. You slide down the chute and into a pool on top of the person who went just ahead of you and didn't get out of your way in time. It's a great conversational ice-breaker, but you only have time for several words before the next slider lands on top of both of you.

There's a small fee for entrance to Dunn's River Park where there are change houses and you meet up with a guide and join a group if you didn't arrive with one. This is also a good place to meet people if you're on your own. During sections of the 200-metre (600-foot) climb up the limestone steps the guides ask you to hold hands, forming a daisy chain. If you're already holding someone's hand it isn't difficult for even the most timid to start a conversation.

The climb and the games you play along the way take the best part of an hour. It's no more strenuous than climbing the steps of a 60-storey building and the surroundings are a darn sight more pleasant. There are some tricky spots and a few places where the rocks are slippery, or the force of the water is strong enough to push your foot out from under you if you don't plant it firmly in the indentations in the rocks.

At any point in the climb you can get out of the falls and follow a trail beside the river through the woods. But that's something nobody ever seems to do. The climb up the falls is a sort of personal commitment. Once you've decided to start it you're darned well going to finish . . . even though you may wonder partway up just what the heck you're doing there.

Anybody who has climbed these falls knows exactly what I mean.

Hong Kong hagglers can't win for losing

Hong Kong

The three Americans had selected material and each had been quoted a price for his custom-made suit, prices varying according to the fabric chosen.

One of the Americans was obviously experienced in such matters. Within minutes he had haggled the cost of his suit from the $240 U.S. he had been quoted, to $180. His companions then also haggled for, and got, equally impressive discounts.

I was in the Holiday Clothing Store in a warren of boutiques just off Nathan Road collecting two suits I had ordered the day before. Arman Chau, who told me, "I manage the store but I am not the manager," had measured me and quoted $250 U.S. for one suit and $200 U.S. for the second.

While I was attempting to mentally convert those prices to Canadian dollars -- which Chau likely interpreted as demurring over his prices -- he offered both for $400 U.S.

I told him he had a deal and returned the following morning for the first fitting. At 7 p.m. that evening I was sipping a cold beer Chau had given me and waiting for the diminutive tailor in the back room to adjust one of my new trouser seams to his satisfaction.

"There's something I have to ask you," I told Chau when the Americans had left and there were no other customers in the tiny store. "I'm here to pay you the balance of the $400 U.S. you quoted me for my two suits. I will gladly pay you the full amount and I am pleased with my purchase.

"But I have to ask: could I have got you to lower your price by haggling with you?"

"Certainly," said Chau, breaking into a wide grin. "You probably would have got both suits for about $340 U.S. instead of $400." He paused a beat. "But," and he jabbed a finger at me for emphasis, "you have bought the best materials and the finest workmanship my tailors can produce. Your suits will not only look good now, but they will look good after you have had them cleaned many times."

He picked up a roll of material selected by one of the Americans. "His suit will look good when he tries it on tomorrow, too. But after he has had it cleaned several times . . ." Chau didn't complete the sentence. His shrug suggested the American would be fortunate to have his suit survive its third dry cleaning.

Chau explained the difference between my suits and those the Americans would pick up the next day was simple economics. The Americans had pushed Chau to the ultimate limit of his profit margin. Their suits would have the cheapest available buttons, zippers, interfacing, thread, padding and lining, items that had been overlooked by the customers as they sought the lowest possible unit price.

To be honest, I hadn't thought about all those other ingredients involved in the manufacture of a suit. I just don't like haggling. If someone quotes me a price for an article or service I simply decide whether I want, or can afford, the goods or service at the quoted price. If not, I look elsewhere.

Most travellers I've met who claim to "know" the Far East, claim that haggling is the name of the game and they boast of various deals they have negotiated.

Chau cautions the shopper not to get too carried away with haggling if the article involved isn't something you can hold in your hand, or isn't something about which you're an expert.

"Don't try it with a camera, for example," he advises. "You might get a very good price, but a very bad lens. Don't try it with gems unless you're an expert in gems and know what to look for. Gems can be easily switched by a less than upright dealer who has made his sale by bringing the price down to a level at which the buyer agreed to pay.

The price may suit the buyer, but the buyer may not get the same item for which he was haggling.

"The best way to shop here," Chau said, "is to go to a reputable dealer; someone who has established a reputation and who values that reputation. Then, decide what you're prepared to pay for the item. If you're pleased by the price, buy it. If you're not pleased, don't buy it.

"It's as simple as that."

The lady's garbage really got around

Budapest
Hungary

Travel to and from the annual meetings of the international travel writers' society to which I belonged for a number of years could sometimes be like old home week when friends from previous travels were encountered at airports en route. This year's congress was held in Budapest, and at Toronto Airport I encountered three colleagues. We flew to New York's La Guardia Airport together and shared a cab to Kennedy Airport.

At Kennedy Airport, there were two more friends -- one from Toronto and one from New York City -- sitting in the departure area bar with a smashing blonde lady, who turned out to be a new society member from Hawaii. One of the Canadian ladies and I joined the trio for a drink, and soon were comparing notes on mid-meeting and post-meeting tours of Eastern Europe each had planned.

When the waitress came by to take new orders, the lady from Hawaii looked at her watch. "We have ten minutes to make our flight," she announced, standing up, "it's been great; see you in Budapest."

She picked up her flight bag and left the lounge followed by the Torontonian and the New Yorker. Pamela, the lady from Toronto, and I, were booked on a New York-Munich-Budapest flight departing two hours later.

It was about five minutes after the trio had rushed off to their flight that Pam noticed the chrome luggage carrier lying beside a chair one of the three had vacated.

"I'll try to catch them," I said, grabbing the carrier and heading for the departure concourse. But they had left their departure lounge by the time I found it.

Pam and I agreed we'd jointly get the luggage carrier to Budapest, and during the congress try to locate its owner who even now would probably be annoyed at having left it behind. Pam carried it aboard the Pan Am flight to Munich.

Next morning in the Munich Airport snack bar, Pam rushed up to me, brandishing the luggage carrier. "It's your turn," she said. "I've been bumped from the Budapest flight and have to go through Zurich. God knows when I'll get to Budapest."

I hauled that damned luggage carrier aboard the Malev flight to Budapest. You've probably seen flight attendants and professional travellers with those carriers. They're a miniature version of the trolleys on which appliance store people deliver your new refrigerator, or stove. You put your suitcase or flight bag on the carrier, and hold it in place with elastic straps.

I've never owned one and don't know how to handle them. There were no straps on this one and it wouldn't telescope down all the way I thought it should, so I had to carry it and my flight bag separately.

Coming aboard the flight the handle of the carrier un-telescoped even farther, and cracked the flight attendant in the shins. That cost me breakfast, even though I apologized several times in my most fluent Hungarian.

There were two long lineups for immigration inspection at Budapest later that morning, because two international flights had arrived simultaneously -- an occurrence most airports appear to pride themselves on arranging.

Glancing across at the other line, I spotted the blonde from Hawaii who had been sitting with my friends at New York.

I crossed the gap between the lineups proudly bearing the luggage carrier which had cost me breakfast and leg space for the previous few hours. As I approached, I noticed the blonde's luggage was neatly strapped to another chrome luggage carrier.

"Hi!" I grinned. "Do you happen to know whether Steve or Al forgot this in New York?" I held out the luggage carrier.

The blonde burst into laughter.

"They didn't leave it in New York," she said between heaves of laughter. "That's my old luggage carrier. I paid $4 for it years ago and it died in New York and I bought this one," pointing at the shiny model on which her luggage reposed.

"You see," she continued, trying to telescope the handle which had banged the flight attendant's shins, "this thing is bent and won't fold up."

Antonio has lovely girls just dying to meet you

Athens
Greece

When you wander out the front door of your downtown Athens hotel you're likely to bump into Antonio -- or George or Peter. There's a warm, wide smile, a hand extended in welcome and the man introduces himself.

"You are from Canada? From Montreal, or Toronto?" Depending on your answer, you'll learn that Antonio lived in your city and that's where he learned his English, which is good but heavily accented. If you tell him you're from Punxatawny, PA, or Tuktoyuktuk that doesn't throw him. He has an uncle in Punxatawny and has personally visited Tuktoyuktuk many times.

Antonio is happy to answer any questions you may have about his city or country and sometimes isn't even in a great hurry to confide that he just happens to own this cozy little bar around the corner where there are some very pretty, but lonely, girls.

For the purposes of research I went with Antonio to the *El Dorado* Night Club at Othonos and Filelinon streets on Constitution Square. I agreed that a beer might be nice and was assured they cost only several hundred drachmas, a few Canadian dollars.

Three attractive young ladies displayed immediate interest in the new arrival Antonio ushered into the otherwise empty and dimly-lighted bar. Antonio introduced me as "my friend from Canada." The barman produced an icy bottle of beer but was upset when I tried to pay for it. "No, no! We trust you here; you pay when you leave."

"Would you like to have a drink with me?" purred a dark-haired beauty, who had materialized firmly against my elbow. "Why don't you buy me a small drink and we can go to a booth and talk?"

We went to the booth and the girl's unordered drink appeared as if by magic; the barman closed heavy curtains behind him as he left.

I soon learned that I was handsome, kind, sensitive, generous, intelligent . . . and that Maria could drink two ounces of lemonade in 43 seconds. She had a terrible thirst. She was also going to lose her job for spending so much time with me (three minutes) if she was only invited to have one drink.

My beer cost 100 drachmas. Maria's lemonade cost 300 drachmas. The scenario is the same all over downtown Athens and the prices are the same at all the bars with lonely ladies, except at the bar for which Peter was shilling, where the customer's drink is 50 drachmas and the girls' drinks are 150.

Peter was an engaging nuisance (who had learned his excellent English in Toronto and had an uncle in my hometown!) So I went with him to the *Carolina* while he explained how his overhead was lower than that of *El Dorado*, which allowed him to charge less.

I recognised the *Carolina.* Last year it was called the *Chicago*. Next year the sign will likely be repainted *Florida*, or *Boston.* Peter's lower overhead may be partly due to location, about two blocks away from busy Constitution Square. But the glance I had at the "girls" from the doorway suggested their age may have had something to do with how much customers were prepared to pay for flattery and expectations about more than flattery after hours.

A Spanish lady in one of the bars told me how the system works -- but only because her boss couldn't understand our conversation in Spanish.

The shills lure men from the street with enticing tales of beautiful girls, and how at this particular bar they're allowed to make dates and leave with the man. In fact the girls work eight-hour shifts and are not allowed to leave the premises until closing time. The girls are paid an hourly rate and small percentage of each drink bought for them.

Should you want to drop in at a bar for nothing more than a drink, have no hesitation in doing so even when the bar is obviously of the type just described. When the first girl approaches, make it very clear you're not going to buy her a drink. After you turn down the second girl the barman will usually signal the others to leave you alone. You can enjoy your drink in peace . . . and watch what happens when Antonio or George brings in another fish.

Or, if you're feeling insecure or inferior, pick a beauty and buy her a few drinks. She'll do wonders for your ego and if you can pace her drinks your bar tab will still be less than an hour spent with most psychiatrists.

Tasmanian Devil aptly-named critter

Taranna
Tasmania, Australia

"That's the nastiest thing I've seen since I had to meet my ex-wife in her lawyer's office," said the Canadian tourist, his eyes wide as he watched the dumpy animal snarl, hiss and growl.

There are lots of jokes about the Tasmanian Devil and the Walt Disney whirling dervish cartoon version makes the critter appear kind of cute and appealing like the ill-tempered Koala bear. But there's nothing cute about the Tasmanian Devil, a raccoon-sized killer with a downright nasty disposition and all the built-in weapons to have its own way against anything short of a military tank.

The carnivorous marsupial used to roam over much of Australia but now is found only in Tasmania, that continent's island state. There are about 3.5 million devils in Tasmania, but since they're nocturnal as well as nasty, the easiest and safest place to see one is in a zoo.

Tasmanian Devil Park is off Highway A9 about 12 kilometres north of Port Arthur (the infamous penal colony). Park manager Mike Copping will let you pet Carla, a baby wombat and you can also see kangaroos, birds and wallabies.

But it is the devils that draw the tourists, perhaps inspired by the hundreds of cartoons the visitor sees of them in tourist literature since Tasmania adopted a cartoon-style devil as the state's logo.

Copping has an old male and a young male devil in a pen with metre-high smooth stone walls and a female in an adjoining pen. The pens have straw-filled caves in which the devils snooze by day until Topping prods them out for the entertainment of visitors.

This day he throws a chunk of frozen kangaroo meat into the mouth of a cave inhabited by a fully-grown devil. "He doesn't want to eat that," Copping explains, "but he's not going to let the other devil get it either."

On cue the younger male shambles around a corner of the cave mouth lured by the smell of the meat. Like a grizzly bear pouncing on a rainbow trout the older devil sprang from the cave and crouched over the meat, eye contact with the younger devil almost crackling above the menacing snarls. "That young'un could probably take it away from him," says Topping, "but neither one of them really wants it enough to fight for."

To make his point, though, the older devil grabbed the meat -- never breaking eye contact with the younger devil -- and shuffled backwards into his lair, there to growl, hiss, snarl and cough like a half-century chain-smoker, at each move made by the younger devil.

A fully-grown devil is like a small bear, just under a metre long with shaggy brown and black hair and irregular blotches of white. The body is stocky, the head large and square and a bushy tail is about one-third the length of the body.

Copping says a pit bull terrier has a jaw pressure of 900 pounds per square inch but a mature devil has a jaw pressure of 3½ tons per square inch. "They'll eat anything; they're like a garbage disposal unit on legs."

But when carrion isn't available they'll kill anything. They have been known to bite the leg off a two-metre-high kangaroo and "have the neck out of it the moment it hits the ground."

Copping offers the photographers an opportunity for a closeup shot. Clad in heavy work gloves he enters the pen of the female and comes at her from behind. One glove grabs the tail and the other the back of the head as the suddenly-awakened beast swings in the air. Copping sets her down atop the wall and ducks back from the paw that takes a swipe at him.

The lady devil struts her stuff -- a show that leaves little doubt there can be a more ill-tempered animal anywhere . . . except perhaps that Canadian's ex-wife.

Travel tip: ***When you don't have to babysit . . .***

Generally people travel to relax. Hauling along items of great value that have to be looked after don't contribute to the process of relaxation. Your wrist watch, for example: if it's an expensive one you might just happen to get it into salt water while cavorting on a beach. It might disappear from that hidey-place in your hotel room or someone could scoop your beach bag while you're swimming. Why not invest in one of those $10 watches which usually tell the time and date just as well?

Warsaw banquet didn't taste quite right

Warsaw
Poland

One should not look a gift horse in the mouth, the cliché goes. But many clichés -- like most rules -- are made to be ignored.

The rain had slowed to a drizzle late that October afternoon and when the lady asked if I'd accompany her on a quick shopping trip to the old section of Warsaw, the idea appealed. It had been a long day of meetings with interminable verbal posturings in a smoke-filled room.

We bundled up because Poland in October has all the raw nastiness of Ontario in December. Old Warsaw isn't. Old Warsaw was bombed to the ground in the last World War but has been faithfully reconstructed. A masterpiece of planning, patience and pride.

Rosemarie was trying to find the store where she had spotted a samovar in the window during an earlier tour. It was around 5 p.m. and the streets were busy with people scurrying home from work.

Not everyone was hurrying. On almost every block there were long queues either outside butcher shops or at sidewalk stands where fresh vegetables were being sold. Some of the queues were fifty or sixty people in length.

We glanced in the windows of some of the butcher shops. One displayed sausages and pork chops. Another had chickens and sausages. A third, with a shorter lineup, had only sausages.

The vegetables appeared to have come from the fields that afternoon; the mud on the carrots and potatoes was still moist. Grocery merchandising hasn't reached Poland yet. Cabbages and lettuce were piled in heaps just as they had come off the trucks – muddy and with bruised and tattered outside leaves.

Unlike the system in most Communist countries -- where you ask for a certain number or weight of fruits and vegetables and must accept the quality of what is doled out to you -- Poles are allowed to choose their own vegetables. It's just as well. Relative to their incomes, foodstuffs cost about three times what they do in Canada.

I ducked into a Pewex store to buy some French cigarettes. The Pewex stores are operated by the Polish government. Various foreign currencies or the Polish zloty are legal tender for the goods which are all imported. But the prices clearly favour the American dollar which was what the people in the lineup were using to buy scotch, French perfumes, wines and brandies, Swiss chocolates, English sherries and lime juice, American cigarettes and chocolate bars and Canadian-made whisky.

Rosemarie found her somavar, demurred about the price and then learned it is against the law to take antiques out of Poland. All luggage, we learned on the way home, is painstakingly searched.

The 600-plus delegates to the international travel writers' association of which we were members, were to be guests at dinner that night of the Polish government's big three Warsaw hotels – the Victoria where we were staying, the Forum and the Grand.

The evening was listed in our convention program as Polish Cuisine Presentation, but it really was a friendly competition between the three teams of hotel chefs.

I've attended a lot of lavish affairs, but have never seen anything like the spread laid out that night. Enormous tables were heaped with literally a ton of food. We later learned there were 110 different main dishes and more than 60 dessert choices.

Each dish was accompanied by an explanation in English printed on cardboard and the list read like the index of a gourmet cookbook: roast saddle of hare and deer; roast whole suckling pig; saddle of wild boar; smoked pork; whole salmon in mayonnaise and jellied fruits; whole stuffed and candied carp, pike, perch and lamb and haunches of blood-red roast beef; an intricate star painstakingly created from hundreds of paper-thin slices of ham.

The desserts were toy houses of gingerbread, lakes of mousse with shores of whipped cream and various buildings and rural scenes of pastries, jellies and fruits.

No expense had been spared; no supplies denied the chefs. Beaming, three-piece-suited government officials and their wives in their finery circulated among the travel writers making sure their glasses remained filled from the two huge bars. There were wines, beer and vodka. Mostly vodka. The bottles nested in solid blocks of ice. The favourite drink of the locals was the finest vodka slightly cut with cranberry juice.

Even when the speeches had been made and the signal given to load up the plates, many guests bypassed some of the creations.

They were just too beautiful to despoil with the serving tools.

Rosemarie and I wound up at the same table. By contrast to those of our table mates our plates looked like those of winners at a TOPS banquet: a sliver of beef, a chip of boar, slice of smoked pork, some flakes of fish, a spear of asparagus.

We toyed with what we had chosen. Conversation at our table died as delegates dug into the heaping plates of delicacies they had selected.

Rosemarie caught my eye across the table. "I can't eat this," she announced quietly. "It just doesn't seem right. It doesn't even taste right. I keep thinking of those poor, cold, grey people and their sausages."

We left the clatter of knives and forks and the tinkle of crystal wine goblets. We sipped cold beer at the bar while those who hadn't tramped the streets of old Warsaw gorged themselves at a feast as memorable to them . . . as it was to us.

Travel tip: *Before you start packing*. . .

▸ Before starting to pack, lay out all items to make sure you've got what you need for all the activities in which you plan to engage. That way there will be no last-minute discoveries you'll have to squeeze in. While everything is laid out, that's also the best time to eliminate items that aren't really needed.

▸ Some thought when choosing clothes for a trip will allow you to get a lot more mileage out of a few items of clothing: a solid or subtly-patterned dress will look like a second outfit with the addition of a sweater, scarf or jewellery; a suit (for men or women) changes into three or four outfits with the aid of a blouse, sweater, shirt; one pair of shorts or trousers should match three or four shirts.

▸ Don't pack anything fragile of value in a suitcase you are checking no matter how carefully it is wrapped. You wouldn't believe the condition in which some suitcases are returned. The airline will repair your suitcase, but they won't pay a nickel for anything in it which is damaged including clothing, the case lining or other items stained or destroyed by liquids whose container has been smashed.

Travel writers know all the answers

Victoria
British Columbia, Canada

The Air Canada office in Victoria was on the ball and 'phoned me at the motel Wednesday night to advise that the 7:50 a.m. Thursday flight to Toronto couldn't get past Vancouver. "I'm sorry, Mr. Scott, we often run into fog at this time of year; we probably won't have a flight leaving Victoria until mid-morning."

That doesn't faze a travel writer; we know all the angles. "Is there an earlier flight?" It made sense to leave Victoria immediately and do the waiting in Vancouver where there are more flights. "There's a Pacific Northwest at 6:40 a.m." I booked it.

It seemed paradoxical to speed on the way to the airport in a pea soup fog, but the airline hadn't called to say the flight was grounded. Maybe the airport was on top of a hill and fog-free. It wasn't. There was time for breakfast -- lots of time; the 6:40 flight took off at 9:30 in bright sunshine.

The fog must have lifted in Vancouver at the same time, because the east-bound flight was long gone when my flight landed. The next east-bound flight was in three hours. That doesn't faze a travel writer. We know all the angles. "Yes, sir, there's a flight to Toronto from Edmonton you can catch if you make flight 301 to Kamloops. It's leaving now. I'll hold it if you run to Gate Seven.

The flight attendant pacing at Gate Seven looked familiar. "Oh, it's you," she called out, "can't you run any faster?" I recalled she had served coffee on the flight from Victoria. I also recognized some of the passengers from the Victoria airport coffee shop who scowled at me as I crept back to my old seat.

Still, those others would be taxiing down the Vancouver runway while my earlier flight from Edmonton was circling Toronto. Being a travel expert certainly has its advantages.

At Edmonton a smiling Air Canada clerk made out the boarding pass for the Toronto flight and told me it would be loading in half an hour. I settled into my novel.

"Oh hell!" It was the woman in the plaid coat who had sat near me a few minutes ago.

"I beg your pardon?" She was quite attractive.

"It's my flight -- it's been delayed."

"Where are you going?"

"Toronto."

The TV monitor showed a capital L beside Toronto flight 154. That number tallied with the boarding pass I clutched and the Air Canada lady admitted it no longer told the truth. Oxygen equipment had been found defective and spare parts were being flown in. There was nothing else going east -- or south.

The only thing going east in Western Canada that afternoon was the flight from Vancouver carrying my suitcase while I had lunch in Edmonton. By the time the Edmonton plane was fixed and got to Toronto the last feeder flight to London would be long gone. Reaching London that night had become an obsession.

That doesn't faze a travel writer. We know all the angles. The girl in Toronto on the rental company's toll-free reservations line said she would hold a car. She wanted to know where I was calling from, and coming from. "You were at Victoria Airport at 6 a.m. and so far you've got to Edmonton? And you think you're going to get to Toronto tonight? I'll hold the car for you until noon Friday." And then she laughed right out loud.

The car was ready at Toronto. "Just go through those doors and you'll find it in the garage," the girl said after filling out the forms. "Hope you're not superstitious; it's in space 13." She laughed. Loudly. It must be part of that company's public relations training; always leave 'em laughing.

Traffic was light at that hour and thinned out past Mississauga. There was lively music on the radio and the satisfaction of knowing I'd be home in a very short time.

The flashing red light bounced off the rearview mirror into bloodshot eyes and a glance at the speedometer showed this one called for major diplomacy. The usual "I didn't notice" routine doesn't work past 150 kilometres per hour. Perhaps some sympathy angle might work.

The Ontario Provincial Police officer provided the opening: "I suppose there's a reason for playing Grand Prix," he offered.

"Well, when I left Victoria this morning at 6 a.m.," I started.

But he interrupted: "Victoria? Well, at that speed I'm not surprised you made such good time."

Six-minute 'war' ends in laughter

Port Said
Egypt

The Canadian public relations man chose a bad time to offer to buy a round of drinks for his table, but the truck stop restaurant in the desert between Cairo and Port Said looked like a safe bet.

Truckers were wolfing down hot meals and men in shabby clothing -- even by Middle East standards -- were drinking Coca-Colas and eating pastries. Besides, the driver who had managed to get our press bus in and out of Cairo without leaving any exterior parts behind, had recommended stopping.

Well, to be truthful, he didn't really recommend anything. The government guide had left us in Cairo, none of us could communicate with the driver and he had simply stopped the bus, gone to a table in the restaurant and ordered a meal for himself.

As we entered the building, a man wearing a heavy black coat and burnoose, with an ancient double-barrelled shotgun over his shoulder, stepped aside to let us pass.

I went into the washroom while the other eight in our group of Canadian travel writers touring the Middle East, settled themselves at two tables.

A grimy, unshaven giant patrolled the washroom. He was there to extract tips from anyone using the facilities. None of us had been able to change money in Egypt and the smallest unit of money I had was worth $10 in Greece. Besides, the giant had rendered no service. I indicated I had no money and side-stepped past him out the door.

"Je-e-e-my Car-r-rter verree good!" beamed the immense proprietor of the filthy restaurant as he banged six bottles of beer onto one table and brought two beers and a Coca-Cola to the adjoining table to which I had fled from the washroom. "Ne-e-e-xon no good!" he said angrily. He opened our bottles before answering my question about price and then announced it would be $20 U.S. for the two beers and Coke at my table.

We told him to take them back. He said they had been opened. We offered to pay $10 U.S., but he was adamant -- and loud. The man with the shotgun stepped inside the door and one of the two German shepherd dogs which paced the restaurant came over and sniffed my ankles. The washroom door opened noisily and the dirty giant glowered at me. One of the ladies at my table found some U.S. bills and paid the $20.

Then the man moved to the next table to try to collect $50 U.S. from the PR man who had ordered the beers. Earlier that day we had bought local bottled beer in Cairo for about $2 U.S. so he'd believed his $20 U.S. would cover the round.

Arguments that we were being ripped off were greeted with raucous laughter and the information that former U.S. President Nixon was no good. The PR man and the truck stop owner argued until the beers were consumed.

The argument was going nowhere so the PR man stood up, put his $20 U.S. on the table and announced we were all leaving.

The others stood up, but with the speed of a rattlesnake the truck stop proprietor grabbed one of the six, pinning his arms behind his back.

"Hostage!" he yelled triumphantly. "You go. We keep him. That's OK. Je-e-e-my Car-r-rter verree good!"

The laughter dropped dead.

The burly Arab had seized the only Jewish member of our group. And there was nothing unprofessional about the armlock in which he was being painfully imprisoned. The man with the shotgun shuffled a little closer. My buddy from the washroom left his station and moved a few steps nearer.

Our group dug into pockets, wallets and purses. I offered Canadian dollars; they were scornfully refused. A Quebec journalist found and offered some South African money from his last trip and it was refused.

In bits and pieces our group managed to make up the $30 U.S. shortfall. Not until the last dollar was on the table was the hostage released.

His release broke the tension and the loud laughter which had accompanied the earlier "negotiations" was renewed.

But we didn't leave a tip.

The Great Barranquilla Bus Race

Barranquilla
Colombia

The buses were side by side now, rocking and roaring and shuddering at perhaps 70 miles per hour.

The girl in the white blouse and green kerchief with huge brown eyes was less than two feet from me -- but she was in the other bus. The bus we were passing. The bus that was on the right side of the road as we hurtled along beside it on the wrong side of the two-lane road towards the blind curve.

Shouts, whoops and jeers almost drowned out the blast of exhausts and cacophony of loose parts rattling over the unevenly-paved roadway. The passengers in the other bus were out for a good time, in high spirits and obviously enjoying the good sport.

Our driver was hunched grimly over the steering wheel, his foot jamming the gas pedal against the firewall where it had been for the past three miles.

The curve was a sharp one and when the oncoming bus suddenly appeared, the closing speed was too great to leave any of the drivers many options.

It was a Sunday in late October and I was travelling from this industrial city to Cartagena on the north coast of Colombia. You can fly to Cartagena from Toronto or Miami but not, apparently, from anywhere else.

It's a distance of about 100 miles and the car rental agency in Barranquilla had quoted an outrageous daily fee plus a mileage charge. Three taxi drivers refused to drop their price below double what a businessman and the hotel manager told me was the going rate and a fourth driver wouldn't quote any price. He said his ancient Dodge wouldn't get there and back.

So I was on the very modestly-priced "Express" bus which cost one-third of the cab fare from my hotel to the bus station.

And that had been a nightmare trip, too. The 23-year-old taxi had more play in its steering than the driver could handle at the rate of speed he chose to drive. He solved that by holding the steering wheel hard left and controlling the veering to the left by constantly tapping the brakes which grabbed to the right. He successfully managed this mechanical ballet through the city's narrow streets which fortunately weren't busy at 7 a.m.

The bus driver was a little man. That makes me nervous in Latin countries. He also looked like the sort of person who would wear a big shiny badge if he was in charge of a municipal parking lot so he could officiously turn away larger men in flashy cars.

He seemed to bear a strong grudge against the transmission of the bus which he attempted to disembowel with each speed shift. He'd passed everything in sight during the first 30 miles of the trip including a bicycle race, donkey carts and all other vehicles. But the driver whose bus we were now alongside wasn't about to be "taken."

I was seated halfway down our bus on the right hand side and twice we had moved up far enough beside the other bus that I could see the driver. Both times we had to fall back as other traffic approached.

The driver of the other bus was a young man with a black Fu Manchu moustache. He wore a white shirt, red bandana and a vaudeville-style straw hat tilted at a rakish angle.

His bus was jammed with young people who appeared headed for a picnic, fiesta or some other fun outing. Some were drinking from wine or beer bottles, others sang to accompany stringed instru-ments and the boy-girl game was on in earnest in some of the back seats.

The driving position of his bus was in the middle of the front seat and he had a pretty teen-aged girl on each side of him. He joked and smiled at the girls as his wreck of a bus hurtled along. Colombia's answer to Juan Fangio was obviously prepared to lay down his life before being found wanting in verve, daring or panache.

The conductor of our bus swore loudly and waved his fist at the other driver each time we drew alongside, a gesture which inspired the other driver to ease to the left into part of our lane and eventually we'd have to fall back.

This would draw cheers and yelps of delight from his passengers.

Our driver, thus humiliated, would drop back and plan his strategy. This invariably consisted of coming up behind the other bus at the highest speed he could coax from his wrecking yard refugee and trying to overtake by surprise tactics. But the other driver could see him coming and would just swing his bus a bit to the left and block the narrow highway. Our driver would slam on the brakes and his 16 passengers would grab for handholds.

It was on a long straight stretch that the buses finally got side by side again. And stayed side by side for about two miles.

There was this pretty girl in the next bus waving and cheering along with her companions. Between us was a small red sticker on my window which read: "Patent device prevents opening in upside down position." Comforting.

My eyes flicked between the girl, the sticker and the empty road ahead.

Life is cheap here. "Honour" -- as in Spain -- is considered more important than life. "Honour," or the defence of it, probably wipes out more motorists in Latin countries than all other crash causes combined.

The bus heading straight for us was moving fast. Its driver hit the brakes so hard it started to swerve sideways.

The road wasn't wide enough for three buses abreast and there wasn't time for any of them to stop before colliding.

At the last moment Juan Fangio swerved his bus to the brink of the deep ditch alongside the right side of the road and ours followed like a lamprey. The oncoming bus took to the ditch at an alarming angle and we rocketed past with millimetres to spare.

The elderly lady in black across the aisle from me continued crossing herself with the hand that didn't cover her eyes.

The rear windows of our bus were covered with dried road spray and I couldn't see whether the third bus had overturned, crashed into the jungle or managed to return to the road.

The speed didn't slacken. Our driver capitalized on the diversion and pulled ahead of the other bus with a triumphant blare of air horns.

Three miles later we stopped in a small village. With taunt-ing blasts from his horns and screams and yells of glee from his passengers, Juan Fangio thundered past flat-out in a whirlwind of dust and debris.

The rear of his bus was out of sight in seconds and we never, thank God, saw it again. He must have turned off somewhere, but our driver kept his foot on the floor the rest of the way to Cartagena, presumably in a frustrated effort to catch up.

Secure in the care of computers

Buffalo
New York, U.S.A.

I was flying to Georgia from Toronto on one of Eastern Airlines' brand new Boeing 757 jets, an aircraft which has proven itself more fuel efficient than earlier jets and infinitely more quiet than any other in which I've flown.

During a layover in Buffalo, Capt. Tolliver invited me to inspect the cockpit. It's an awesome display of knobs, buttons, dials, and levers, but Tolliver said he flies the plane by pushing only four buttons. "Of course you have to know the correct sequence of those buttons," he cracked. "That's why I needed an extra year's training."

The 757 is run by 40-odd computers which have more than 400 sub-computers and I suggested to the captain that the crew's greatest challenge on flights now must be fighting boredom.

"Not at all," Tolliver replied. "We play computer games," and he asked his co-pilot to call up a flight pattern for the western United States. Up on the screen came a colourful diagram showing Denver, Salt Lake City, Phoenix, Santa Fe, and Las Vegas.

"We'll bomb Salt Lake," the pilot said, counting to three. Each fumbled with buttons. The co-pilot's trajectory hit Denver. The pilot got Salt Lake City; a comic strip cloud appeared beside the city containing the word "bang."

I was feeling more confident about the rest of the flight on the computer-operated aircraft until a flight attendant came into the cabin. "We're low on water, captain," she said. "Since we've got time, can we top up the tanks?"

The pilot picked up a microphone and asked the control tower for water. "We can't connect with your aircraft," was the reply.

"Can't you use such-and-such an alternative method?" the pilot asked.

"Negative," replied the tower. "The computer is down."

I returned to my seat to enjoy the balance of the flight on the wonderful new aircraft that is kept in the air by 450-odd computers.

Tarzan's magnetism didn't work for 'Dad'

Sitges
Spain

The man towering over us appeared to be about six feet, eight inches tall, but his hands seemed to dangle below his knees. He'd caught me dozing in the blazing sun and I asked him to repeat the question.

"I say," he began in an Australian accent thick enough to caulk knotholes, "might I borrow your marvellous dog and take him for a short walk?"

I sat up for a closer look at the stranger and realised he'd been part of a group we'd met the previous night in one of the many bars of Sitges, a Spanish beach resort an hour's drive south of Barcelona. "It's me, Tony," he said, recognising my faint glimmer of recog-nition. "Last night you indicated Tarzan might enjoy a little walk, particularly since you still can't get about too well."

I glanced over to where Tarzan was dozing in the stifling shade of a beach cabana. He's one of the oddest-looking dogs one could ever hope to see. He's supposedly a Griffon von Deen Basset, measures four feet from nose tip to tail tip and 16 inches in height. His hair is white with the wiriness of a goat except for a brown mandarin moustache just ahead of his white beard. He's got webbed feet and legs like those on Victorian chairs. Floppy ears and sad brown eyes hang down but most of the time his pointed tail sticks up ramrod straight.

He wasn't enjoying the heat of Spain where I was recuperating from a ski injury and nor was he enjoying the curtailment of exploratory walks.

Tony was equally odd in physical appearance. He was in his late fifties and appeared to have been built of leftover bones which were too long to fit anybody else. His nose was too long, his arms were too long and his toes were longer than my fingers. Kneecaps, elbows, wrists, ankles and knuckles appeared to have been contributed by a much larger donor and added by a careless sub-contractor.

Although he was between 6'-6" and 6'-8" he wouldn't have weighed over 150 pounds.

Walking the dog for some reason then obscure seemed important to Tony. He didn't look like a dognapper, so I untied Tarzan and handed Tony the lead. "We'll be here for another hour," I told Tony, "have fun."

As he loped off down the beach like some exaggerated and minimally upholstered robot, my companion, Wendy, observed that Tony seemed to be a pleasant sort of person in spite of being physically "the ugliest man I've ever met."

Tarzan, who can outrun most rabbits, galloped behind Tony at the limit of his taut leash.

In less than 20 minutes Tony returned at a slower pace holding Tarzan's lead in his right hand and the hand of a statuesque brunette in his left. Tarzan collapsed in the cabana's shade as Tony introduced "my friend Sylvia from Manchester." He enquired if we'd be on the beach the next day, Wednesday, and wandered off arm-in-arm with Sylvia.

The next day he borrowed the dog and brought back Alice, a stunning redhead who held Tarzan's lead -- and Tony's hand -- when they came to our cabana. The usual introduction was made and the pair wandered off. Tarzan snorted irritably and appeared to pass out from heat prostration.

On Friday Tony and Tarzan returned from their walk with a smashing German girl -- I believe her name was Ingrid. Ingrid couldn't speak English, but nodded eagerly when Tony introduced us. Tony's German vocabulary appeared to encompass less than a dozen words, but Ingrid accepted his jumbled invitation to a beach-side bar.

We spent Saturday around the pool of a friend's villa and didn't see Tony until that night when we were at the curbside table of our favourite bar.

"Good gracious," he exclaimed, "I was afraid you'd left town. Where's Tarzan?" Wendy explained we'd left him to enjoy the cool marble floor of our hotel room.

Tony was alone that night, looking more spooky than a stretched Vincent Price in a horror movie. Harsh street lights cast severe shadows from his outsize beak of a nose across one side of his face.

"Tony," I asked, "how come you know so many lovely young ladies -- like Ingrid . . . you can't even speak to her? And you said you'd only been here a few days . . . "

"Ah, yes, well you see," he eased into his answer, "that's why I so enjoy walking Tarzan down the beach. He seems to sniff them out and then the birds always ask what kind of dog he is, and then we're talking, and they start patting him . . . and, hey presto! It's absolutely amazing.

"You see, when a chap looks as I do, he needs some sort of ice-breaker. I can do just fine once a conversation is started . . . " he broke off to ogle a passing pectoral impossibility.

"I say," he brought his eyes back to our table, "I don't suppose you'd consider selling the little chap?" Wendy's look provided the answer.

"Well then," he signalled a passing waiter to refill our drinks, "perhaps I might walk the little fellow as long as you're here?"

That was fine with us and Tarzan and Tony continued getting their regular exercise until my leg healed and we returned home.

The experience was beneficial for Tarzan; I've been walking him ever since -- even since I returned to Canada a few years ago.

To date I've been approached by a precocious eight-year-old girl who claimed Tarzan wasn't a dog and challenged me to prove otherwise, two elderly tourists seeking traffic directions and a drunken derelict who panhandled me out of a dollar and then belligerently demanded to know what kind of a nut would keep a short-legged goat for a pet.

Travel tip: *Cigarettes still have their uses*

Even if you don't smoke, having a package of cigarettes with you while driving in a Third World country can often save you a lot of time. You'll save the time when you reach a military check point and casually offer some to the soldiers who are having a look through your car and personal belongings.

The soldiers earn only a pittance and on some lightly-travelled highways don't see much action, let alone such interesting things as foreigners. They have all sorts of time to browse through your things while you wait in the heat. A few cigarettes rapidly establish that you're a friendly person and the reward for that is usually a quick once-over search with a lot of smiles and friendly gestures all around.

Wee Scottish burr confounded Colonials

Cairndow
Loch Fyne, Scotland

The way the six of us hit it off was almost like a chemical reaction although our ages ranged from my lovely companion's 20 years to George's late seventies.

And we had so little in common:

John, early forties, was a bar steward at a gentlemens' club in Southampton, England and very serious about everything. His blonde wife, Vivian, was mid-thirties, shapely and loaded with vitality.

George was a "joiner" from Ardrossan, Scotland. In an accent so thick I could only understand every third word, he explained a joiner is a Scottish carpenter. His wife, Flo, had frizzy white hair, always wore tweeds and had that rosy-cheeked outdoorsy look that made her look years younger than she probably was.

I was a thirty-two-year-old Canadian weekly newspaper publisher.

The six of us met after supper on a Tuesday in April at the Cairndow Inn where we were the only guests. Cairndow is in west-central Scotland near Inveraray in County Argyll at the head of Loch Fyne.

Supper had been one of those awkward meals. The six of us sat at three little tables in the dining room as far away from each other, it seemed, as we could get. There was a lot of whispering during the meal. George and the elderly waiter were the only two who spoke in normal voices.

But when we gathered in the residents' lounge for after dinner drinks, voluble George broke the ice by making introductions.

It was also George -- after first learning Wendy and I weren't Americans -- who signalled the aged retainer for a round of drinks, insisting we all enjoy a very special malt whisky he'd discovered was stocked by the inn.

John bought a round of doubles and then it was my turn. The ladies drank gin. We were now on first-name terms and Harold, the waiter-cum-barman whose raised eyebrows had betrayed apprehension at the rapidity with which drinks were being ordered and consumed, was invited to join us for a "wee dram."

When the cook came to tell Harold she was leaving for the night, she was urged into a comfortable chair and given a "clachan-dichter," which George ponderously explained was "one for the cobblestones," presumably the Scottish equivalent of North America's "one for the road."

Everybody became quite jolly except John who became more dignified, proper and almost pompous with each successive drink. He wore a sports jacket, white shirt and tie and every few minutes "shot" his shirt cuffs and tightened his tie. If Vivian hadn't eventually coaxed him to remove the tie, he likely would have strangled.

The evening babbled on -- George leading the conversation by expounding with incredible recall the colourful history of the area, and helping us map out a tour of ruined castles for the next day. The more he drank, however, the heavier was his burr. By the end of the evening I was able to understand only every sixth word.

We went to our rooms when Harold excused himself and began setting breakfast tables in the adjoining dining room.

Warm greetings were exchanged less than two hours later at breakfast and then each couple went off to do its own thing. In John's case, this was dry fly fishing in a nearby brook, dressed in business suit, white shirt and tie.

Scotland that spring was enjoying what the natives called a heat wave. The temperature got close to fifty degrees Fahrenheit during the afternoon and when we returned from our wanderings for tea, John and Vivian were actually sunbathing in the inn's garden.

That evening was a repeat of the first except that George abandoned his discourse on Scottish history and launched full-tilt into his other hobby -- whiskies. Despite the fact he'd enjoyed a half dozen of them before he started, George could identify the brand of any whisky placed before him, even naming the glen from which it came.

Pretending to go to the washroom, I sneaked outside and got a bottle of Canadian rye whisky from the car which I gave to Harold, instructing him to serve some to George the next time he ordered a drink.

George tasted the neat whisky appreciatively and smacked his lips. "Och," he observed, "t'is nae a malt." Another sip confirmed it wasn't 'northern' scotch . . . and yet another nip determined it wasn't from the south, either. By the time he finished the double dram he'd explained in great detail everything the whisky wasn't and concluded it must be Canadian rye whisky because it wasn't Scotch, Irish or American bourbon. He said he'd never before tasted Canadian rye whisky.

John was missing at breakfast the next morning.

At 4 a.m. Vivian had gone to bed and John said he'd be there minutes later. He'd had so many whiskies Vivian had again removed his tie to prevent strangulation. But in the morning when Vivian awoke, John wasn't in their room.

Vivian was on the verge of calling in the local constabulary when a rumpled, bleary-eyed John shuffled into the dining room. A chambermaid had awakened him, he explained, when she checked an empty room to be sure it was in order. That room was identically located, but one floor below, where Vivian had been waiting for him.

"But John," Vivian asked in embarrassed anguish, "what if there had been someone sleeping in that room? You'd have frightened her half to death."

"There wasn't," John replied, ladling fresh cream over his hot oatmeal.

Harold and the cook joined our group in the lounge again that night. To save many steps, Harold had brought some bottles from the bar and instituted an honour system under which we poured our own drinks and kept track of them on a tally sheet. Harold remarked that thanks to bar sales on the previous two nights the Inn wasn't likely to suffer too heavily if somebody forgot to mark down a round.

George had taken a great fancy to Wendy and she was intrigued by him, though she had confided to me after their first meeting that she couldn't understand a word he uttered.

It was on the third night that the showdown came.

Wendy was sitting between George and Vivian on a huge sofa sipping her gin and lemon and minding her own business. Suddenly George's buzz-saw mumblings stopped and he looked questioningly at her from under his wildly-unkempt white eyebrows.

She sensed he had asked a question and -- as she'd done for the past two evenings -- smiled prettily and nodded assent.

There was another barrage from George directed at Wendy followed by another very pregnant pause during which he waited for an answer. She smiled sweetly and agreed with him.

"Och its no wha' ah wantid to noo," George trumpeted impatiently. "Ah wannit ta nae if smokin' cigarettes keeps yae slim."

John and I translated and Wendy answered the question.

George resumed rolling rs into his whisky tumbler, muttering something about Colonials not understanding the Mother Tongue.

I couldn't resist it.

"Wendy, didn't you understand what George asked?"

"No."

"Didn't you understand anything he said?"

"No." She looked directly into my eyes, pleading.

But I couldn't stop. "You mean you haven't understood a thing he's said during the past two days?"

She flushed crimson and nodded.

George flushed scarlet and snorted.

But for the rest of our memorable stay in that charming inn with the delightful, warm guests, Flo played the role of interpreter despite George's strenuous protests that his "wee" touch of an accent should cause no difficulties for anyone.

Thanks to Flo we were finally able to enjoy a six-way conversation.

Airline tips: *Check most of it*

▸ If you have to check one piece of luggage you might as well check all of it -- except for that flight bag with vital toilet articles (like prescription medication, cash, identification, reading material, etc.) The one case you're allowed as carry-on luggage has to be stowed under the seat in front of you where the designers provided just enough room for your legs. If the plane is full you'll have to share the limited space with that case for the whole flight because regulations prohibit stowing anything heavy in the overhead racks.

▸ Check in early at the airport. Seats are usually assigned on a first-come, first-served basis. Late check-ins often get the least desirable seats and can sometimes even be bumped from an overbooked flight -- even though flights aren't supposed to be overbooked.

▸ If its your first flight, tell the cabin attendant. Most will be happy to help get you settled, explain the individual control buttons for lighting, air, seat adjustment, call button, selection for music channels and volume control for music or movies.

B.C.'s logging roads no place for city folks

Princeton
British Columbia, Canada

The rental car was up to both axles in loose, sandy gravel, but the driver of the logging rig that had forced me off the road obligingly stopped and hauled the car back on the road with a heavy chain.

"Thanks," he said as he swung down from the high cab. "There wasn't room for both of us and I sure couldn't have stopped this rig." He said his load of pine logs weighed about 60 tons.

According to the official British Columbia highway map I was about 20 kilometres west of Summerland in the foot of the Okanagan Valley in south-central B.C. The map showed a narrow, broken, black-and-white line linking Princeton to Summerland. This appeared to be about 30 kilometres shorter than the red-line route from Summerland through Penticton, Kalenden, Keremeos and Hedley, to Princeton.

I'd been on the road since 6 a.m. in a bid to make Vancouver by early afternoon and the chance to save 30 kilometres and four communities had appeal.

The gravel road out of Summerland sported one faded signpost indicating Princeton and then wound and climbed like a dusty snake up into the evergreen ridges of the Cascade Mountains. The only sign of life for the first few kilometres was whisky jacks flitting across the road and when I slowed at the first fork, a cicada shrilling from high in a big spruce.

There was no signpost at that fork, but the main road was obviously to the right because that was the most heavily travelled. The decision was just as easy at the next fork; the heavy traffic entered from the left.

Same at the third fork which led up to the right from an open valley and climbed a dusty washboard up the side of another ridge. In spite of the loose gravel I was making just as good time as on a paved, police-patrolled highway. Lose some time on the switch-backs; make it up on the straights through the cool, lonely forest.

Been There Done That

The huge chromed front of the red truck loomed suddenly on my side of the blind uphill curve. I'd been expecting something on all the other curves and the flip of the steering wheel was reflexive. There was just room to sink the car in the soft gravel ahead of some boulders and a row of trees.

The trucker went through a whole lot of gears and his rig disappeared in bucketsful of heavy yellow dust. He backed close enough to attach the tow chain.

The car wasn't damaged but the next 15 kilometres were covered at a more sedate pace. The road followed a pine ridge and got narrower as its surface deteriorated. As it started downhill the road entered a large clearing -- and ended.

In the clearing, whole trees that had been dragged from the forest were being stripped of their limbs by a bulldozer. A snarling machine like a mechanical, one-armed crab was hoisting the stripped trunks onto a truck.

The road that ended here had so obviously been the main Summerland-Princeton route that I hadn't bothered to confirm it with the first truck driver. The rental car had B.C. plates so he probably assumed I worked for the logging company and had some reason for driving into the logging preserve.

The men taking a break around the fire of pine boughs allowed as how this wasn't the road to Princeton and hadn't been for the last 30 kilometres. "You went wrong down there in the valley when you turned right the second time . . . and you been goin' wrong ever since," one of them laughed from around a dead roll-your-own butt.

"Lucky you picked this one," another observed. "You could follow some a them roads around and around for days without gettin' nowheres."

The man with the dead cigarette stuck to his lip told me which fork to look for on the way back down the valley, "but you'd best wait a few minutes and follow that trucker down. He'll be loaded in a couple of minutes. That way you can be behind him in case he meets an empty comin' up. Them buggers just go flat out and don't look out for nobody or nothin'."

The truck driver said he'd signal the fork I needed by making his second stop there to tighten his load. Even a quarter mile behind him the dust hung so heavily along some sections of the road I needed the wipers to clear the windshield. It was a slow trip but he spotted the plume of dust from the up-bound truck well before meeting it and we were both pulled off in a wide place when it hurtled past in a shower of stones and dust.

The driver told me he didn't think there were any other heavy logging operations between the fork where we parted company and Princeton. Just stay on the main road, he said, and keep checking with anybody you meet that it is the main road.

I reached Princeton a mere four hours after leaving Summerland on the 80-kilometre shortcut which registered just over 145 kilometres on the car's odometer. I was late for the Vancouver appointment, but balanced that against my glimpse at B.C.'s logging industry and acquisition of another valuable travel lesson.

Don't take back road shortcuts in logging country unless you're darn sure somebody has put up signposts. The usual "reading" of a gravel road's traffic volume just doesn't work in logging country.

It only hurts when . . .

Sitting at a desk answering a telephone isn't necessarily as sedentary an occupation as it may sound. In fact a travel agent friend injured herself while doing just that recently.

A valued customer telephoned and asked the agent to book him a three-week round-trip ticket to Australia any time during June.

"Sure," she said, "I'll call you right back with the dates. By the way, do you have your visa for Australia?"

"No," the customer replied. "I'm charging my trip on MasterCard."

"I think I busted something inside trying not to laugh while I told him Canadians need a visa in order to be admitted to Australia."

Travel tip: *The old multi-use trick . . .*

Some thought when choosing clothes for a trip will allow you to get more mileage out of a few items of clothing: a solid or subtly-patterned dress will look like a second outfit with the addition of a sweater, scarf or jewellery; a suit (for men or women) changes into three or four outfits with the aid of a blouse, sweater, shirt; one pair of shorts or trousers should match three or four shirts.

Super salesman's enthusiasm knew no moral bounds

Kingston
Jamaica

I figured the tapping on the plate glass window was probably the caramel-coloured hooker with a better offer, but when I'd ignored it for a few seconds I heard the heavy door scrape open. "P-s-s-s-t. Hey, mister! . . . wanna buy some ganja? It's real good stuff!"

I was at the empty end of the cavernous lobby of the Sheraton Hotel and the boy had somehow sneaked past security guards and through the shrubbery of a courtyard to make his pitch. I knew ganja was marijuana because signs at the airport warn visitors about using the stuff in Jamaica and spell out the stiff penalties for doing so.

The kid took me so much by surprise I didn't ask him the usual questions about his interesting line of work. But the next night, half a block from the hotel, he materialized beside me, having, as far as I could determine in the gloom, stepped out of a dense hedge.

"Hey, mister, feel like some ganja tonight?" When I told him that wasn't my thing he extolled the virtues of his Jamaica Gold which was available as a special favour at only $50 an ounce. "$50 Jamaican?" I asked.

"U.S.," he replied with a hurt look on his face.

He tagged along continuing his sales pitch for at least 100 metres before becoming convinced I really didn't want the stuff and wasn't just trying to lower his price. He said he was 15 years old, bribed the hotel guards to get access to guests and had singled me out after noticing a small Canadian flag decal on my suitcase when I was checking in. Canadians were his best customers, he said.

"How about a girl? Would you like a nice girl?"

"If I want one I can find my own, thanks." In the half block before my friendly, neighbourhood pusher had come along I'd declined three gracious offers -- including the persistent lady who'd made her unsuccessful pitch the previous night.

"Them broads around the hotel?" The look of disgust on his young face was comical. "No, man, I mean nice young stuff," he said earnestly. I lit a cigarette in lieu of laughing out loud.

My would-be procurer rhymed off a string of models and their options like a used car salesman moving in for the kill. It was an intriguing pitch and very difficult to realize the salesman was only 15 years old. "There's not even any commission in it for me," was his bottom line. "I'm just setting it up for you because you're a nice guy; you're a doctor, ain'tcha?"

I told him I wasn't a doctor and didn't want "a neat, young chick," thanks. I was just out for a walk because the hotel's air conditioning was broken. I had reached the end of the second block and turned to go back to the hotel.

Super salesman tagged along. It was the off-season and most wealthy *gringos* are wise enough not to walk the streets of Kingston alone at night. I represented a potential bonanza for this lad . . . if only he could come up with some product or service he could sell.

Suddenly he grabbed my arm. "Hey, man, I got you figured out now!" he said excitedly. "You don' want no ganja or coke; you don't want no chicks and you ain't bar-hoppin'. Are you gay, man, 'cause I'm gay. For a good price I could meet you in your room . . ."

I didn't backhand the kid because his private enterprise initiative was refreshing. Besides, his sales pitches weren't even as insulting or in as bad taste as many which find their way into my living room at home via the TV set.

Incidentally, the kid didn't make a sale.

The customer can *always* be satisfied

Singapore

When I told the store keeper that I didn't like his mother-of-pearl carvings and therefore didn't want to buy those he was offering, he dived until his counter and reappeared to shove another huge tray into my face.

"These are very rare and valuable carvings," he coaxed. "These are made from *father*-of-pearl . . ."

Officer's bark carried no bite

St. George's
Bermuda

Bermuda was the last stop on a 13-day, 10-country swing through the Caribbean and I looked forward to an uncomplicated and brisk customs and immigration clearance at the airport, a good dinner and some sleep.

The customs officer would see my Canadian passport and probably just whistle a fellow colonial right through the red tape with a welcoming smile.

The black lady ahead of me had joined my flight in Nassau and the huge customs officer with the bristling moustache wasn't missing a cranny of her capacious boxes and bags. There was lots of room on the low counter for my single suitcase and I decided to save him some time by having it ready for inspection.

Two outside catches and a three-digit combination lock open my suitcase; inside there are two catches on each of two dividers. I opened the suitcase, flipped open the divider catches and stepped back.

The customs officer withdrew his moustache from one of the lady's burlap bags and glared at me. "Don't open your luggage, sir," he barked in the finest of military parade ground voices, "until commanded to do so by an officer of Her Majesty's Customs Service."

A sarcastic wisecrack died in my larynx. He was about six and a half feet tall. There seemed no point in explaining I had only been trying to save him some time. I stepped forward, snapped the four catches closed, slammed the case shut, banged both latches and spun all three of the lock tumblers.

"There," I thought darkly, "and when you want me to open it I'll fumble the combination a few times -- maybe even pretend to forget it for a while -- because you can search through that suitcase until your moustache turns white and you won't find anything I'm not supposed to have."

The woman from Nassau was told she could start re-packing her luggage. I felt a sinking feeling as the huge customs officer turned his attention to me.

I don't like hassles with customs officers and this one was obviously in the mood to throw his considerable weight around. Customs officers work on shifts. Quitting time or coffee breaks are the only times which inspire most of them with any sense of urgency. They don't care how long it takes a traveller to re-pack the suitcase they've turned upside down and inside out.

This one fixed me with a wide, warm smile. "Have a pleasant visit in Bermuda, sir," he said, patting a customs clearance sticker on my locked suitcase.

The caramel mousse

Ixtapa
Mexico

The distinguished-looking American business executive and I just happened to wind up in a corner together during a coffee break of the meeting we were both attending at a ritzy resort here. We had developed a nodding acquaintance through the first few days of meetings and numerous cocktail parties, but he seemed to feel our isolation from the group required a conversation.

"I woke up this morning," he started with no preamble, "and all I could smell in the room was a sort of caramel smell. I couldn't find out where it was coming from." He sipped his coffee.

"I went into the bathroom to shave and nearly had a heart attack when I looked in the mirror. I had some sort of rash all over one side of my face. It looked terrible and I panicked that I might have caught some strange disease down here.

"When I got up the courage to look very closely at my face, I found out where that caramel smell was coming from. The maid must have left a chocolate on my pillow when she turned down the bedspread. I was very tired when I got into bed last night and didn't notice it. I must have slept on the damn thing all night."

All it took was a bed to put expert in his place

Quebec City
Quebec, Canada

During the several get-togethers when we planned The Big Weekend there was a fair bit of good-natured banter about how lucky Brian and Irene were in having their weekend in Montreal and Quebec City personally escorted by a travel expert. Not only a travel expert, but a bilingual expert on Quebec.

I wasn't particularly interested in going to Montreal where it sometimes seemed I spent more time than at home, but I was delighted at the prospect of having some company on a trip because loneliness is the greatest scourge of the travel writer. The walls of all those single hotel and motel rooms seem eventually to just close right in on you.

"Do I turn here for the airport?" I asked Wendy as we drove out of London that Saturday morning. She and the others chuckled indulgently at what they supposed was a weak joke. Then Wendy called out: "What are you doing? You should have turned back there!"

I turned around, explaining as I did so my request for directions had been serious.

"I always take cabs to the airport. Cab drivers seem to think you are going to miss the last flight that week. I usually go to the airport with my eyes closed. You usually meet my returning flights and drive me home. When I've been away for several weeks I only have eyes for you . . . and that's why I don't know how to get to the airport even though I go there a lot."

"Park over there!" commanded Brian, pointing to the airport lot. A few minutes earlier he had mentioned he had never before been to that airport.

We had to change planes at Toronto. I had memorized the number of the Toronto-Montreal flight and sneaked a glance at a video display terminal on the way past to find out from which gate our flight was leaving.

We had traipsed a hundred yards or so when I heard Wendy behind me saying to Brian: "Where the hell is Dave going now? We're supposed to leave from Gate 74 and he's heading for Terminal One." I waited for them to catch up.

"My God!" was Wendy's greeting. "How do you ever get anywhere if you can't even find your way around an airport you must have been through a hundred times?"

"We've got all kinds of connection time," I said with what I hoped was an appropriate degree or irritation, "and there's something I want to pick up in the book store."

"The book store *and* the departure gate are both this way," Wendy said turning around. To Brian she added: "Maybe you'd better drive in Montreal -- if we get there."

The air conditioned rental car was ready at Montreal's Dorval Airport. I drove us flawlessly to the downtown hotel by a scenic route over Mount Royal during which we stopped to tour St. Joseph's Oratory. The rooms I had arranged at Montreal's finest hotel were perfect.

My only oversight was in not having made dinner reservations . . . but the place I thought they'd enjoy (where you bring your own wine in a paper bag and the highest-priced entrée is about $10) doesn't accept reservations.

They didn't want to go there, anyway and by the time they'd sifted the yellow pages and debated the merits of each ethnic restaurant advertised, I knew we were in trouble.

We wound up having roast beef in a chain restaurant outlet after waiting an hour for a table in the adjoining bar which didn't stock any of the liquors I ordered. Dinner and wine cost $147 more than it would have at that fabulous little Greek restaurant.

The weather was great the next day and we drove to Quebec City. I babbled happily about French cuisine as we thundered along that flat, boring highway on the South Shore. I hoped I could coerce the group into one of the superb French restaurants which abound in Quebec City where we had planned a quick lunch en route to Ste. Anne de Beaupré and Montmorency Falls.

We stopped at a place advertising French cuisine and I had translated about half of the entrées from French to English for our group before Wendy nudged me painfully and hissed, "the right-hand page is in English!"

We decided to order à la carte. Brian and Irene disregarded my gentle reminder that the place wasn't a seafood restaurant and both ordered shrimp cocktails to start.

The waiter assured me the paté was made on the premises so Wendy and I ordered that with French bread.

The shrimp in the cocktails were four inches long and Brian and Irene assured us the sauce was piquant and exquisite.

The paté was a thick slice of something reminiscent of Spam, Spork, Spick -- one of those tinned luncheon meats that can only be rendered palatable by the imaginative addition of all sorts of garnishments. The bread was stale.

Fate works in strange ways and this time conspired against me to salvage what remained of The Big Weekend. I awoke the next morning with what was later diagnosed as pneumonia.

While Wendy and Brian and Irene went sightseeing and shopping -- unencumbered by a bilingual Quebec travel expert -- I stayed in bed for two days under every blanket, bedspread and coat I could find and perspired away 15 pounds.

They'd look in every now and then and tell me about the great time they were having and I'd drift off into a coma-like sleep for hours at a time. It was a bit rocky getting home with that high fever and fatigue, but a few more days in bed there finally threw the bug.

All in all the trip was a great success. Wendy and Brian and Irene had such fun that they're planning a long weekend in Toronto . . . next time I'm out of the country on a travel writing assignment.

Travel tip: *All for one, one for all*

When two or more people or a family are planning a vacation trip, a little advance planning goes a long way.

Let each participant spend some time alone jotting down on paper the specific things he or she hopes to see and do on that trip. Then get together with your lists and determine what common preferences can head up the master itinerary.

This precludes a shy or easy-going individual being deprived by an over-bearing member of the group of what he or she has long wanted to see or do. It also ensures that each member of the group will get to see or do at least some of the things that mean a lot to them, instead of just being along for the ride.

In search of a 'cuppa'

Melbourne
Australia

The hotels of Australia and New Zealand follow the civilized custom of many hotels in the United Kingdom of equipping every guest room with an electric kettle and packets of tea, coffee, sugar and cream, or whitener. The tray of goodies is in the room of any hotel with class; the trick is to find it.

If you don't know this is the custom of the land, you might never find the coffee makings in some hotels unless you went looking for an extra blanket or were paranoid and hunting for electronic eavesdropping devices.

On my third morning in Melbourne I bumped into a couple I knew from Ottawa in the lobby of the five-star hotel where we were staying. Wes and Joan were going the same way and I fell in step, chatting. In the second block, Joan grabbed her husband's arm.

"There's a place that might have some!" she said with the eagerness that must manifest itself when a hurting drug addict recognises a pusher. "God, I hope so." She pointed at an unprepossessing restaurant across the street.

"I'm just dying for a decent, hot cup of coffee," she explained. "That stuff from room service," she confided, "is awful and it's always lukewarm by the time it gets up to the room. I need a decent cup of coffee to get me started in the morning. Would you like to join us?"

"Had mine in the room," thanks, was my response along with an explanation about the tea and coffee kits provided in each room.

But one wonders whether a scenario such as this might have been going on in the hotel's kitchen that very morning:

"'Arry! It's them bleedin' Canadians in Room 701 again. They want another pot of coffee -- nothing else. Fancy 'avin' more money than brains or bein' too damn lazy to plug in a kettle for a 'cuppa'!"

That nasty cannon ball could knock your eye out

Macon
Georgia, U.S.A.

They call it the Old Cannonball House and it's one of the must-see places on the tour of Macon which calls itself Cherry Blossom Capital of the World. The story goes that in 1864, General William Tecumseh Sherman -- whose memory is not revered in these parts -- decided to blow the cupola off the town's grandest mansion.

Sherman lined up his cannon, fired the fuse . . . and missed, by several hundred metres. The cannon ball hit a sidewalk, bounced through a Greek style pillar of another residence, smashed though a parlour window and rolled into the hallway where it remains.

My volunteer guide at the museum was a member of the Daughters of the American Revolution and although her father had fought in the American Civil War, she insisted that historians are wrong to call the "skirmish" a war and it should be more correctly described as the "late, great disturbance."

"Now you write that down, young man," she insisted, pointing at my notebook. "We can't have people up there in Canada talking about a civil war when there never really was one."

And then she got started on the story about Sherman's cannon ball. This is a vignette that doesn't translate well into print since both the lady's fervour and rich Georgia accent are missing.

There we were looking down at the cannon ball on the hallway floor. It was solid black iron the size of a turnip. The guide waved her arms about as she worked into her story the miraculous luck of the lady of the house who had escaped being hit by the errant ball. She apparently had left the front parlour moments before the ball struck, to dress for a social engagement.

"Why, if she had been standing there where she had been looking out the window when that cannon ball came through the wall, she might have . . . well, it might have taken her eye out!"

Japan's Bullet Train is *always* on time

Fukuoka
Japan

One of the most interesting magazine assignments I've ever had was to go to Shofuku-Ji temple on Japan's southernmost island, Kyushu, and interview a Canadian who was nearing his 10th year of training in the Rinzai sect of the school of Zen Buddhism.

It appeared likely then that Brian Burke-Gaffney was about to become the first "round-eye" (Westerner) ever to be made a roshi (abbot.)

Burke-Gaffney had told me during a couple of telephone calls that I would be allowed into the monastery to see how and where he lived and -- as best a Westerner could understand -- what Zen Buddhism was all about.

The day with Brian meant ducking out of a tightly-structured crash tour of Japan with the Japanese Tourist Board and when I mentioned my plans to the tour leader, her reply was succinct: "Absolutely not. You will stay with the group."

So I left the hotel at 4 a.m., got a cab to Tokyo Airport and the flight to Fukuoka I had told Brian I'd make. The day with Brian was fascinating. So was lunch with the other monks and tea with Brian's roshi who was kind enough to set some time aside for the occasion.

It was dark when Brian and I left the monastery for the Bullet Train station. The small group with which I was touring would be in Kyoto that night and I would have a room at the hotel. All I had to do was sneak back there, join the others for breakfast and hope not too much fallout would result from my missed day.

Before going to Japan I had read a thick book about the Bullet Train. It told me the train's time tolerances were two minutes either side of its schedule. Brian got me a first-class ticket to Kyoto, took me out to the platform and showed me where to stand.

"I have to return for prayers," he said. "Do not get on any train that stops here until it is exactly 8:03. There's a clock on the wall there; check it with your watch. If you get on an earlier train it will take you to the wrong island. Do not get off the train until it stops at 11:23."

We shook hands and he left. The Seiko clock on the wall agreed with the Seiko watch on my wrist. So I didn't get on the train that pulled up at 7:59 and left before the minute hand moved to 8.

The next train didn't show up until 8:07. Something had to be wrong, but I climbed aboard anyway. After all, the next train would be even wronger, I reasoned.

It didn't look like a first-class car. Whenever I showed my ticket to people they smiled, bowed and offered me a seat. The train roared off into the night. After the expensive taxi ride to Tokyo Airport, the even more expensive plane ticket and this train ticket, I was low on yen and had no more travellers' cheques.

Not to worry, I decided. I could check this train's progress against my map and the names on the stations where we stopped. If the train started heading in the wrong direction I could get off at least partway to Kyoto and possibly have enough cash for a taxi to Kyoto.

That scheme blew up at the first station. It had pastel-coloured ceramic tile walls like the Toronto subway, but the only sign for its name was in Japanese.

I had wandered the length of the railway car trying to find someone who spoke English, French or Spanish -- yes, I tried them all! I was received by bows, smiles and nothing I could comprehend.

The train hurtled on through the night, occasionally stopping at stations whose names might have been easier to correlate to my map had they been in Greek.

The stress built.

But there was a bright spot: the best meal I had during those eight days in Japan. A vendor working the aisles of the train sold me three bananas and two bags of peanuts.

The bananas and peanuts were the first things my system was able to handle in that long day.

The coach was hot and I'd been on the go for more than 19 hours. It was hard to keep the eyes open, but they were glued to that Seiko watch. At 11:23 p.m. the Bullet Train was going flat out through open fields.

It stopped at 11:29. I got off at what had to be the wrong station because that train cannot vary from its schedule by more than two minutes. A Seiko clock at that station agreed with my Seiko watch. I was separated from the group whose leader by now would be seething with rage; I was low on cash and probably several hundred kilometres away from Kyoto.

The first 11 taxi drivers at the cab rank apparently didn't understand me when I asked them to please take me to the Century Hotel in Kyoto. They just beckoned to whoever was behind me in line to get into their cab and I knew I was in real difficulty.

The 12th driver laughed right out loud. "Light dare!" he said pointing to a tall building half a block away. The building wore a huge neon sign in Japanese characters. "Dat is you hotel," the driver said, bowing. "You no need me," and he beckoned the man behind me into his cab.

As I stumbled gratefully through the lobby, a voice hailed me by name from the adjacent lounge-restaurant. It was our tour leader and a couple of the travel writers having a nightcap.

"How was your day in the monastery?" was her friendly greeting. "Come and have a drink and tell us all about it," she smiled.

It was a happy ending to a stressful day. But no Japanese official could ever explain how the Bullet Train could possibly have left Fukuoko four minutes late and arrived in Kyoto six minutes late.

"Impossible," they said. "Your watch must have been wrong."

Travel tip: *Ugly, but always there*

I saw the luggage in Dallas when the couple was checking in at the airline counter and while I was waiting for my suitcase at Toronto that luggage came up too. It was nondescript soft-sided luggage like millions of others and it had certainly been around. But it stood out vividly in the heap of incoming bags.

When the couple from Dallas came to collect their luggage I asked the man how long he'd been using the luggage with his name written on both sides in two-inch-high letters like the ones you can buy for sticking on mailboxes or the outside of houses.

"They're ugly, aren't they?" he chuckled. "But my wife and I travel a lot and we just don't want someone mistakenly picking up our bags at an airport or train station. Those letters have been on those bags for over six years now. The trick is to use some alcohol to get the surface of the bag really clean and dry before sticking the letters on. Once they're on there, nothing can rip them off."

Resort you can't afford can still entertain you

If you can't afford to go to the hotel whose brochure has been lying on your coffee table for the past few weeks, don't just heave it away with a long, sad sigh and turn your mind to other matters. There's a game you can play with that brochure and win, lose or draw you'll feel a lot better about not being able to make that trip.

Gather your family and friends around you some evening, make sure each has a cup or glass of his or her favourite libation at hand and take turns translating for one another what the brochure writer really meant when he used those special words they teach at Brochure Writing School.

Right there at the start, for example, where the resort is described as ***unspoiled***. That usually means the place is a $100 taxi ride from the nearest airport and the only shopping within 35 kilometres is in the resort's own store. ***Secluded***, on the other hand, means you won't be able to find a taxi driver at the airport who has ever heard of the place.

If the resort describes itself as ***quiet***, don't be surprised to find that the other two guests are honeymooners . . . and they will not want to hear any of your jokes or help you prop up the bar far into the night. If the brochure uses the phrase ***quiet and cosy***, chances are good you'll be sharing a bathroom with the honeymooners.

There are other catch-all phrases to beware. A resort described as ***large, vast, immense***, or having some enormous acreage, usually means a place where you need a map to get from the front desk to your room. If a place so described is also ***popular***, they'll have run out of those maps by the time you locate the front desk.

Descriptions about dining facilities can be equally misleading. ***Gourmet cuisine*** sometimes means management gives the chef a sufficient budget to buy sauce, gravy and glaze mixes while ***charming*** usually assures a table cloth, or at the very least, freshly-printed menus . . . to show the new prices.

Dining rooms described as ***elegant*** usually have a flower on each table; ***sophisticated*** often means a candle and ***romantic***, is often both flower and candle. Beware dining establishments billed as ***quaint***. That can often mean you're likely to find a lizard eating the flower on the table.

These folks at the Brochure Writing School are nothing if not inventive. They can take a word like ***modern*** and teach it as meaning that a hotel was built in the last half-century. ***New*** in their vocabulary means the place has been renamed this year after last season's cockroach scandal, horrendous over booking fiasco or food poisoning of guests. ***Brand new***, on the other hand, means the premises will reek of paint and carpet cement and you may have to spend the first few nights in a beach chaise while the furniture for your rooms clears customs and then is uncrated.

The list goes on and I wouldn't want to spoil all your fun. But it should be pointed out that not all these adjectives translate negatively.

Friendly, for example, means you will get a smile from the bartender after you've waited a half hour to be served. He was chatting up that little number in turquoise at the other end of the bar and he's sure enough smiling!

Courteous staff means that when you arrive at the dining room at the precise time you booked your table, the maître d' will tell you "***please*** take a number ***Sir*** (or ***Madam***) and we'll call you from the bar in an hour or so."

You can then take your business, if you wish, to a ***fast-food*** restaurant. The pre-cooked, frozen, pre-packaged food is ***fast*** for the owner to cook; it usually also lodges ***fast*** in the pit of your stomach and remains there for days.

Or, you can call it a night and head back to your room. If it's an ***elegant*** room you won't want to sit on the chairs because they're too uncomfortable; but if it's ***spacious*** you and your companion will both be able to unpack at the same time. If it's a ***deluxe*** room, chances are good the plumbing will work. If you sprung for a ***super deluxe*** room, your television set will probably work and perhaps even one of the bedside lights.

But enough!

Get to the game and enjoy!

I've left you a ***bounteous assortment*** (at least three) of travel brochure adjectives with which you can amuse yourself and friends while whiling away a summer afternoon or evening at considerably less than the ***budget*** ($200 U.S. per night) resort you've decided you can't afford this year.

Cordon bleu

Encamp
Co-Principality of Andorra

While we explored the tiny Co-Principality of Andorra on that lovely spring day, the narrow corkscrew roads that went either up mountainsides or down mountainsides, frequently crossed small, vodka-clear, rushing rivers. The source of those cascading torrents was obvious; in whatever direction one looked up, there were deep snow fields and glaciers capping the peaks and ridges of the ancient Pyrenees Mountains that closed in on all sides.

Where the road shoulders made it safe to do so, I parked my sports car near the arched stone bridges and walked back to gaze into the pools of some of the rivers. Always the waters were moving too swiftly, or their surface was too rippled by currents, to spot any fish lurking, or dark shadows darting after drifting food.

The rivers dropped so sharply down the steep, jagged valleys that I wondered if any fish could fight their way upstream to those pools. I knew the rivers ran into northern Spain and wandered through stony deserts to eventually empty into the Mediterranean. These were gorgeous trout rivers, but what trout ever swam out of the polluted Mediterranean and made its way several hundred miles up into mountains as steep and forbidding as these?

We didn't know it at the time, but with that uncanny luck that dogs my travels, we had checked in the previous afternoon at Andorra's most expensive hotel. The clue should probably have been that at dinner we were the only guests, but our every whim was instantly obliged by a staff of five, imperiously commanded by a maître d' with astonishingly exacting standards.

Another clue might have been that there was no dilemma about tipping so many servers; the manager had explained when we were checking in that a twenty per cent gratuity would be automatically added to all bar and meal charges during our stay. If m'sieur wished to show appreciation for particularly superb service he could, of course, leave more cash at the bar or dining table. The implication was clear that only the worst of boors would not avail themselves of this opportunity.

Ramón may have been curt with his staff, but he was more than gracious with us. He was Spanish, but spoke excellent French -- all the better to accommodate well-heeled visitors from nearby France -- so we could communicate easily. He livened our first meal in Andorra by telling us, with our encouragement, all sorts of fascinating information about this little-known historical enigma on the map of Europe. The stories took time; I had to translate each for my unilingual companion.

The second night, after we'd ordered three or four courses and several wines to accompany them, Ramón was solicitous about our sightseeing tour.

Did we go to that little place he had suggested for lunch, and was it to our liking? Had we gone down to the weekly market at Seo d'Urgell, the northernmost town of Spain that abuts the Andorran frontier to the south? Had we seen the famous Chapel of Saint Michael of Engolasters, so revered by ecclesiastical historians?

It wasn't until he was supervising the serving of our coffee that I remembered the tumbling rivers with those black, froth-flecked pools.

"Fish, m'sieur? Fish? Andorra is world renowned for her famous blue trout!"

"Blue?"

"Yes, m'sieur. M'sieur will have noticed the rivers are seldom exposed to the sun because the valleys they traverse have such steep walls. And the waters from the melting snows are always so cold." When I finished translating this information for my companion, Ramón was poised.

"Does m'sieur perhaps enjoy the sport of fishing? I have heard it is a sport much loved by those from your country." (Ramón had enquired that morning about our Ontario licence plates. He said he had never heard of a country called Ontario. He was particularly impressed by the crown emblem when it was explained this was the *sombrero* of the British queen.)

Among the very few items that had not been stolen from my car in transit from Halifax to LeHavre was a brand new and very expensive four-piece pack fly rod, its reel, leaders and dry flies. It was the perfect rig for those small rivers with the steep walls and limited space in which to cast.

It happened that Ramón was a keen fisherman; it happened that he could have some free hours available the next morning if I wished to fish with him. He could show me where the famous blue trout lurked, and how to entice them to my fly. We should leave right after breakfast so he could return no later than 12:30 to supervise his staff at lunch.

I wore crepe-soled sandals, shorts and a short-sleeved cotton shirt. Ramón wore black trousers with their razor-sharp crease tucked into rubber boots, a stiffly-starched, long-sleeved dress shirt and, so help me God, black bow tie. In deference to the warm weather, or perhaps the informality of the occasion, he eschewed the suit's satin-lapelled jacket and sported a rakishly-tilted Basque beret.

We took my car, its convertible top down, followed the corkscrew highway down to the capital town of Andorra la Vella and then up into the La Massana valley. Just past a series of three narrow tunnels hacked through the ancient cliffs, Ramón told me to park on the wide shoulder. We gathered our equipment and scrambled down slippery scree from the tunnel excavations to the river that thundered and crashed through a narrow gorge.

The world-famous Andorran blue trout have a lifestyle similar to any other kind of river trout. They find a niche in a pool where they don't have to fight the current while they scan that pool for any goodies that the current may bring. When something looks yummy to them, they dart out of their hidey-hole and grab it.

One of them grabbed a tiny, dark bunch of fuzz and hairs I drifted through the first pool before Ramón had rigged his line. The little fish was about eight inches long, so there was no protracted drama of playing it in the pool. I wet my hand and gently disengaged it from the hook. The trout, still as death in my hand, had the black back of what we know as a "brookie," or "speckle," but the black continued much farther down the sides. The trademark bright spots on the sides were there, too, but the colours were very pale.

I was preparing to release the fish when Ramón seized my arm. "No! No!," he exclaimed. "In here!" and indicated the wicker creel he had carried down from the car.

"But I have no use for it and it is so small," I explained.

"Non! Non!" Ramón almost shouted. "*Muy bueno*! *Muy bueno*!" He was so excited he lapsed into his native Spanish.

I handed him the fish and it disappeared into the creel. I hoped he had a wife and kids who would enjoy the trout, or perhaps a girl friend. I enjoy an occasional hunk of swordfish or shark; sometimes a piece of a big salmon -- if I've caught it. But I don't enjoy messing around with sardine-sized panfish full of bones, no matter how professionally they're filleted or cooked.

We worked about a half mile of the small river, pretty well matching each other, fish for fish, although whenever Ramón wasn't watching, I released the little ones, or let them escape from the hook if they could.

I cursed having none of the de-barbed fly hooks I normally use in Canada. They let you see what you've hooked and if you want it, it becomes a real match of skills. If you don't want the fish, give it some slack and it's gone with minimal injury. If you want to keep it and it gets a split-second of slack, it's gone just as fast.

When the sun slid onto the pool we were sharing, Ramón flicked up his still-immaculate white shirt cuff to check his watch. He signalled it was time to leave. We hiked back down the bank of the river and scrambled up the scree to my car. Ramón was glowing with pride. We had eight "fantastic" fish, he said, just as he had promised when he offered his services.

"I hope you and your family enjoy the fish," I told him, "because I don't want them." Ramón just beamed.

I took my companion to lunch at another dining room in a small hotel we'd noticed the day before. We spent the afternoon sightseeing and browsing several stores in a quest for toothpaste.

Ramón was all smiles when we entered the dining room that evening. He explained there would be no need for menus. Since we were now buddies, his micro-second wink implied, we'd get preferential treatment. He said that since we seemed to be so interested in Andorra and the hotel was not busy in this season, he'd prevailed upon the chef to provide an exquisite menu of traditional Andorran fare.

We did our best with the first course which I later learned was thin slices in aspic of everything that can be scraped from a boiled boar's head, including a generous scattering of bone chips. The entrée was, of course, grilled Andorran blue trout. They arrived with great theatrics on an enormous covered platter surrounded by lemon slices and were served with tiny boiled potatoes under a layer of paprika, and white asparagus. They had been cooked whole, and the eyes of several glared at us as the server flourished them around before transferring them to our plates.

Ramón pranced and beamed as though he had orchestrated delivery of Europe's crown jewels. The carefully-veiled glare from my companion telegraphed a reminder that she enjoyed fish even less than I. And that she held me personally responsible for the culinary outrage that now rested before her, focal point of every eye in the room.

We struggled gamely with the presentation which had been expertly cooked. When a trout has been expertly cooked, the flesh falls from the skeleton, leaving slabs of bone-free flesh. That's the theory. In practice the bone-free flesh averages three bones per mouthful, one of which inevitably lodges between tooth and gum.

Nor did the "world-renowned" colour of the trout ease our discomfiture. As promised by Ramón, the white flesh did have a faintly bluish cast, as faint as that you'll sometimes notice in freshly-fallen snow at cold temperatures and under certain light conditions.

Ramón hovered, soaking up fraudulent compliments and false benedictions as we choked the carefully-chewed bones down with too much white wine. Enough of those damned fish, we hoped, to make it appear as though we had enjoyed the staff's special effort.

Dessert was flan, a tasteless custard awash in a burned-brown-sugar sauce. But it contained no bones.

After coffee and a suitable interval, a beaming Ramón presented the account with a flourish, apparently still believing he and his staff had excelled themselves in delighting our palates.

The charges eclipsed by more than double the most expensive offering on the hotel's over-priced menu.

The evening's salvation was that a café down the street was still open when we fled there to attack their attractive display of sandwiches and pastries.

Travel tip: *Super meal worth five-minutes' research*

If you hanker for a really good meal when you're travelling, don't ask the kid who's filling your gas tank for suggestions. Take a moment to drop into some prosperous-looking establishment and ask the manager or owner for his or her advice.

Chances are he or she will be flattered and delighted to offer suggestions.

If you spot one, pop into the Chamber of Commerce or local equivalent and folks there will also be only too happy to steer you to some place that will provide you pleasant memories of their town . . . to which they hope you might someday return

Sibelius inspired the fantasy; Finland fulfilled it

Helsinki
Finland

There were rules in the house where I grew up and one of them was that on winter Sunday afternoons when the weather was too cold or stormy to go skiing, the drawing room belonged to Father. He closed the big double doors, stretched out on the oversize chesterfield facing a blazing wood fire and spent the afternoon listening to classical music.

Classical music, I was told at about the age of seven, wasn't even as nice to listen to as church music. So I never kicked up a fuss about not being allowed to share the concerts.

On one of those Sunday afternoons I was sent to the drawing room to fetch something. I eased the door open and tiptoed into the room. Father was lying there with his eyes closed.

Coming from the speakers in the big old radio to which he'd wired up the record turntable, were the most exciting sounds my young ears had ever heard. It was loud and turbulent and its crescendos soared and crashed like ocean breakers. But as regular as waves was a plaintive theme, repeated and repeated and growing in insistence and volume.

I couldn't move until the final thundering crescendo was over . . . and if there had been any hairs on my seven-year-old neck and back they would all have been standing on end as they do now whenever I experience that piece of music.

"Was that classical music?" I asked my father when he got up to change the record. "If it was, I really like classical music!"

"Yes," I recall him saying, "if any piece of music is a classic, that one is. It's called *Finlandia* and was written by a man named Jean Sibelius who lived in Finland and was very proud of his country as his countrymen were proud of him and the music he wrote.

"During the last war when the Russians were invading Finland," Father continued, "there was a town the Russians were trying to capture. They had shelled it from a distance and were rolling towards it in their tanks. Only one radio station had escaped the bombing and stayed on the air. For hours and hours as the tanks rolled ever closer, the radio station played *Finlandia* over and over again.

"The music so moved the Finns of that area that they made a last-ditch effort to save their town. Five hundred men saddled up their horses and they rode off to repel the Russian tanks with the music of *Finlandia* ringing in their ears. They were all killed and the Russians captured their town." But that music lives on, Father said, and that's why it is called "classical" music. It is music that will always mean something to people, whether it inspires them to love, to hate, to happiness or bravery or whether they simply enjoy listening to it over and over again.

Jean Sibelius got me hooked on classical music and I've been grateful to him ever since. I've also tried to check out that incredibly romantic story my father told me years ago. But I have yet to confirm it anywhere. Finns I have asked about it during several visits to their country say they have never heard that story.

So I'm writing it off as classical licence; some quick thinking by a father who wanted to surely set the hook in an impressionable child and invented a romantic tale to show there is more to real music than just melodically arranged notes.

That winter day back in southern Quebec I vowed to visit the country where, and about which, *Finlandia* had been written. And as I grew older, the way in which I would visit Finland became ever more elaborate. By the time I was in my early 30s it had become a full-blown fantasy.

The tour of the country would be in a convertible sports car with a tape deck playing a never-ending tape of *Finlandia* at full volume. A beautiful blonde with green eyes would be at my side. We would wait outside the border of Finland, if necessary, until the weather was nice enough to cross the country with the top down on the car.

A mad fantasy? The product of a warped mind? Could Sigmund Freud have had a heyday analysing this one?

I didn't care.

And that chance finally came. The sports car was a mustard yellow Fiat Sport Spyder with a black convertible top. The blonde was even more lovely than the lady in those fantasies I'd been nurturing for almost three decades.

It was August and we entered Finland from the north, having driven there from the Mediterranean coast by way of the entire length of Europe to its northernmost point in Norway.

The day my fantasy was fulfilled the sun was shining and it was almost hot -- for Lapland.

The tape of *Finlandia* was put in the tape player after we cleared the few formalities at the Finnish border. As we travelled south I gradually increased the volume of the music and the speed of the car.

The blonde later said she would never again drive through Finland -- or anywhere else, for that matter -- at 170 kilometres per hour while having her ears assailed by such loud music and her hair nearly torn from its roots by the wind.

But it was wonderful. The seemingly-endless stretches of pine forest and the rushing streams and rivers were beautiful. We passed herds of reindeer and later found friendly people with whom to swap hand signals -- since we had no common language in which to converse.

A few years later I returned to Finland and again paid homage to Jean Sibelius.

I went to Sibelius Park in the northwest quarter of Helsinki to see the extraordinary monument to the dead composer that was erected in 1963. Ella Hiltunen, the sculptress, used up seven years of her life building this enormous tribute to Sibelius. In order to do so, she first had to learn how to weld.

The amazing sculpture is probably symbolic of a massive pipe organ. A huge bust of Sibelius glowers at it from across a large patio.

Real music can move real people in strange ways; perhaps Hiltunen was also playing out strange fantasies that a brilliant composer had inspired.

Travel tip: *Don't be obvious*

Too many travellers carry large wads of cash and are careless about flashing it in amusement areas, restaurants and other public places.

Carry cash in at least two pockets with a smaller amount in the pocket from which you draw to pay. As you run low, inconspicuously top up the pocket from which you are paying.

The con games of Santo Domingo

Santo Domingo
Dominican Republic

I should have let the first shyster rip me off.

But I didn't like his style and after catching him in the first two lies, I decided to bail -- out of the frying pan and into the proverbial fire -- as it turned out.

It was after 10 p.m. when I lined up for immigration clearance at the airport here. I had been travelling by car, bus, planes, shank's mare and taxis in 95-degree heat since 4 a.m. that day and a bath, meal and bed were priorities.

A sharply-dressed young man standing beside a large sign announcing "Dominican Republic National Tourist Bureau" introduced himself by name as a representative of the Bureau.

"Where are you staying?" he asked. I gave him the name of an hotel listed in guide books as moderately priced and in the historic section of this city of five million people.

"No good! No good!" he exclaimed. "Besides it is now closed. I see from the label on your bag you are a travel writer. I will get you a good government rate for travel agents at a hotel I know. It is downtown. After you pass the immigration and customs we will go there by taxi and I will arrange everything for you, OK?"

Many Caribbean islands have tourist bureau officers at the airport to assist travellers -- particularly travel writers and travel agents -- whose goodwill does no harm to their tourism industry.

"OK," I said, "and a lady will come with us, too. We will leave her at the hotel downtown where she has a reservation and then go to the hotel you recommend."

He looked puzzled. "But you are alone?"

"Yes, but I sat with this lady on the flight from Haiti. She's buying shoes for her boutique. She has many cases and was going to take a bus. I offered her a ride since I'm going downtown too. If this hotel you recommend is downtown it can't be far out of our way."

"I will meet you outside with a taxi," the man said, and left.

While queuing for customs I consulted my guidebook about the hotel the man had recommended. The book located it in the far northwest corner of the city.

The Haitian lady who had been my seat mate on the flight was waiting outside customs with her five huge, empty suitcases.

"I can speak to these people in their language," the lady told me in French. "I will get you a good price for the taxi."

"That's all been arranged by the government tourist board," I told her. And there was the chap from the tourist board chatting with a large, smiling black man beside a car that was conspicuous in the taxi rank because it bore no signs indicating it was a taxi.

The Haitian lady jabbered at the driver in patois, then turned to me and said, "he is going to charge you $25 U.S. to go downtown. That is twice what it should be. I will get another taxi."

She tried two others and was quoted $25 U.S. by each. "They're all in it together," she said, "you may as well take the first one for $25."

It's a long ride from the airport to downtown Santo Domingo and as we drove the tourist board representative extolled the many virtues of the hotel where, he said, he had reserved a room for me.

Something didn't ring quite true. Tourist board reps don't "sell" hotels. They sell cities, regions and their country. Under cross examination this man admitted he did not represent the Dominican Republic Tourist Board, but represented the hotel.

"You also told me your hotel was in the Old Quarter," I reminded him. "It's in the northwest, isn't it?" He admitted it was.

"Then you've lied to me twice so I'm not staying at your hotel. I want to stay in the Old Quarter so I can photograph it tomorrow."

The Haitian lady wanted to know what was going on. I told her in French.

"Why don't you stay where I'm staying?" she asked. "It's two blocks from the Cathedral of Santa Maria. It isn't fancy but it's only tonight, so what does it matter? And it is not expensive . . . "

So I bailed out of the slick rip-off into a series of little ones that just went on and on and on.

Mr. Smooth from the airport and his driver were less than gracious when the fish they thought they had snared hauled his suitcase out of the "taxi" at the Hotel La Fama. They flung the bags of the Haitian lady into the street and shouted remarks at her which appeared to make her black face a few shades darker.

I helped her get her bags across the street and into the tiny, dimly-lighted lobby.

She jabbered at a man behind the desk who took a key from a

hook and indicated I should follow him. That room was down a narrow alleyway of cracked concrete and puddles of liquid that didn't smell like rain water.

The room was a dank cell with two single cots each covered with a sere sheet. Moisture oozed through the corners of the walls. The bathroom had a toilet with no seat, a cracked basin with one rusty tap and an unpainted concrete shower stall.

"No thanks," I said. "I'll take a taxi to another hotel."

But there were no taxis. The hotel had no telephone with which to call one and there were no other hotels nearby -- I was told.

I could see through that lie instantly, of course . . . but after hauling a heavy suitcase through wet, dark streets that more closely resembled North American alleys, I realized someone had finally told me the truth. There were no taxis and there were no other hotels.

So it was back to La Fama. By then the rate for that dank cell had doubled. The young Haitian man who showed me to the room had some English and told me it was very bad people had taken advantage of me twice. He would look after me the next day, he said, by arranging a tour after first negotiating a favourable price with a taxi driver. To get rid of him I told him I'd pay him to get me to the government's tourist information office at 9 a.m.

Screaming and loud crashes woke me around 6 a.m. My neighbour was throwing her shoes and then an empty bottle at cockroaches. I'd seen several mouse-sized ones in my cell, but have learned if you leave them alone they won't bother you. If you throw things at them and score a direct hit, they make a nasty mess.

I decided to get the hell out of Hotel La Fama and take my chances with a taxi to the tourist board which surely could arrange a driver for a quick look at Santo Domingo before a flight that night to Puerto Rico. But my self-appointed guide was even at that hour lurking in the lobby and had my suitcase in his hand before I knew it.

I let him haul it half a dozen blocks to a restaurant and then to the tourist office which was closed. We learned from the owner of a posh clothing store next door that the tourist office had been closed for some time pending the swearing-in of the new president.

So it was a taxi tour in a decrepit Austin at $70 U.S. for what remained of the day. The driver was a nice old chap who didn't appreciate the way my "guide" was issuing orders to him. Nor did I appreciate having to translate the guide's information to me in French to the driver in Spanish and the replies from the driver in Spanish back to the "guide" in French. When the "guide" went to a washroom, the driver and I left him there.

The balance of the tour was enjoyable, the city-wide games of automobile "chicken" notwithstanding. The driver explained his rate was not a rip-off. When cruise ships visit in the winter, rates for the city tour are $70 U.S., four tourists per taxi.

It was just my bad luck, the driver pointed out, that I didn't have three friends with whom to share the fare.

Preoccupation in Toronto, ripples in Dallas

Dallas
Texas, U.S.A.

My seat mate on the Air Canada flight to Dallas was en route to Houston -- the next leg of our trip -- and he swore softly when the announcement came for us to show our boarding passes. It was the first time he had spoken since leaving Toronto.

"This ought to be interesting," he said, showing me his boarding pass which had the confirmed destination clearly marked LAX for Los Angeles. "I went through a bit of hell trying to get on this flight," he said. "Fortunately I also have a ticket for Houston."

The steward did a double take: "You've got to be kidding!" he told the Texan. "This plane isn't going to Los Angeles."

"Neither am I," drawled my companion, "but I've had a heck of a time trying to get home to Houston on this boarding pass."

A female flight attendant came along to find out what was wrong. She and the steward exchanged puzzled looks over the boarding pass. Then the steward brightened and suggested to the flight attendant: "Preoccupation?"

"Preoccupation," she agreed after a pause, and they moved on.

"There won't be any trouble getting my bags from LA," the Texan observed wryly, "there are two direct flights a day."

Some time later he rummaged through his pockets and found two claim stubs for Houston. Despite a Toronto airline clerk's "preoccupation," the Texan and his luggage were reunited in Houston.

Tobogganing the streets of Madeira

Funchal
Madeira, Portugal

Everything is either up or down in Madeira. The main airport, a half hour's drive over corkscrew roads from the capital, Funchal, used up the most level part of this coast and the runway is only long enough to handle 707s.

The steep hills that are the volcanic heritage of this dot on the map 545 km west of North Africa and 978 km southwest of Lisbon, cause many problems. But they also provide a novel entertainment for tourists as unique to Madeira as is climbing Dunn's River Falls in Jamaica, being pulled in a rickshaw when visiting China or riding one of those ill-tempered camels to Egypt's Sphinx.

Tobogganing -- as it's called here -- started as logically as the first settlers solved the logistics of hauling supplies inland from the shore and produce from inland to the shore.

They used crude sledges dragged by mules or horses. It was hard work going uphill but on the descent the driver could sometimes give his feet a rest and let the animals pull him downhill.

As this capital city expanded, a network of cobblestone streets stretched up the sharply-sloping hillside. The flint-hard cobblestones had less friction than the mud pathways and a man on a sledge could enjoy an exhilarating ride down . . . at least until he failed to negotiate a curve and rammed into a house or stone wall.

Over a century ago an early tourist watched farmers enjoying the slide as they dragged their produce down to market. He paid one of the men for the privilege of hurtling down a chute-like street and so launched a tourist business which flourishes today.

But like most things that turn into an institution, the excitement is gone because the excitement used to lie in wondering how badly you'd be hurt when your ride ended -- wherever that happened to be.

There's no guessing nowadays. The sleds have a wicker bench mounted on them which seats three slender adults. Each sled is guided by two men who run alongside holding guy ropes to keep the sled from slewing off course. The runners wear Madeiran dress -- straw hats, white shirt with red bandana and white trousers.

It used to be possible to slide non-stop down six kilometres of Funchal streets, but road repairs have temporarily cut the run in half. It costs about $4 per person for three kilometres of sliding and when the 6 km run is back in operation it will be $7 per person – plus tip for your breathless runners.

Tobogganing is a Madeira must, of course. You can get a taxi from your hotel to the restaurant high above Funchal near the start of the run. After coffee or tea and Madeira cake, make arrangements with the men who run the toboggans.

Then, with the brakes of your taxi squeaking behind you at a discreet distance, you make the toboggan run.

The roadways used for tobogganing are flanked with riots of colourful flowers but the highlight is the view of the harbour over which you get ever-changing vistas as you descend.

If you should happen to feel just a little silly as you rocket down the steep roadway in your wicker chair with the runners panting and perspiring alongside, take heart. You're in good company. People like Sir Winston and Lady Churchill and George Bernard Shaw are reported to have regularly enjoyed tobogganing down the streets of Madeira.

And nobody laughed at them.

Airline tips: *For the smoothest flight*

▸ The best seats on aircraft for the smoothest ride are right over the wings. Other good areas are those in the front row of each section and often by the emergency exits, because they have more leg room. Avoid the last row because seats usually don't recline fully there, are often the last to be served drinks or meals and are usually near the washrooms which means a lot of traffic

▸ Keep your seat belt fastened throughout the flight regardless of whether the seat belt is on. Aircraft can suddenly encounter unexpected turbulence and bounce passengers right out of their seats without warning. A passenger on a Canadian flight was killed some years ago when his flight hit turbulence and he broke his neck after hitting the ceiling.

There's potassium in them that hills

Fredericton
New Brunswick, Canada

"It seems like a very simple solution to me," the heavy-set man at the next table said. "One of you will just have to kill the other three."

We were in an elegant Fredericton restaurant, scheming -- perhaps a bit too loudly -- about how we would sell non-existent minerals from our gold mine to the Nicaraguan government for cheques we couldn't cash because they would bounce. But we could use the government cheques to raise collateral for such management expenses as a modest fleet of Ferraris for weekends and Rolls Corniches for use during business hours.

Four of us had just won the opportunity to go claim-staking with a representative from New Brunswick's department of natural resources and a local prospector. Anybody can stake a mining claim in Canada, but when you're just getting into prospecting it helps to have a couple of experts along.

The gimmick which had fired -- perhaps even crazed -- our imaginations was the brainchild of New Brunswick's director of tourism who believed some travel writers meeting there might want to get out into the bush and stake a claim.

Don Carroll, co-ordinator of information services for the mineral resource division of the department, thought Helen Newman was just plain nuts. "You expect a bunch of journalists from Vancouver and Toronto and Montreal to go tramping around in the bush? You must be mad."

But Carroll dutifully turned up at a dinner, explained the claim-staking process and said he'd take two or three of the group out into the bush in two days' time to stake one mining claim. Anyone who wished to participate should put his or her business card into his miner's panning dish for a draw. From the group of 35, Carroll was astonished to find 20 cards.

Carroll lined up his brother Wayne to accompany the group because Wayne, a motor mechanic who maintains heavy mining equipment, spends a lot of his spare time at serious prospecting.

My card was first out of the pan, followed by those of Toronto-based youth columnist Lucy Izon, Toronto photographer Mike Dobel and Christine Aikenhead of CN Marine.

By claim-staking day it was evident to tourism and resources people that four claims would have to be staked. In New Brunswick there can only be one owner of a mining claim and the only solution we'd reached about who would own the claim was that the most eager would have to kill the other three. We had kicked around the possibility of forming a consortium around the one claim, but none of the four really trusted the other three.

"It's the only way," counselled Montreal film producer Don Forsyth. "They've been doing it in the movies and on TV for years. You have to claim jump or kill the partners. Since you're all novices you probably won't get the claim-jumping right. You'll have to kill the others."

So on claim-staking day Carroll had four prospecting licence application forms waiting at the Bathurst office of the department of natural resources. Such a licence is available to anyone on payment of a $10 fee and includes 10 sets of four aluminum tags with which to mark the boundary of each claim which is 400 metres square.

We crammed into a department station wagon and drove about 30 kilometres northwest from Bathurst into the hilly bushland of the Tetagouche Lakes region.

Carroll stopped the wagon on the shoulder of a gravel road beside an outcrop of grey rock sprayed with bright blue paint. That marked the westerly limit of the Anaconda Gold Mine, he said and some of the old claims had opened up beside that mine. We flipped to see whose claim would get staked first. Izon won the first flip.

Claims must be staked in a precise manner. You start at the northeast point of the area you intend to claim. There you mark off the trunk of a handy tree about 1½ metres above the ground. If no tree is handy, you have to find a two-metre section of one, square a couple of feet of it and plant it upright by piling rocks around its base.

To the top of the stake's south side you nail the aluminum claim marker. Underneath that with a felt-tipped marker, you print your name, the full date, exact time, number of your claim and the number of your prospector's licence. You then walk 400 metres due south, marking your route by tying strips of orange or yellow plastic ribbon to tree branches every 20-30 paces.

The 400-metre sides of the claim are measured by double paces; you count one every time your left foot hits the ground. A man will cover the distance in 250 double paces; Carroll decided Izon would do it in 260 double paces. Izon used an old claim marker we found by the roadside to start her claim and then we trudged up the side of a hill. It was fairly easy going on the first 400-metre leg because that parallelled the limit of the Anaconda Mine that had been marked by blue paint. Wayne guided Izon by constant compass checks. Izon counted her paces. Don tied ribbon to the trees and Aikenhead, Dobel and I wise-cracked about becoming mining magnates in between gasping for breath as we kept climbing.

A handy tree was squared off when Izon reached her 260th double pace. The pause while she chopped her marker gave us a long enough rest for the black flies to find us and stake their claims. From the second stake we marched 400 metres west and the fourth leg was due east back to the point from which we had started.

Izon's claim was staked in about an hour and we decided while hiking the fourth leg of her claim that the only way we could stake the others in the time available before the claim office closed, was to split into two groups.

Wayne and I headed into the bush to stake my claim. While we were doing that the others measured off the 400 metres from the western limit of Izon's claim and marked the spot where Wayne and I should come out of the woods after marking my 400-metre square. We were back in about half an hour and Wayne brought us out of the bush within three paces of the 400-metre point.

It was near there that Wayne found a quartz-like outcrop from which he chipped samples. "This looks really promising," he said, stuffing the rocks into a bag. "I've passed this place often and if I'd thought it had mineral content like this I would have staked it myself."

We guarded the samples until the others staked their claims and then we hightailed it to the department's office in Bathurst to register the claims before the office closed. There's a lot of writing required to register a mining claim but the office staff was patient and appeared to enjoy helping a group that was clearly destined to soon make major financial waves the length of Toronto's Bay Street.

From the claims office we drove for more than an hour to meet up with our group at another motel. When we entered the motel office, Aikenhead carried the mineral samples wrapped in a yellow rain slicker and cradled in her arms like a baby.

"Do you have a safe here?" I asked the bewildered receptionist. "We have some valuables." She summoned the manager but by the time he arrived we were convulsed with laughter.

The mineral samples spent the night under Dobel's bed and the next day he took them home with him to Toronto for assay.

Dobel obviously hadn't counted as strongly on his mineral wealth lifting him above the level of office drudgery as some of us had. When news of a major gold discovery in New Brunswick some months later reminded me of our claims, I telephoned him to ask the results of our assay. He apologised for not having taken the samples to an assay office and promised to do so that day. That weekend I cleaned the garden mud from my spade and shovel to have them ready for the move to New Brunswick.

Several weeks later I received a letter from Dobel. With twitching fingers I ripped it open, snatched out the contents and found two sheets covered with chemical symbols and very small percentage figures. Attached was a letter that read:

"Dear Dave, at long last, here is the assay on our mineral claims. The assayer interpreted all these numbers for me, to wit, 'your bag of rocks is . . . a bag of rocks!!!' There is no silver present, nor much of anything else.

"There is a high level of potassium which usually indicates a gold-bearing area but precious little actual gold. We would have to dig up, transport and smelt 1,000 tons of rock just to get one ounce of gold! I don't think that would be a profitable operation.

"I think I'll continue the search for wealth among the silver molecules of my film emulsions. Best regards, Mike." There was something stapled to his letter. Perhaps a serious note that he had been kidding about the .001 gold content of the samples?

My luck ran true. It was a sizeable bill from the Toronto assay company -- which I'd agreed to share.

Travel tip: *Act your age*

Don't sign up for a trip that is beyond your physical capabilities, but keep in mind there are many places available, even for the handicapped.

If you're not in tip-top physical shape you should not, for example, book a ski package to the Alps. Not only are the pistes longer there, and generally steeper than anything in North America, but the air at those altitudes is much thinner.

Speakers' Corner brings them out of the woodwork

London
England

The earnest young Japanese man with the large bible tucked under one arm had the undivided attention of about sixty people.

"Your city is cold, uncaring and unfeeling," he cried, flinging out one arm for emphasis. "There is no love evident here in London . . . no compassion for strangers and none of the human warmth our Lord taught . . . "

"Don't you listen to his rubbish! Don't any of you waste your attention on this man's blatherings. I can save you . . . for I am the Lord. Don't listen to this man. He is one of my patients. If you want to be saved come 'round to my clinic Monday morning and I'll save you . . . "

The Lord and Saviour was elegantly tailored and had an aristocratic bearing. He was bare-headed against the vicious damp cold of that January Sunday in Hyde Park and a solid-gold clip held his silk necktie in place.

A Pakistani woman told him he was interrupting the speaker.

"And you, woman, are interrupting the British way of life!" retorted the Lord and Saviour, hitting his stride again. "You Pakis, you Wogs, you Chinks . . . I beg your pardon, sir," he bowed from the waist to the neighbouring speaker, "I believe you are Japanese."

He continued in a vicious tirade of racial bigotry the more amazing for its cultured delivery.

"Whom do you wish to listen to?" he demanded when almost all races but white, Anglo-Saxon Protestants had been insultingly banished from his England.

"You tell us!" somebody in the crowd cried and the man with the solid gold tie clip and full-length cashmere coat walked off a dozen paces followed by most of the Japanese fellow's audience.

"I bear that man no malice," the young Japanese man explained to his diminished gathering. "The Lord cannot be in his heart because he is full of hate . . ."

Been There Done That

It was just another incident at Speakers' Corner in Hyde Park, forum for over 100 years for anybody who wants to get up on a soapbox and speak his mind on any subject.

It all started in July of 1855 when feelings were running high against the Sunday Trading Bill and a mass protest meeting was planned. Police forbade the meeting and none was held there until October 14 when a carpenter spoke. History, unfortunately, does not tell us what he said, but he returned for the next few Sundays and spoke without incident.

In 1862 a meeting in support of Garibaldi ended in bloodshed and there was a full-scale riot in 1866 when Police Superintendent Sir Richard Mayne ordered the park locked up to prevent a meeting.

Londoners, angered at being denied their right to meeting, tore down the wrought iron fences. In 1872 the commissioner of works set out an area of the park for meetings and it was decreed that anybody might express himself on any subject provided he "not offend public order and decency." There is also one unwritten law: the British monarchy is never spoken against.

Speakers' Corner has over the years become a tourist "must" and an interesting afternoon's diversion for many Londoners. There's no admission cost and no charge for speaking.

People with tales to tell, causes to boost or axes to grind show up on Sunday afternoons with boxes, chairs, step ladders or even telephone directories to stand on and deliver their messages.

It's a verbal free-for-all with no holds barred. While the speaker is free to express his views, the audience is just as free to disagree and the verbal jousting can get quite intense.

The Socialist Party of Britain has a stand there each week and the speaker hands out copies of the party's organ, *Socialist Standard*.

Just as well he has the pamphlets to hand out. He usually can't get a word in edgewise over the heated heckling, jeering and insults of the crowd although many of his quips, retorts and verbal ripostes are clever.

The churches are there, too. The London Secular League, the Methodist Church, West London Mission and the Catholic Evidence Guild. There was something for each of the 1,000 onlookers milling through the park that Sunday.

A young, bearded man was selling his ideas for the Campaign for Homosexual Equality. The Palestine Liberation Organization was drumming up recruits and receiving abuse from the crowd for its efforts.

A hippy in outlandish clothes, mounted on a stepladder and flourishing an incorrectly-spelled sign pleaded the case for being a hippy: "I wash windows for a living and don't cost anybody anything. If I want to wear clothes like these and make free love on the floor of my flat, why shouldn't I? Do you object to making free love?" he asked a passing lovely . . . but she blushed and quickened her pace.

Spectators wander from speaker to speaker photographing everything, looking as though they wonder what they're doing here.

Off in a quiet corner, Robert Ogilvie rambles on to a small crowd of his disciples about spiritual existentialism. He's a little gnome of a man with a Scottish accent, black beret, filthy trench coat and neatly-trimmed white beard.

The thrust of the portion of his delivery I caught was about his love for "our beautiful English language -- the language of poets and kings which, when properly spoken, is like music to my ears."

But in the next sentence he dropped an horrendous grammatical clanger.

I wandered off to hear what the Freedom Fighters were planning to fight about next. They had attracted the attention of three bobbies and the crowd was swelling. It looked as though they must have come up with something quite controversial.

Not a Newfie joke

Deer Lake
Newfoundland, Canada

None of the Canadian delegates to a meeting of international travel writers here was overheard asking about exchange rates on Newfoundland money.

But one of the group, struggling out of a Corner Brook liquor store with several bottles of Screech was heard to comment ruefully that he should have waited to make his booze purchase in the duty-free store at the airport here from which most delegates flew to their Canadian home towns.

The night the Mexican cab driver played impresario

Cabo San Lucas
Mexico

Two sides of the hotel dining room were open to the warm night air and, part way through the entrée, I started hearing mariachi music filtering through the lush vines which screened one side of the area from the dusty vulgarity of the town outside.

The first few numbers registered only as piped-in background music. But then, during one peppy number, I realized the sound track also contained the noises of tires screeching on asphalt, unmuffled motorbikes, dog fights and shrilling children -- those ubiquitous sounds that remind you each time you waken where you are.

Just as some children will follow a marching military brass band anywhere, I'll track down a good mariachi band wherever it's playing -- particularly if the trumpet player is good.

So as soon as I could convince my wife Wendy that she really didn't want dessert, we were out on the dusty main drag of Cabo, heading toward the most likely source of the mariachi music.

That turned out to be a vacant corner lot a block up the street, the town's unofficial *zocala*, or central square. An enterprising local chap operated a taco stand on wheels there, and I'd noticed earlier in the day he was doing a brisk business with tourists and locals alike.

This night there was a small queue waiting for his savoury offerings. And a few steps away, a nine-piece mariachi band in full traditional Mexican regalia was strumming, stomping and blowing up a beautifully melodic storm. The band had its back to the street and the small crowd and was playing to an audience of three people who were seated on a plank supported at each end by two cases of beer.

There was a tough-looking *hombre* at each end of the plank on either side of a woman whose apparel and demeanor did little to suggest she spent her Sundays teaching scriptures to local children. The trio swayed to the rhythm of the music, the men prevented from falling off their plank only by the arms they had intertwined around each others' shoulders behind the woman.

The band played beautifully. The trumpet's notes were clear and sweet and the tonguing was superb. The singers' voices blended perfectly and where many amateur groups fail, they successfully resisted the impulse to try to overpower the instruments with their voices in the choruses of some of the peppy, popular numbers.

We loitered on the far corner of the street for a few minutes, but during that time one of the men on the plank got up and scuffled with a closer bystander, making it clear that the command performance of the mariachi band was for his lady -- or the lady he was sharing with his buddy -- and kibitzers were not welcome.

We strolled past several times and then noticed an open-fronted bar directly across the street with empty tables facing the square where the mariachi band still made sweet music. Neither of us wanted one just then, but we ordered beers and sipped at them while savouring the music of the band from across the street.

Half an hour later, Wendy said she wanted to get back to the novel she was reading, and I walked her back to our hotel. The music followed, and strains of it came in through our open window. "Go ahead," she said after watching me trying to concentrate on my book for a while. "Go back to that bar; I'll be fine."

So I went back to the same table, ordered a beer and watched and listened to the group that was still going strong across the street. There were no other customers and after exchanging pleasantries, the owner brought his beer over and sat down at my table.

"You like the mariachi music?" he asked.

"Very much," I replied. "What's the special occasion?"

He explained that the man on the far end of the plank was a taxi driver who had made a lot of money and was celebrating. "But they are all very drunk," he added, somewhat unnecessarily as the taxi driver was again lurching about trying to clear away onlookers.

"Very, very drunk," the bar owner said. "They are paying 600 pesos (about $4.30 Canadian) for each of those songs. Tomorrow, the driver will have no money. But, tonight, he's having a good time."

The bar owner left me then to help his assistant pull down shutters and ready the premises for closing. When he began shutting the iron grillwork which would barricade the front of his establishment, I got up to leave.

"No, no, you don't have to leave," the bar owner said. "I just have to close the bar. You can stay here and listen to the music as long as you like. It's very beautiful, isn't it?" When he and his assistant had finished their chores, they brought three cans of cold beer to the table. We chatted, sipped the beer, and enjoyed the music.

I had noticed the village police cruiser earlier that evening. A 20-year-old Chevrolet with no muffler, only one headlight and *Policia* painted across the trunk attracts the attention of a *Norde Americano gringo*. The police car had been chugging and rattling past the little square about every 15 minutes during the evening. Now it idled into a parking space, the uniformed officer shut off the motor and got out.

"Will there be trouble?" I asked the bar owner.

"Probably not," he replied. "They're not breaking any law; the cop probably just wants to hear the music. It's very good," he added again with pride. The officer lounged against the side of his car, tapping the toe of his boot in the dust.

When the assistant finished his beer, the bar owner sent him for three more. I suspected the bar owner was treating me to the beers, but not wanting to presume on his kindness I pulled out a few 100-peso notes and let him see me counting them under the table.

"No, no," he said, pointing at the notes, "no money. You will drink with us, please."

Halfway through that can of beer, the taxi driver fell over backwards from the plank where the three were seated. This time he didn't get up. At the end of that number, his companion apparently told the mariachi band that there was no more money, because they packed up their instruments and straggled off down the street.

The two survivors -- the second man and the woman -- supporting each other with arms around their shoulders, set off down the main street as though battling invisible but very high seas. Strollers got off the sidewalk at their approach, and eventually they lurched out of sight into the gloom.

I thanked my benefactors for the ringside seat and the beer and strolled back to the hotel. A few weeks later, I bought some mariachi records in a music store in Guadalajara.

I play them at home on weekends. The artists are good; the recordings are clear. But the sights and other sounds are missing: the palm fronds whispering in the night sky, the smell of hot dust from the street, the chatter of children playing games along the sidewalk, the snapping sound of the tab on an ice cold can of *Tecate* beer.

I'll always be grateful to that very drunk taxi driver in Cabo San Lucas for fond memories of that fabulous evening concert . . . an evening he probably doesn't even remember.

Yes, there are some know-it-all travel writers

Jerusalem
Israel

Every time I've toured a foreign country in the company of North American travel writers there's always been at least one for whom the trip is the fourth or fifth to the city, region or country. This has often been a bonus because the journalist on his previous trips has found the correct answers to those questions that some government guides won't answer, or won't answer honestly, and we share information.

But that benefit has to be weighed against the sometimes pompous, pedantic, bombastic or condescending dissertations that sometimes flow unbidden and unwanted from some travel writers who have seen it all before.

There were seven of us in the stretched Mercedes taxicab on the three-kilometre trip from the Jerusalem Hilton Hotel to the Jerusalem Sheraton Hotel where we had been invited to a late-night cocktail party.

Sure enough, one of the group was on his fifth trip to Israel. From door to door he scarcely paused for breath, pointing out all the landmarks as we sped through the dark, wet streets. This clearly annoyed the driver who had politely tried a number of times to point out more significant sites and to correct some of the lecturer's apparently erroneous information.

As the taxi pulled into the Sheraton's forecourt, the travel writer (who I'll call Wally) loudly announced: "I'll look after the taxi; you have to know how to deal with these blokes or they'll hold you up for whatever they think they can get away with."

We piled out of the taxi and Wally strode around to the driver's door. "Look here," he said, pulling out a roll of banknotes and starting to count them, "I'm not going to pay you one shekel more than four thousand."

The taxi driver held up his arms as though fending off a blow. "No, no," he protested, "too much, too much."

"If you don't like that you can call the police," the travel writer argued, clearly deaf to the driver's protests. "I know how you blokes operate. You call the police; I'll wait right here." He continued counting hundred-shekel notes from his bankroll.

I'd been to Jerusalem before, but kept my mouth shut; you can usually learn a lot more that way. But one of the first-timers to Israel jumped in and told Wally, "the cab fare should only be about 300 shekels."

"Yes! Yes!" the driver agreed. "Four hundred is enough."

Wally folded up his bankroll and started counting again. "Yes," he said, "of course. Slip of the tongue. Just got back from Italy, you know . . . wasn't thinking; here you are, my good man," and he handed the driver 400 shekels.

We all chuckled at the incident, but it didn't end there.

Wally and his wife left the party at the Sheraton long before I did.

The next day I bumped into Wally between business meetings at the Hilton Hotel.

"If you don't mind me asking," Wally enquired quietly, "how much did you pay for your cab back here from the Sheraton last night?"

"The driver asked for 250 shekels for five of us," I answered, "but because he was honest I gave him 350."

"H-m-m-m-m-m-," Wally harrumphed. "We had a driver who demanded 2,200 shekels. I offered him 500 and told him he could call the police if he wasn't satisfied. He decided to settle for the 500."

Travel Tip: Early bird can avoid some worms

If you have long distances to cover by car in a Third World country, consider packing up the night before and leaving at, or before, dawn. It's cooler then and you'll also make better time because you'll be on the highway before the donkey carts, overloaded trucks and buses and most of the drivers who might have had too much to drink by mid-afternoon. If you don't have confirmed accommodation reservations plan on stopping early -- no later than 3 p.m.

Not easy to be a customer

Roseau
Dominica

When the advertised tour of the island was cancelled because not enough people signed up, I tried to rent a car in which to do my own exploring. It wasn't easy . . . but the price was, ultimately, right.

The hotel manager put me in touch with Albert Astaphan who owns two of the very few rental vehicles here. But Astaphan wouldn't rent a car for just one day. "I charge only $85 (E.C.) per day (about $40 Canadian) and a new tire costs $250. "So if you break a tire because the roads are so bad, I have lost money."

And Astaphan wouldn't rent a car for one day and charge me for two days. "That wouldn't be fair to you," he explained. He was intractable.

So I found two hotel guests who had just checked in for a week's stay and eventually talked them into what must have sounded quite implausible.

The deal was that one of them would put up the $100 U.S. cash deposit against damage to the car and rent the car for two days. I would pay for the two days rental if, on the second day, they would drive me to the airport on the far side of the island.

That would give them the use of the car for the rest of that day. Meanwhile they would be welcome to join me on a fast-paced tour of the island.

Astaphan didn't mind renting a car to one of the ladies for two days. He was late picking us up at the hotel and then he had to change a soft tire on the four-year-old Toyota.

With all the confusion and delays he never did get either a deposit or any payment.

The "shared" rental system worked well. The two ladies from Boston appreciated having a male companion with them as we explored the island and I enjoyed their company.

On the second day we drove across the island to the airport. I had paid the car renter $80 U.S. for the two days rent and asked her to please get a receipt for the two-day rental when she returned the car to Astaphan.

"I'll bet if you keep the car for a third day and return it undamaged he'll probably only charge you for the two days," I suggested as we parted company at the airport.

About two weeks later I received a letter from the lady who had rented the car. She said she had kept the car for the third day. She enclosed a receipt from Astaphan for $62 U.S. . . . and her personal cheque for $18 U.S. because Astaphan had charged her only $62 for three days car rental although he had originally quoted $40 U.S. per day.

I haven't figured that one out, either. But I've decided Astaphan's rental rates and methods of doing business are somehow refreshingly more than fair.

Wanna see your luggage again?

Luggage goes astray as inevitably as night falls, but there are some things you can do to lower the odds on it happening to you. And even if you've read this sort of advice before, take a moment to brush up on the pointers; they could save exasperation and untold inconvenience.

▸ If you wish to transport some item of exceptional value you can sometimes purchase excess valuation insurance (EVI) from the airlines at check-in. Carriers may refuse to sell EVI on some items like antiques or expensive musical instruments, so it's wise to check with their local office before taking the item to the airport.

▸ Never pack anything in baggage you are going to check that you absolutely can't get along without at your destination -- passport, tickets for on-going travel, reservation guarantees, prescription medicine or drugs or medicines you may not be able to get at your destination without a local prescription.

▸ Check in on your flight as early as possible. Late arrivals may catch the flight but often their luggage doesn't. If your itinerary involves changes of aircraft or airlines have your tickets written up to allow ample time between connections for checked-through luggage to be transferred.

In the hands of an expert

Rotorua
North Island, New Zealand

The 10-pound brown trout got away. Let's get that fact right up front in this story about a most unusual fishing trip, and be done with it.

It was just after 11 p.m. and fishing guide *extraordinaire* Mike Scott had pulled out the last stop in his effort to help the Canadian visitor catch a trophy-sized trout.

Scott operates Ty-llyn Fishing Lodge on Lake Rotorua on New Zealand's North Island, two blocks from what is probably the world's best trout-fishing river. He boasts that any guest catching a brown trout weighing less than eight pounds, does not pay for that day's accommodations, meals and guide service.

"There will be one under the bank there, just below that little bush that sticks out. Drop your fly about one-third of the way across the river with enough line to drift it a couple of feet below that hole. Then bring it slowly up -- but not too slowly or the current will take it into the bank and you'll snag those bushes.

I knew this was it.

The fish weren't rising and Scott said nobody had caught anything for several weeks. I had unsuccessfully worked the upper half of the river in late afternoon on my own and for the past two hours Scott and I had been beating the waters again. He'd shown me several dozen hidey-holes, but nothing had come roiling up out of them.

To reach this last-chance hole, we had tiptoed down a private laneway lined with No Trespassing signs.

Scott assured me he had permission from the owner to use the property to gain access to the river, but we must be careful not to wake the residents.

Close to an open bedroom window we had to scale a smooth brick wall about six feet high to get to the river bank. We somehow managed this silently in the dark while wearing chest waders without breaking the fly rods, ripping the waders or slipping into the deep, black, fast-flowing water.

I worked the line out across the river to a length that would exactly reach the precise spot I had to land the wet fly and then made the cast.

"Well done," came a deep-voiced whisper from somewhere in the darkness. "Perfect."

Fly fishing is an art form. It's a passion, a way of life for some and it can be every bit as much a snob sport as falconry or fencing. For a bumbling colonial who grew up thrashing the waters of northern Quebec with a $10 split-bamboo fly rod, that simple "well done" was enough to make the whole expedition worthwhile. The words came, after all, from the world's third-ranked fly fisherman.

The fly snaked out and settled on the water like dandelion fluff. My eyes couldn't follow its drift in the darkness, but by gauging the current, I knew when it was in position and started to retrieve it.

The fish hit exactly where Scott said it would and exactly how he said it would -- like a Mack truck.

I struck. It was like setting the hook in a tractor tire mired on the river bottom.

And then the line went slack. The leader had parted from the line. It must have snapped, because the world's third-ranked fly-fisherman who had rigged my rod would most definitely have tied the proper knot . . .

The angry trout jumped half a dozen times after that in the middle of the river, trying to shake the hook.

And that's how we know it weighed exactly 10 pounds.

Travel tip: A word to the wise . . .

When travelling in foreign countries it's a good idea to carry some of the local currency in small denominations to cover the cost of tips, snacks, drinks and other minor purchases.

Keep that cash in a separate pocket, or area of your wallet or purse -- if you must travel with a purse.

When you're making those minor purchases you can then bring out the $20 or so of local cash without having to display your credit cards, travellers' cheques or larger supply of Canadian or U.S. cash.

Travel experiences you really can't write about

It's unfortunate that many of the fun things encountered on the travel beat can't always be shared with readers.

One of the funniest travel stories I've heard in years, for example, can't be definitively tracked down. So in fairness, it can't be reported in complete detail.

This happened a few years ago and was recounted by a travel writer colleague who was there and swears it happened. A certain country (which has to be nameless) had, fairly or unfairly, acquired a sordid reputation for bandits. There were reports of tourists being stopped at gunpoint and relieved of their cash, jewellery and cameras.

The tourist industry of that country was slumping as these reports circulated in the lucrative North American travel market.

So the national tourist board invited a group of travel writers to visit the country, savour its food, enjoy its sights and overdose on its liquors. All red-carpet treatment. The trip was carefully orchestrated in hopes the journalists would go home and write glowing accounts of the friendly natives, superb food, colourful history and stunning sights.

On Day Two the journalists were bused out of the capital city to visit one of the scenic wonders before enjoying a gourmet lunch. They wandered around taking photographs, buying souvenirs and interviewing tourism officials.

Then it was time to get back on the bus to go to lunch. That's when they discovered bandits had stolen the press bus!

And in it, of course, press cameras, passports, jackets, purses, flight bags and all those other things people carry on a day's outing.

The lady who told me the story said all the personal items were later returned to the journalists and the bus hijacking was explained as some sort of "misunderstanding."

Officials of the country where she said it happened assured me they knew nothing about the incident. So you'll have to guess at the country; it would serve no purpose to name it because by now that country's government has almost certainly passed a law banning the theft of buses being used by members of the foreign press!

Another funny story happened this year . . . and I was there.

I was meeting with the tourist board representative of a major

Canadian tourist destination who was taking me on a whirlwind tour of her city's newest tourist attractions.

I know the city well, but it saves a lot of time to have someone along who has all the answers and knows all the short cuts. I could take notes as she drove between points of interest and parked without hassles in reserved parking areas.

By pre-arrangement we met at one of her city's finest restaurants for breakfast. She was a few minutes late for the meeting.

"Good to see you again," she enthused with a big, warm smile, settling into the restaurant booth.

"I'm sorry the weather is so lousy, but the forecast says the rain should stop by noon. How are you? Don't you think the décor of this place is fabulous? They do terrific eggs Benedict here, in case you haven't ordered yet."

"They must do something well," I answered with a smirk, "because they seem to serve a widely varied clientele."

"What do you mean?"

I pointed at a baited rat trap tucked into the far corner of an adjacent booth near the kitchen door.

"Oh my God!" she wailed. "Oh God, please don't write anything about that! Harold (the restaurant owner, and not his right name) will have a fit."

Harold did indeed have a fit when the tourist board rep told him the next day a travel writer had spotted a baited rat trap in his restaurant. "What did Scott say?" was Harold's immediate concern.

"He said he couldn't decide whether the word rat-trap should be hyphenated," the tourism official replied.

Harold reportedly also wailed, "Oh, my God!" He also, unfortunately, fired two employees that day.

Since the rat trap has gone and new standards of cleanliness are in place in Harold's restaurant, there seems no constructive merit in identifying the restaurant, or the city.

Travel tip: *Go for the comfort*

All footwear you're taking on a trip should be well broken in. The same applies to clothing. Pack only outfits you know are comfortable.

Reminder of man's inhumanity

Stutthof
Poland

There was drizzle and fog and that kind of dampness that reaches to the bone marrow the day we visited the concentration camp here, about 50 km from Gdansk on the Baltic Sea.

Even now, only a few decades after the remaining prisoners were liberated by the Soviets, it's a depressing place. It's a place that wrenches at emotions and nerves. The visitor sees the triple-tiered bunks in the long, roughly-constructed frame buildings where prisoners slept six to each tier of a bunk; a space about six feet by four feet.

Within sight of all of the living quarter windows are the gas houses where 85,000 of the 120,000 prisoners died and the furnace building where their corpses were incinerated after the Nazis ran out of space in the mass burial grounds nearby.

The visit graphically answered a question which someone had asked at the outset of the tour – why any government would preserve such a ghastly reminder of man's inhumanity to man and treat it as a tourist attraction.

We were glad to get back to the warmth and immediacy of the press bus.

The guide was the last one on the bus and asked whether anybody had questions before we left Stutthof.

The lady from New York near the front of the bus raised her hand. "How much does it cost," she called out, "to get into the concentration camp?"

"It isn't used any more," the guide answered. "It hasn't been used since the Soviets liberated it in 1945. It is just kept as a reminder to people of what can happen when there is not peace in the world."

The lady from New York did not pursue her question.

Swedish parties are turnabouts

Goteborg
Sweden

It wasn't International Women's Year when a friend and I attended a weekend party at this North Sea summer resort, but North America's 'Why Not' ladies would have had their eyes opened.

The entire bash at the cottage where we were house guests was just as the most rabid female libber would have arranged things in her wildest pipe dream.

The attractive green-eyed blonde with whom I was travelling through Europe was not my wife, but for a variety of reasons Wendy wore a wide gold band on the third finger of her left hand and most people assumed we were married.

Our host Tómas believed we were married and there seemed no worthwhile reason to disabuse him of this notion. Tómas told us the party would be typical of those held by young Swedes at seaside resorts all summer long. There would be about a dozen couples. We'd have a typical Swedish dinner of sea food accompanied by gallons of iced beer, akvavit and song followed by dancing.

We helped Tómas set up for the party and then loafed around a crackling wood fire listening to a hard rain rattle on the porch roof and sipping *Falcon* beers, a local brew similar to Canadian ale.

That's when Tómas explained what he called "the Swedish way of doing things."

"Wendy," he started, "I hope you won't misunderstand what I'm going to tell your husband, but it's just the way we are and you both said you wanted to come to a real Swedish party. There are a few married couples coming tonight but most of the girls are single." He paused for a massive infusion of vodka and grapefruit juice, a concoction he said he used as a "primer" for parties.

"You should try some of the girls," he told me earnestly. "If some girl takes a liking to you you should go along with her. It doesn't mean anything, but here in Sweden the girls do the choosing. Let me know what you think of the system tomorrow.

"I know, I know," Tómas hurried on, fending off a comment Wendy hadn't been about to make, "It's not the way you do things, but it's the way we do things . . . and it doesn't mean anything . . . and some of the girls are beautiful."

"If he does . . . what do I do?" Wendy asked Tómas.

"That's up to you," Tómas answered. "In Sweden the girls do whatever they want . . . and with whomever they want. And they're used to getting their own way. I think Dave should try a couple of them . . . if that's what they want."

The party started at the sort of tempo Canadian parties achieve only after the bar has been open three or four hours.

The guests arrived singly, in couples and in small groups and mostly by taxi despite the cottage being about seven kilometres out of town. Swedes who drink don't drive their cars to or from parties.

Tómas' guests were all Swedes in their late 20s or early 30s. We had been impressed for some time by his command of English, but learned that night he was the least fluent in English of all the Swedes present.

Each arrival was introduced and most apologized for having less than perfect English, despite grammar and vocabulary superior to that of many Canadians. The Swedes spoke their own language until either Wendy or I came within earshot at which point they'd switch -- even in mid-sentence -- to English.

The girl who decided she'd fancy an interlude with the pear-shaped Canadian tourist was a nurse with ice-blue eyes and honey-coloured hair . . . not that liquid, amber-coloured honey sold in jars, but the whipped, creamed variety that comes in tubs. She was about 5'-7" tall and the balance of her staggering physiognomy cannot be described with objectivity or justice in the pages of a book designed for readership of all ages.

Hers was the face and body of red-blooded mens' wildest fantasies. She arrived with a boy friend.

We discussed nursing. Canada. Sweden.

The boy friend moved off to talk with other people after Ingrid made it very clear she preferred a two-way conversation.

We discussed socialism. Her glass was empty then and yes, she'd like another, but came with me to the bar while I mixed them.

We discussed me . . . because all my questions about her drew answers that snapped right back to that topic.

Through no fault of Ingrid's we were separated at the dinner table, but she'd managed to get three or four people between her and the boy friend and her frequent glances and bold winks left no doubt she'd staked out a claim.

And the moment people began getting up from the shambles of broken lobster shells, empty beer cans and bread-crust-littered wreckage that was the dinner table, Ingrid was suggesting quietly into my ear that we should dance.

The party roared on . . .

Sunday's breakfast was a more subdued affair. Tómas was not pleased with either Wendy or me because neither of us knew the name of the sultry brunette brooding in his kitchen. Tómas had found her in his bed when he awoke and had been trying to find out her name without asking her, a move he felt might be just a tad gauche.

"I saw you with that blonde," were Tómas' opening words to me. "You lucky devil! I had my eye on her, too, but she certainly seemed to take a liking to you from the moment she walked through the door. She's been going out with Nels for almost a year.

"How was she?" Tómas went on, apparently oblivious to Wendy's presence.

"I wouldn't know," I had to tell Tómas. "We just talked . . . and she was very interesting to talk to." Tómas looked disgusted.

I had insulted Ingrid, he pointed out, although he hoped she might write off my peculiar behaviour as idiosyncratic of Canadians, whose life-style apparently is not well known in Scandinavia.

When Tómas returned from taking the buxom brunette home, he chided me again for "failing" Ingrid and leaving him with explanations to make at the next party where she showed up. He also grumbled about the nuisance of taking his over-night roommate home.

I couldn't understand the attitude. Where we came from, I told Tómas, 90 per cent of the men at any given party would have exerted every technique in their repertoire to get the girl to where she had more than willingly gone.

That, Tómas explained, was the problem. Had it been his idea, he would have been delighted. But it was the girl's idea. In Sweden it was always the girl's idea, he said and that's why so many Swedes marry girls from other countries.

The phone rang. It was the brunette. Yes, Tómas said, he'd take her to the discotheque that evening.

"I need a vacation," he sighed, after hanging up the phone. He said his vacation -- like those taken by most Swedish bachelors -- would be to Poland. There, he said, with a trace of envy in his voice, the men do the asking and "the girls know their place."

It's probably hard for most virile male Canadians to work up much sympathy for Tómas and his "harassed" confreres. But it was interesting to talk to the Swedish men and learn how bitterly many resent their ladies' liberated lead in romantic matters.

We Canadian males often yearn for the sort of situations that were available at Tómas' party, but many might wonder at the reaction of Tómas and his friends.

If a conclusion is to be drawn, it is likely that the male ego or psyche is generally receptive to the female taking the lead or even calling the shots in many fields of endeavour. But it would seem the male feels compelled to take the lead in at least one key area.

Travel agent swears it's true

A travel agent friend in Montreal swears this story is true. It doesn't translate on paper as well without the French accent:

A large and very drunk lumberjack wearing a raccoon coat lurched into her travel agency. He approached a pretty young girl behind the counter who had just started working at the agency.

"I wan', please, a ticket for de plane so I can go and see my fren' in Christ Church," the man slurred.

The girl made out a round trip ticket to Christ Church and the man paid cash from an immense wad of bills he pulled from his pocket. Clutching his ticket he weaved out of the agency.

Four days later the girl looked up from her desk to see the same man, just as smashed, lurch through the agency door, still wearing his raccoon coat.

"Did you have a good time in the Barbados?" she asked brightly, although suspecting that something must have gone wrong because she had sold the man a 14-day round trip ticket.

"It was OK," he said, "but I couldn't find my fren' d'ere. H'I look all over dat place and den some guy tol' me dere's anodder one of dose Christ Church place in New Zealand. So will you make me, please, a ticket to go dere?" No anger. No rancour. No complaint.

The man paid for the second ticket with cash, staggered out of the agency and hasn't returned.

If that didn't provide you with a chuckle, take a moment to picture our pickled Quebec friend lurching around in the steaming heat of Barbados in his raccoon coat, looking for his friend . . .

Ounces of prevention can make you hungry

Budapest
Hungary

It was Thanksgiving, so the group of 16 Canadians attending a week-long meeting in Budapest decided we'd get together that evening for a Canadian Thanksgiving dinner. Arrangements were made for a small, private banquet room upstairs at the Citadella Restaurant.

We had a distinguished guest with us at dinner that night, an internationally recognized Canadian medical doctor who has devoted his life to protecting North American travellers from diseases in foreign lands.

The doctor is suave and dashingly handsome and it didn't surprise me to notice when we sat down at the banquet table that he was flanked by the two single female members of our group, each of whom was hanging on his every word.

An hour and a half later, the waiters got around to bringing wine and bread to the table. "No wine," announced the doctor, covering his glass so the waiter couldn't fill it. "Please bring bottled mineral water. You can't be too sure about the wine here," he said to the ladies beside him, "and alcohol isn't good for you, anyway." Both ladies sipped furtively at their wine.

Almost another hour later the waiters came to take dinner orders, by which time we had learned there would be no traditional turkey for our Thanksgiving dinner, but there were many appetizing options on the menu, most of which we had managed to translate.

"I understand the Hungarians do great things with chicken," one of the single ladies said to the doctor as her turn to order from the waiter neared.

"Tsk-tsk-tsk," admonished the doctor wagging his forefinger at her. "Botulism! It can be very bad here. Sometimes fatal. The fish is usually safe; it's what I'm having." They both ordered fish.

The waiter paused behind the lady on the doctor's other side, pen poised over his order pad. "I'll have the shellfish combination," the lady told the waiter and the doctor swung towards her, forefinger upraised. "Red tide!" he exclaimed. "Very dangerous. Probably ptomaine."

The lady's complexion paled. "Of course," she said. "I'll have the fish."

The gypsy violins thundered and wailed around us and the waiters kept bearing wine and bottled water and a procession of wonderful dishes -- to most of us.

Later I met the doctor's dinner companions in a coffee house near our hotel. They were attacking their strudels and pastries as though they hadn't eaten for hours, which indeed turned out to be the case.

"That fish was awful," one complained. "I don't like fish anyway, but the doctor was just so handsome and smooth and I was trying to impress him."

"I was trying to impress him too," the other chimed in, "until he wouldn't let me have any salad. By then I said to hell with it, but I had already ordered all sorts of other stuff I didn't want."

I didn't tell the ladies that Colleen to my left had raved about her chicken, that John to my right had loved his venison and that my blood-rare chateaubriand had been ecstasy . . . except for what the waiter insisted was sauce béarnaise, but which was really tartar sauce, and which might have given a spark of flavour to their fish.

That little, white bag

A friend recently told this story on herself about an embarrassing situation on her first flight. She got settled in her seat and while waiting for the plane to take off, rummaged in the pouch on the back of the seat ahead of her. She discovered a motion sickness bag.

"I decided getting sick was probably part of the deal or they wouldn't have provided the bag," she explained. "I sat there holding that damn bag at the ready until we were up in the air and the flight attendant came around to take orders for drinks. She asked me if I felt sick and thought it was very amusing when I told her I didn't, but explained why I had the bag ready."

The travel junkie's wonder drug

Salema
Algarve, Portugal

Even the pre-school children playing in the golden sand were quiet. They had toy dump trucks and were building a network of roadways. Occasionally the sound of a vocally-simulated gear change danced past on the light, salt-scented breeze.

The fishermen's morning's catch was being Dutch-auctioned under a tin-roofed building open on two sides, but the drone of voices carried only a few dozen metres. Small waves from the blue Atlantic washed the beach, tumbling grains of sand as each receded with the swishing sound a paint brush makes on rough wood.

It was mid-morning in this fishing hamlet a billion miles from Ontario, and 15 kilometres west of Lagos in the Algarve, Portugal's southernmost province.

The sun beat down through a sky of unreal blue, undiluted by even a wisp of cloud. In the narrow margin of shade under the gunwale of a green and yellow and blue fishing boat, a mongrel dog snuffled and snored in a deep sleep. Several metres away his master and a companion enjoyed their pipes as they cleaned a fishing net on the gunwale of their red, purple and aquamarine boat.

I had strolled to the beach through the warren of narrow, cobblestone alleys that is the hamlet of Salema. Strolled was the word because the settlement's construction predates cars and trucks and the narrow streets accommodate only motorbikes, fish barrows and bicycles.

The tiny, freshly-whitewashed stucco homes each share a neighbour's wall, creating something like meandering motels that Jack might have built.

Each unit is different from the next; some with flower-filled window boxes, another with religious tiles set in the walls, one with a blue door and the next with a mauve door. Some have one floor, others two.

The alley that is the main street angles up a hillside approximately parallel to the beach below. After walking to the top of that street I crossed over to a pathway and came down again, past the back doors and patios and kitchen windows that overlook the beach.

From every second or third open window wafted tantalizing odours of lunches simmering over wood stoves. On many of the alternative patios wives of the fishermen sat in the sun cleaning the fish and peeling the vegetables that would be lunch and carrying on animated conversations across the gaps.

The cobbled pathway past the patios was bordered on the seaside by a low stone wall over which the women pitched fish heads, innards and bones.

The village cats seemed to be allowed only as close as the seaside of the wall. They waited patiently there for their treats, stripping the offerings to the bones. The system seemed to have worked for generations. The bleached fish bones of decades were heaped along the far side of the wall, bleaching in the sun and slowly turning to powder.

Just west of the white-walled cluster which is the village of Salema there is a new bar-restaurant at the top of the beach.

From the wooden terrace you can see the village on your left and watch the ant-sized tractor pulling the fishing boats to and from the surf. Straight in front the beige beach melts into the blue Atlantic which disappears in a sky the same colour. To the right the beach crescent ends in sandstone cliffs which plunge 50 metres into the sea.

From the empty terrace this day the village and the beach and the sea and the sky and the cliffs are frozen in a silent panorama no film or brush can capture. Time stands still.

With all those props as signposts the imagination starts a journey. One of those unexpected journeys that can divert the course of a life as suddenly and inexorably as a heart attack or a maiming automobile crash.

The new bar-restaurant is used by some villagers, but was built for the convenience of the few tourists who drive the winding three kilometres down from the coast highway to see what that dot on the map of the coastline looks like close up.

Perhaps if those tourists hadn't shown up I might have eventually managed to find a way to blend into that panorama -- for keeps.

But their touring van snorted into the parking lot by the beach and the doors clattered and slammed as they leaped out with their cameras to frame the colourful boats on the beach and the weather-beaten faces of the fishermen at the auction and the whitewashed homes.

I looked with a start at the wristwatch I'd forgotten I was wearing. And across at the rental car in the parking lot that had to be jockeyed another several hundred kilometres that day to keep up to the itinerary.

I dragged myself back to reality.

But I took from Salema what the kids would call an upper. A tiny capsule of a re-usable drug in the form of memory. I can pop that memory pill again and again whenever there are some spare minutes.

They're habit forming, but not harmful to your health. They don't impair anything . . . except the user's appreciation of what North Americans call civilization and progress.

Airline tips: *One is all right . . .*

They keep offering it to you, but experts agree the less alcohol you drink in flight, the better. One drink may help you sleep better, but more will just exacerbate your dehydration problems. Be sure to drink lots of water or fruit juices.

Time to be picky . . .

The longer the flight, the more meals you're likely to be served. The smart traveller eats about half of what's served. Don't feel guilty about just picking at that sometimes excellent food; it's going to be thrown away whether you touch the tray, or not.

Try to keep moving . . .

On long flights it's wise to move around the aircraft whenever you get a chance even though this may annoy some other passengers. The walking increases your blood circulation and helps reduce the possibility of blood clots forming in your system.

Let your wishes be known . . .

If you plan to fight jet lag by sleeping on a long flight, try to get a window seat so seat mates won't be clambering over you. Make a point of informing the flight attendant you plan to sleep and do not wish to be awakened for meals -- or specify which meals you do want.

100 rum shops to serve 6,000

Hillsborough
Carriacou, Grenada, Windward Islands

There are more than 100 rum shops but only one gasoline station on this tiny island. Those statistics may suggest that the 6,000 residents of this speck on the map usually are too smashed to drive, but that's not the case.

"There is less drunkenness here than on most of the other Caribbean islands," says Oliver Bullen, owner-manager of the island's biggest hotel. "A lot of people drink a lot of rum, but apart from the occasional tourist, you seldom see a drunken person."

You don't see an unhappy person on Carriacou, either, or anybody in a hurry except the odd yahoo in a car or van bent on sustaining his imagined macho image by hurtling past other motorists on the blind curves of the one-lane roadways.

Carriacou and Petite Martinique are diminutive dependencies of Grenada and not widely known. When U.S. troops invaded Grenada in 1983 in what locals call "the intervention," islanders had to wait a week until U.S. troops found their island and came to "liberate" them from Communists. When the marines finally arrived they found smiling natives offering pop and beer instead of armed Cubans.

Hillsborough is the port of entry, seat of government and only town, population 600. The main street parallels a beach and the stroller will notice that the first floors of some buildings are of stone and the second of frame-and-shingle construction. The thick stone walls indicate the first floors were 18th-century warehouses.

From almost any point on the island you can see offshore islets and islands, one of them the large French island of Martinique.

A number of Grenadians, hearing I was going to Carriacou mentioned that many islanders supplement their incomes by smuggling. Whatever they do smuggle – if indeed they do smuggle – isn't offered to day-trippers. Discreet inquiries by my driver failed to turn up any French cigarettes to augment my dwindling supply.

The *je ne sais quoi* of Ireland's Blarney Castle

Blarney Castle
Ireland

A lot of them come to laugh or joke or just to cross another name off their list of places to see.

But most leave in a different frame of mind. They leave having done something they never believed they would and something they were prepared to kid their companions about if they did it.

They return to their cars or buses in reflective mood and paying closer attention to the other people making their way towards the Blarney Stone they have left.

There are the North Americans, brightly dressed and bristling with cameras, flight bags and binoculars. There are the western Europeans – the Dutch, Belgians, Germans and French -- looking as though they feel out of place and as if they aren't quite sure why they are here, but nevertheless determined to visit something as integral to Ireland as the Eiffel Tower is to France.

And there are the Irish, many of whom help make up the estimated 250,000 visitors each year to this castle and its famous Blarney Stone. They come in all shapes and sizes and ages and from all economic strata. Some live in Ireland, others are a generation or more removed and come to visit from all corners of the world. But they come in an endless stream to what appears to be their mecca and many seem driven by the same remorseless determination that brings believers to Lourdes or Ste. Anne de Beaupré.

Some come in wheelchairs, on crutches or with walkers or canes. For some the ten-minute stroll from the car park to the foot of the ancient castle keep is an agonizing journey of over an hour. And that has to be followed by the climb up 120 steep, well-worn stone steps to the top of the castle and the object of what seems like their pilgrimage.

Kissing the Blarney Stone is an expression which has become firmly rooted in the English language and at the back of many people's minds is the thought that some day they might like to do it. It's the sort of thing they joke about when they're saying goodbye to friends at the airport.

Somehow the joke seems out of place when you get here and are following the pathway through the lush meadowland under spreading tree branches and over the wooden footbridge across the chuckling River Martin. Ahead and high above the treetops towers the keep of the third castle on this site, built in 1446. The first castle in the 10th century was of wood, later replaced by a stone structure subsequently destroyed.

The Blarney Stone is a block of limestone four feet, one inch long by one foot one inch wide and nine inches deep built into the battlement about two feet from the top. The stone is said to give the gift or oratory in exchange for a kiss.

One legend is that it was once known as Jacob's pillow and was brought here from the Holy Land during the crusades and another is that the stone was a gift of gratitude from Robert Bruce who had been aided in battle by the MacCarthys, owners of the castle.

The most popular version is that the MacCarthy who reigned in Munster during Queen Elizabeth's time and who was able, literally, to talk the noose off his head, caused blarney to enter the English language as meaning in conversation, "fair words in soft speech."

In his dealings with the Queen -- while professing to be her loyal Baron of Blarney -- MacCarthy never fulfilled any promise he had made or agreed to. Procrastination followed dalliance; delay and subterfuge followed device and evasion until eventually in disgust the queen is reported to have cried out: "Blarney, Blarney, what he says he does not mean. It is the usual blarney."

It's difficult to photograph the stone; more difficult to kiss it, because it is below the walking area of the battlement and under the top part of the wall. To reach the stone with your lips, empty your pockets of valuables, turn your back on the wall in which the stone is located, sit on a blanket provided by an attendant, and lean away back and over. When your head is well below the level of your heels you can look up at the stone and kiss it -- if that's your thing.

If you dare let your eyes roll back, you get a magnificent, though upside down, view of the rolling countryside surrounding the castle.

If you get there, you might hang back from doing what you may consider is making a fool of yourself in front of strangers. But you'll always be drawn to the stone in time and you can always fall back on one of those phrases which echo off the ancient stones all day long: "Well, what the heck, I climbed all those steps . . . I may as well give it a go . . ."

Having given it a "go," you'll wait to watch others go through the ritual.

Then it's slowly back down those 120 winding stone steps. Slowly, because you don't know who's labouring up them just around the corner. It may be a giggling teenager from Edmonton or it might be an old gentleman in his eighties, taking it one step at a time, gasping and wheezing like a TV wrestler, face purple as an eggplant but determined to make it back to the stone again if it's the last thing he does.

Do your laughing about Ireland's Blarney Stone before you go and see it. When you get there, something will get to you.

Travel tips: *A list of don'ts!*

- Don't forget that your welcome anywhere will usually be in a direct ratio to your approach to strangers and a big, pleasant smile is not only the best, but also the most useful, item you can take with you.
- Don't wander around in a foreign country while displaying symbols of wealth. If you're travelling with friends you don't have to impress them with material things. If you're hoping to make new friends, being loaded down with expensive jewellery isn't going to help you meet any nicer people than you'd otherwise meet. If anything, the reverse is true.
- Don't forget that each of your credit cards has the same value (or liability) as a $1,000 or $20,000 bill. Look after them accordingly. If you plan to travel on plastic, check with your travel agent to make certain your cards will be accepted where you're going. Some major hotels and restaurants in certain countries still accept no credit cards.
- Don't get into an un-metered taxi *anywhere* without first being quoted a firm price to your destination.
- Don't be uncomfortable. If it's a long flight or train trip, take off your shoes, loosen belt, necktie, girdle (?). If nobody is sitting beside you the arm rests usually fold back out of the way and you can spread out -- maybe even have a good snooze.

Thai hotelier offers souvenir price list

Khanchanaburi
Thailand

The hotel industry calls it shrinkage; so does your neighbourhood grocery or hardware store. I call it theft, but then again I'm forever being taken to task for calling a spade a bloody shovel.

I fail to see the logic of our so-called enlightened society which loses billions of dollars a year to people who steal things, but which cannot bring itself to call such people thieves. I learned at my mother's knee -- and across my father's knee -- that when you take something which is not yours, you are stealing. You are a thief.

Society doesn't like thieves and since the dawn of civilization has always made laws about private property and established penalties for those who break those laws.

The hotel industry says people who steal towels and bed spreads and ash trays are "pilfering," and the items they take home with them are "shrinkage." The hotel managers and owners know precisely who removed the items and where they live. The thief had to provide his name and address, and often his business address, before he was given a room key. The front desk has an imprint of his credit card . . . and the credit card companies can sure find their card holders when they want to!

But hoteliers tell me they don't press charges to recover goods stolen from them because if they did, the thief (sorry, pilferer) won't stay at their hotel on his next trip to town. Who wants a thief on the premises, anyway? Today an ash tray; tomorrow a $1,000 TV set.

And what's with this "pilferage'' euphemism? It's like calling a man with half a dozen convictions for rape an incurable romantic. Or calling a pickpocket, a loans officer. (On reflection, anyone who has had recent dealings with a Canadian bank could justifiably question that last example).

The manager of *The Rama of River Kwai Hotel* in Kanchanaburi, Thailand, has not only a sense of humour, but one of reality.

North American hoteliers would do well to solve their 'shrinkage' and 'pilferage' problems by following his sensible example.

In the stationery folder in the drawer of the desk in each room of The Rama Hotel is a card printed in Thai and English. The English version -- complete with spelling idiosyncrasies -- follows:

"Any of our souvenir-minded quest are desirous of keeping any item of the supplied and small articles which we provide for the comfort and convenience of our quests. During their at the hotel, please inform the room attendant, and the management, we will glad to provide you at the cost prices as listed below:"

There follows a price list of every single thing inside the four walls of the room, including such souvenir ideas as the telephone (about $29 Canadian); wastebasket ($2); bed cover ($100); coat hangers ($6 each); and the room service menu, a bargain at only $2.50. The bed, chairs, dresser, mattress, wall-to-wall carpet and bathroom sink were also included.

No cost was posted for the price list which I brought along for reference!

A check of items on the list against those still in my room indicated the previous occupant had taken advantage of the shopping facility. The floor maid didn't understand my discussion about the missing vacuum flask ($20); wooden tray ($5); vase ($1.25) or file -- presumably nail file, ($6).

But they didn't show up on my bill at checkout time.

I thought the Thai hotel manager's idea was brilliant.

It lets every hotel guest know where he stands since some hotel guests apparently sincerely believe they are expected to remove (steal, pilfer, spirit away, cause to shrink, etc.) all glasses, ash trays and light bulbs, for starters.

But this chap wanted them to stay in the room, or be paid for and with the price list there's no confusion. Remove whatever items you wish, and they'll turn up on your bill when you check out.

Modern hotels do a marvellous job policing their mini bars; why can't they get just as tough on those who steal other items so I don't have to keep paying more for hotel rooms? It angers me that just because hotel managements are reluctant to embarrass thieves I have to pay through the nose for a hotel room and then drink my nightcap out of a plastic cup.

Who got the tip?

Camaguey
Cuba

In some countries you have to do it their way. Cuba is one of those places. So it was that a solemn trio accompanied me to my hotel room.

With me were my guide, my driver and a tourist board functionary. Each of us carried a large suitcase.

The room contained two narrow single beds, a bedside stand, dresser, table and two chairs.

The four of us and the luggage filled the room. I joked about who would sleep with whom. It must have lost something in the translation because nobody laughed.

The men started leaving the room, one of them explaining they planned to check into their own rooms.

"Whose luggage is this?" I asked, pointing at three enormous suitcases that weren't mine.

"It's all yours, isn't it?" said Miguel, the guide.

"No. I thought it was yours. I thought you were all moving into this room." The three men looked thoroughly bewildered.

I looked at the tag on the nearest suitcase. It was an Air France tag bearing a Paris home address. The next belonged to somebody from Whitby, Ontario. The third was from Ottawa.

"They were with you in the lobby," Miguel started to explain. "I thought they were yours."

"What did you think I brought for one week in a hot country?"

Miguel didn't answer and showed the tags to the others.

"We had better get these back to the lobby," Miguel said. "People will be looking for them." Each man took a suitcase and we trekked back to he lobby.

Mercifully the lobby was empty when we left the three suitcases in the middle of the marble floor.

Swiss rent-a-cop on call but off-duty

Trun
Switzerland

There was no possible way to avoid a collision so in the micro second of decision I decided to ram the car at fault even though that meant a head-on crash.

The small house trailer we were towing seemed to shove my car forward despite the fact we were climbing a grade and the car and trailer tires were locked against the flinty road surface.

The driver of the car we were going to hit just sat there and watched us slide into him. He'd started a left turn across our lane into a parking lot and had plenty of time. But for some reason he froze partway through the turn. My choices were hitting him, a fast-moving car passing him on his right, or a row of parked cars on my right.

The six sliding tires and uphill grade slowed my car from perhaps 50 to about 15 miles per hour before its front corner plowed through his grille and radiator. But the impact was still enough to wreak havoc with the interior of the trailer and hurl our bewildered dog from the back seat against the dashboard.

It was 11 a.m. and a dozen people ran out of the restaurant attracted by my blaring rally horns, screaming tires and the crash. Nobody was injured.

The other driver appeared to be in his late twenties and very shaken. He spoke Switzerdeutsch but his message would have been clear in any language: "It was my fault . . . I'm sorry . . . are you all right?" He produced his international insurance green card and began filling out an accident report form. A pretty girl named Reta who had come from the restaurant spoke excellent English and translated for us. She explained the other driver was willing to pay for damages on the spot if I could name a price.

Across the street from the restaurant was a Fiat garage and the owner had been among the first on the scene. Reta thought we ought to be able to get an estimate from him on the damage to my Fiat, but it was an export model and the puzzled dealer said he had never ever seen one like it. "Thousands of francs," was his closest guess, "but I don't know how many."

He understood my French and agreed to call the police after I insisted three times. I refused to move my car until the positions of both were chalked on the road.

The policeman had to come from the next village which gave us all time for coffee at the restaurant. The policeman finally arrived with his roof light flashing and siren beep-booping.

He glanced at the cars and the skid and chalk marks before coming into the restaurant. By that time the other driver and I had completed our accident report forms. His was in German. Mine, issued in Andorra, was in Catalan, but the forms had identical layouts and we assumed the wording would be the same on each.

Reta translated the other driver's report. He admitted full liability and his sketch of how the crash had occurred couldn't have been more honest.

We signed the forms while the tall policeman looked on.

"Very good," he said when the formalities were completed and he shook hands all around. "Now, who called me?"

I told him I had.

"Then you must pay me five francs.

"Why?"

"Because I had to come here when you called. The five francs will help to pay for the gasoline." I paid him five francs.

"Now will you please sign this accident report as a witness?"

"No. The other driver has already signed it and admitted the accident was his fault. You don't need my signature. Besides, I'm not on duty."

The policeman was right about the other driver's signed "confession."

Within a mere ten months his Swiss insurance company repaid me for the hefty sum I'd paid to have my car repaired.

Travel tip: *You're our ambassador*

Wherever you go you're an ambassador for your own country and the guest of another. It's not only polite to do things the way they're normally done in your host country, it's part of that enriching travel experience

Been There Done That

Easterners wrote the book on southern hospitality

Pointe au Loup
Magdalen Islands, Quebec, Canada

There are few places in the world more isolated than where Ross Newcombe's rental car ran out of transmission fluid. It happened between Havre-aux-Maisons and Grosse Île in this archipelago in the Gulf of the St. Lawrence roughly equidistant from Newfoundland, Cape Breton Island, Gaspé, Prince Edward Island and Anticosti Island.

The paved road at that point follows a 25-kilometre-long sand spit at times only 100 metres wide and inhabited only by sea birds and whatever else lives on sand, flotsam and sea grass.

But Newcombe, a Montreal-based customer service representative with Continental Can Company, knows these islands and their people.

"I knew what was wrong with the car so I just raised the hood and waited. The first car along stopped and the driver said he'd get me some fluid. I didn't want every car after that to stop, so I left the car and tried to get out of sight on the other side of the road.

"About five minutes later I saw a big beer truck backing down the highway. He must have backed that truck up at least a mile.

"The driver asked me what was wrong and whether he could help or give me a ride into town. When I told him everything was under control he asked me if I'd like a beer. I said that would be nice and expected he'd toss me a bottle. Damned if he didn't give me an ice cold case of a dozen *Laurentides* beers."

Newcombe said he enjoyed several of the *Laurentides* before the Samaritan returned with the transmission fluid and the only payment the man would accept – was a cold beer.

When the car broke down on the way back from his client call at Grand Entry, Newcombe still had some beer to reward the man who drove him to the nearest garage.

"People who talk about southern hospitality should visit the Magdalen Islands," Newcombe told me later. "You never lack for food or accommodation or help here."

He said his predecessor in the job arrived on one visit and couldn't get a rental car. He used a taxi to make his calls. "About halfway to Havre Aubert the driver looked at his watch, noted it was almost noon and said they should stop for some lunch. He drove to his home, told his wife to set another place and poured his passenger a large whisky. After lunch – and another large whisky – they continued their journey.

"Can you imagine that happening in Montreal, or Toronto?"

Scott's travel maxims

- Rental cars only break down on weekends or in the towns and cities where the agency from which you rented, is not represented.
- On an itinerary with many connecting flights, the flight for which you make the biggest scramble is the flight which will be delayed the longest
- That "simply fabulous" little bar or restaurant which a friend has discovered and raved about will be closed on the day you visit.
- The customs officer with the sweetest smile, or most absent-minded manner, is the only customs officer at that port of entry who will ruthlessly pull all your luggage apart.
- The exotic foreign dish about which a friend raved will be the worst meal you have on your trip. Similarly, if you take someone to a restaurant you have touted as fabulous – because it was, last year – there will be a new chef and the meal will be the worst of your trip.
- If you are embarrassingly low on cash, you will never discover until checkout time that the hotel/motel where you stayed does not accept any credit cards.
- If your seat mate on any given flight to a destination where you don't know anyone, is gorgeous, approachable and very friendly, she will disembark one stop before, or after, you do. (I am sure the same thing happens to ladies who draw a handsome, friendly man as their seat companion.)
- The flowers, skiing, snorkelling conditions, coloured leaves or sport fishing were the best they have ever been in a decade – the week before you arrived.

Susie's wardrobe lacks neat stuff from Aswan

Aswan
Egypt

They were passengers on one of those luxury boats that cruise the upper reaches of the Nile River in southern Egypt . . . one of those five-day trips that run about $4,000 U.S. per person, not including airfare to Egypt and home.

Everybody on the cruise got to know Harry and Susie. . . well, just because they were both so loud. Their voices were loud and so was their clothing. Susie favoured large, flowered prints in purples, tangerines, pinks and chartreuses. Harry had electric blue trousers, Kodak yellow shirts and white penny loafers. They were in their early sixties and passengers in the dining room within three tables in every direction soon learned Harry was doing "real good" with his shoe store back home; so good he was thinking about opening another outlet.

When Harry's business finally took off, he and Susie decided they'd travel the world. Last year they had "done" Europe on a four-week tour. The year before they had "done" the entire Caribbean on a two-week cruise. Now it was time for some classic destinations and their travel agent suggested this cruise which stops all along the Nile River and offers side trips to the wonders of the ancient civilizations.

There were stops at Karnak and Luxor and tours to the pyramids and temples where visitors can go inside the ancient tombs and marvel at the floor-to-ceiling hieroglyphics which depict the life of the pharaoh buried there and the things he hoped to achieve in his life after death. At all these places Susie was a hit with the pedlars. She bought beads and bangles and trinkets; onyx, wood and alabaster carvings, post cards, table napkins and brass ash trays.

The serious shoppers on the cruise boat were saving their cash for Aswan, the turn-around point of the cruise.

That's where Susie's travel agent had suggested she spend some time shopping for clothes. Egypt's cotton is world-famous, he assured her, and the workmanship exquisite and skilled. So Susie told

Harry she was going ashore early that day to buy some dresses. Harry said he'd pass on the shopping trip; the weather was cold back home and he'd just soak up some of that lovely hot sun on the upper deck.

All the people at the tables around Harry and Susie's table were on time for dinner that evening because it was usually at dinner that Susie showed Harry the treasures she had acquired during her daily shopping expedition.

Susie showed up for dinner in a turquoise blouse adorned with yellow and lavender flowers the size of peonies, a garment that had clearly not been purchased in Aswan. The diners waited patiently but there was no show-and-tell from Susie's shopping trip.

As the stewards were clearing away the entrée dishes, a tablemate could wait no longer.

"Did you have any luck shopping in Aswan?" she asked.

"Naw," said Susie scornfully. "I musta been tuh every store and stall in town. But all their clothing here has the same kinda crappy patterns like on all a them walls in the old buildings we been lookin' at all week."

In good company

Las Vegas
Nevada, U.S.A.

A Toronto travel writer colleague found himself in some humourous situations recently when he was in Las Vegas gathering information for travel articles on that destination.

His wife didn't want to make the trip again but his 18-year-old daughter, Diane, was delighted to accompany Dad on his rounds of the casinos, night clubs and dining spots.

"We fitted right in," my friend told me. "There are hundreds of middle-aged or elderly men squiring beautiful young women around the Las Vegas night clubs. But I bet I was probably the only one who could honestly tell anyone who might have wondered out loud that the young lady on my arm really was my daughter."

Something got lost in the translation, comrade

Moscow
Russia

I was the only Canadian in a group of travel journalists visiting Russia and found the briefings that Americans gave each other prior to going, and during the visit, often amusing. Americans always seem to want to do the right thing when they're in a foreign country, but their thinking seems often warped by Hollywood's version of reality.

In this case it was bugged telephones, spies lurking around every corner, infiltration by KGB agents and all sorts of other sinister plots.

So it was we were instructed never to refer to Russians by that apparently pejorative word. They were Soviets, we were told and they lived in either the Soviet Union or the U.S.S.R. The Russians I met, however, insisted they were Russians, except for some from Moscow who preferred to be called Muscovites.

A couple of exchanges took place in Moscow that convinced me more than ever that international travel is the key to world peace. If more North Americans had one-on-one contact with Russians, we'd understand them a lot better and rapidly develop a great deal more respect for them. That would translate to a lot of materials being diverted from rocket and missile manufacture to tour buses and hotel construction.

More personal contact with Russians would also show up our abysmal lack of knowledge of who they are, where they're coming from and what they're attempting to achieve.

In Moscow we had a lady guide whose fund of knowledge about Russia and whose reserves of patience both appeared to be limitless. At one point our bus stopped at the highest point in Moscow from which there's a lookout over half the city. I was getting off the bus as one of the ladies who had already seen the view was trying to get back on, out of the wet snow that was falling.

"Don't bother going to have a look," she snorted within

earshot of the guide, "there's nothing to see and you can see it all in a minute."

The view she had dismissed was spectacular. True, it was savagely cold and damp and couldn't be photographed because of the overcast and the snow, but as far as the eye could see in a 180-degree sweep, the exciting architecture of the city was spread below.

There were the gilded, onion-shaped domes of the churches and crenellated stone spires of others, buildings in just about every architectural style and colour of building material ever erected. Through it all wound the Moscow River beneath a dozen bridges of various designs. It's the sort of view to which you have to give the same kind of detailed attention you'd happily devote to an Hieronymous Bosch painting.

When I got back on the bus, one of the non-smokers in the group was haranguing our guide, Marina, about her cigarette-smoking habit. Marina never smoked on the bus; but whenever she disembarked it wasn't long before she lighted up.

Marina listened patiently to the zealot's arguments about health, air pollution and wasteful expense. When he finally paused, she smiled sweetly at him and answered: "Like your Mark Twain, I have quit smoking many times."

Later that day we attended a meeting with officials from Intourist, the tourism arm of the Soviet Union. Press kits extolling the wonders of the Soviet Union's tourist areas were distributed and the vice-minister of tourism explained through an interpreter how Intourist's efforts have been increasing the numbers of tourists to her country.

"In these strained times with threats of nuclear confrontations, tourism can play a great role in world peace," she concluded, and the hand of an American journalist immediately shot up to ask a question:

"You've said the Soviet Union now draws 60,000 American tourists each year," he said, "but what steps are the Soviet Union taking to balance that out by sending tourists to the United States?"

With no hesitation and a poker face, the vice-minister replied: "It is difficult for us to encourage tourism from the Soviet Union to the United States when Aeroflot (the Soviet airline) is not granted landing rights in the United States and when our cruise ships are not allowed to call on U.S. ports."

There were no further questions.

Helping hand deserved better than a Mexican *gotcha!*

Taxco
Mexico

The young Canadian couple said they thoroughly enjoyed the old-world charm of the silver-mining town of Taxco, high in the mountains of the interior. They were climbing a long set of stone steps up the steep hillside that overlooks the beautiful spired church of Santa Prisca.

"Near the top of the steps," the man recounted, "we caught up to a little old lady from the village who was unsteadily making her way down. She was all bent over and using a cane and so unsteady that she had to get both feet on each step before starting on to the next.

"I felt sorry for her and motioned that I'd like to help her down. Eventually she accepted my arm but even then she had to move very slowly.

"It seemed to take forever before we got back down to the square; it probably took 15 minutes to get her down those steps which my wife and I could have handled in a couple of minutes.

"The moment we reached the square and I let go of her arm, her hand shot out under my nose, palm up, waiting to receive money."

"What did you do then?" I asked, starting to break up with laughter.

"I was so astonished," the man said, "that I just reached into my pocket for a bunch of change and put it in her hand." He had to stop for a moment while his wife and I hooted with laughter. When we paused for breath, he resumed his story.

"She just took the money and walked off. She didn't even thank me!"

A really safe parking place

Seville
Spain

They grow oranges here . . . and thieves. For breakfast you're served an orange-flavoured drink made from water and orange crystals. After breakfast you learn about the thieves.

The concierge/bellboy from the Dona Maria Hotel earned himself a good tip the night before when I checked in. He moved an immense trash bin on wheels so I could park legally in the square in front of the hotel and behind the Cathedral y Giralda which dominates the core of this venerable Spanish city.

The rented Opel was about 15 steps away from the front door of the local police station in front of which there were never fewer than two officers each time I passed, day or night.

When I carried my suitcase out to the car in the morning the first thing I noticed was broken glass all over the back seat. I gave silent thanks to the hotel receptionist who had insisted when I checked in that nothing be left in the car even though it was parked outside the police station in a high-profile public place.

The thieves had been thorough. From inside the car they went through the back seat to the trunk and made off with a pair of new running shoes. They had ripped open the glove box which contained nothing of value and torn off a plastic plate on the dashboard behind which a radio is normally installed, though this car had none.

Three policemen were chatting as usual in front of the police station 15 steps away so I signalled one to come over.

"Yes," he agreed, looking at the shattered glass. "You have bee robbed. You should call the police." He shrugged and ambled back to his colleagues. These officers, despite carrying revolvers, merely direct traffic, I later learned.

The Avis office was only a few blocks away so I walked. (When you get a free and legal parking spot in Europe you hang onto it – even if that means taking taxis to and from the other parts of the city you may wish to visit).

When I made my report to the man at the Avis office and asked for another car, he laughed. Then he pulled out a street map of Seville and started making marks on it. He showed me how to get to a place that would replace the window "in less than half an hour."

"You will pay for it there," he said, "and they will give you a receipt. That amount will be deducted from your bill when you turn the car back in at Lisbon. Don't bother wasting your time going to the police unless you need documentation for an insurance claim. They will waste at least half of your day and do nothing for you."

Puzzled, I asked, "Don't you need information about where this happened, or when, or . . .?"

"You are in Seville," he shrugged. "I assume it happened here. This is a way of life in Seville. You are the tenth customer to come in this morning and report a broken window. That is why I laughed when you asked for another car. I never have an extra car available here."

He said his daily average of smash-and-grab reports is between 15 and 20. "The people who do it are on drugs and they will steal anything they can sell for a few pesetas. Somebody must have surprised them or they would have taken your spare tire and the tools."

Dirt cheap

Charlottetown
Prince Edward Island, Canada

The bouncy, pleasant lady who runs the gift shop at Charlottetown's airport is doing a land mine business in real estate.

For 50 cents she'll sell you a small plastic bag of red soil to which is stapled a hand-written tag that reads: "Red soil of P.E.I."

"You want to believe people are buying them!" she laughed. "They just keep me digging. Just see, you'll buy one before you leave."

Wrong on one count, lady, but it wasn't long before a fellow passenger killing time between flights forked over 50 cents for a bag of soil.

Bahamian pot luck

Nassau
Bahamas

"Hey, man, wanna buy some real good Colombian gold?"

"What's the going rate?"

"Ten dollars a bag, man. I can getcha some great hash, or coke . . . "

The uniformed police officer lounging in the shade of a doorway within earshot didn't appear to hear the young black man's pitch.

"No thanks," I told him and continued along Bay Street, the main drag of this capital city of the Commonwealth of The Bahamas.

The black man didn't follow. He had his eye on a paunchy American from a cruise ship who was wearing a rakishly-tilted hat obviously just purchased from the nearby native straw market on Rawson Square.

Before the end of the block there was another soft voice in my ear with the same offer and on the return trip on the other side of the street, a third sales pitch. No hard sell -- just the quiet message that *anything* in the drug field was immediately available. The prices quoted didn't vary, but boasts of the quality of the wares embraced most superlatives.

I mentioned the incident that night to a fellow resort guest from Los Angeles and his eyes lit up. "I've heard they got great grass here -- and *anything* else," he said. "Where was this cat?"

Next day I watched the buy.

The American told the black man he wanted a $10 bag of marijuana. The vendor said he was just a runner but that if the buyer stayed where he was -- in the blinding sun of the town's main street -- he'd bring the bag. He was back in less than ten minutes, took the $10 bill and stuffed several ounces of marijuana wrapped in a scrap of kraft paper into the American's shirt pocket.

The American bought cigarette papers at a tobacco store and returned to the resort.

The Bahamian government tour guide didn't want to even discuss drugs until the questions became insistent. "They very rough on drugs here," he finally said. "One joint cost you a fine of $500 to $1,000 the first time you get caught depending on what kinda mood de magistrate's in. Hash or opium or those others cost you a whole lot more. That's why we got no drug problems here."

He wasn't surprised to hear I'd been approached three times in two blocks along Bay Street. "Oh yeah," he said, "some of the boys sell it to tourists from off the cruise boats, but they don't use it."

At dinner that night the man from Los Angeles and his friends appeared very relaxed and gusts of laughter exploded at their table throughout the meal.

"Yeah, we smoked it all up," he confided later at the bar. "It sure smelled good but it was lousy grass. It was cut with something. We're flying on the rum. That Bacardi rum is only $6 a litre . . . and it sure ain't cut!"

Sorry ma'am, no parachutes

An elderly family friend named Eva was making her first airplane flight. Her companion who had flown many timcs later regaled friends with Eva's experience. The flight attendant had helped with the unfamiliar seat belt buckle and was turning to leave when Eva grabbed her arm. "Where is my parachute?" she deman-ded. "Is it under the seat?"

The flight attendant explained parachutes were not supplied to passengers on jet aircraft . . . which did little to allay Eva's worst fears about what might happen in the event of an engine failure at 35,000 feet.

Travel tip: *Make sure that deal – is a deal*

Watch out for the super accommodation deals offered on highway billboards. Their claim of accommodating two people "from $29.95," or whatever, is usually true. But if you don't specifically request that accommodation while checking in you may find yourself being legitimately billed for perhaps $39.95 or more . . . because you have been assigned a better or larger room.

There'll always be an England

London
England

The neat metal sign on the condom dispenser in the public lavatory read: "manufactured to British Standard No. BS3704."

On the adjacent wall in meticulously-printed black felt pen, somebody had written: "So was the Titanic."

That amusing graffiti speaks volumes about the enigmatic, proud and often eccentric Englishman.

His taxes, cost-of-living and commodity prices are soaring and his wage-increase prospects have been frozen by Parliament.

He watches the remnants of the great British Empire dissolve like an ice cube in a hot toddy. And -- as insult added to injury -- awaits fragmentation of the ironically-named United Kingdom itself, driven in no less than five different directions by determined separatists.

He watches once-cherished family heirlooms carried off his island by the truckload to the shops and homes of European and American collectors, and writes despairing letters to *The Times* about each sale of an historic family home to nouveau-riche Arabs.

Words like stoic, tenacious or stubborn come to mind, but Stiff Upper Lip has to head the list.

It's an overworked cliché, but it's a way of life for the hard-core Englishman; the type who wouldn't consider for a moment leaving the rheumatic fog of his homeland for brighter prospects in a more friendly environment.

The type who hates the climate but walks his dog three miles every Sunday afternoon come rain, sleet, fog or snow.

Even the expatriates haven't forgotten their homeland. A few years ago I sat shivering one August in the damnably cold dining room of an hotel in Caernarvon, Wales. An elderly gentleman wearing a full-length black cashmere winter overcoat stamped in and called his order to the waitress on the way to his table which overlooked the fog-shrouded harbour.

"Bring me two double whiskies," he demanded, downing the first in one gulp when it came to his table. He remained scowling out at the mist and drizzle for the duration of my breakfast.

He didn't appear to be a drunk, or even enjoy his whisky, so on leaving I asked the waitress about him.

"Oh yes," she said. "Funny man, isn't he? He's very rich and lives on Long Island in America but he grew up here and comes back every summer for several months and just sits there staring at the fog, muttering about it. Nobody can understand why he comes here if he hates the weather, but it's the only thing he ever talks about."

As in Canada, there are different classes and income groups in the United Kingdom. There's Old Family With Money; Old Family Without Money; professionals earning money and the "working class" which never manages to earn -- or hold on to -- enough money to live comfortably.

Harsh taxation hasn't yet wiped out all of the Old Families With Money, but in recent years many of Britain's lovely old estates have passed from the families that could no longer keep them up, to wealthy foreigners, or the state.

But the Stiff Upper Lip is so far holding out against the crushing costs of the welfare state Britain has become and even defying the lack of central heating in many homes and hotels. There are still bowler hats and brollies to be seen on the streets and even the occasional chauffeur-driven Rolls or Bentley occupied by English-men, though the majority of the limousines contain dark-skinned people wearing turbans or saris.

The quaint double-decker buses still belch clouds of exhaust fumes through the crowded streets as do the clattering, chattering diesel-powered Austin taxicabs. The guard still changes at 11 a.m. outside Buckingham Palace and tea is taken at 4.

But there is the odd chink appearing in Great Britain's facade. Since the time of Charles II (in the 1600s) a curious superstition has surrounded the ravens which used to abound at London's famous White Tower.

The superstition is that when there are no longer ravens in the tower, both the tower and the British Commonwealth will fall.

There were half a dozen ravens wandering around the tower grounds when I visited there recently but I noticed they didn't fly off when chased by children.

"Yes, sir," one of the tour guides confided. "Their wings are clipped . . . and we feed them ground beef each day."

When ya gotta go . . .

Derwent
Tasmania, Australia

We had to keep up to our schedule, so in fog and rain we drove for hundreds of kilometres through some of Tasmania's finest scenery. The lunch stop was clearly going to be the highlight of this drab day and we were grateful to find a lovely old pub in the hamlet of Derwent. A pleasant lady pulled draft beers for us and pointed down the hallway when I asked for directions to the washroom.

I found it down the murky hallway and noted with disgust the door bore one of those cutesey signs, in this case a top hat and cane. Cute -- and often confusing -- pictures, silhouettes and pictographs on the doors of public conveniences, rile me. More maddening still, this door was locked. Why hadn't that stupid barmaid given me the key before I made that long hike down the hallway?

I traipsed all the way back to the bar. "May I please have the key to the mens' washroom?"

"It isn't locked, love."

"Yes it is. The door with the picture of the top hat and cane on it?"

The barmaid looked puzzled and then started to hoot with laughter. It was a full minute before she could speak.

"That's not a top hat and cane, love. That's a bucket and mop! That's where we keep the cleaning things. Now wouldn't you have wondered about us Aussies if the door hadn't been locked and you'd gone in and found just a bucket and a mop?"

Travel tip: *Inventory is good insurance*

Keep a list of all your valuables and the means to identify them (camera and lenses serial numbers, wristwatch serial number, etc.) This will help in the event of a loss or theft and aid in keeping track of what you have taken with you so nothing is left behind.

Joie de vivre in Quebec

Quebec City
Quebec, Canada

Dusk was nudging daylight out of Québec City's steep, narrow streets and rush hour's frenzy was in recess until daybreak.

Some sparrows were squabbling high in an ancient elm, but the only other sounds were the fading cackle of some tourists and the click of the old man's cane and shuffle of the gimpy leg he dragged after him along Rue Ste. Anne.

I passed him and turned down Desjardins Hill towards Brasserie Gaulois where the waitresses are pretty, the beer flagons are always capped with foam and the folk singer has more lilt than a Strauss waltz.

They were coming up Côte de la Fabrique which angles onto Desjardins at the monument to Cardinal Taschereau.

There was no traffic on Desjardins so when the dozen young men and women crossed Côte de la Fabrique they strolled up the middle of the roadway.

Some were arm in arm and others held hands, but there were no missing links and they were all singing. They were singing loudly and in harmony and their simple folk song carried clearly the length of the block:

"C'est dans le mois de mai,
En montant la rivière;
Que les filles sont belles,
Que les filles sont belles au gue . . . "

(That doesn't translate into anything particularly sophisticated in English, but with a touch of poetic licence is:

"It's in the month of May,
Going up the river;
Oh, the girls are pretty;
They are full of the joys of spring . . . ")

I stopped in my tracks and looked around for a policeman because I was only several days removed from Ontario where singing in the streets -- no matter how harmoniously -- is considered a threat to the peace.

"Et que tout les amants
En montant la rivière
Y trouvent leur maîtresse . . . "

(Translation:

"And all the lovers
In going up the river
Will find there, their mistresses/lovers.")

There was a policeman, wandering down Côte de la Fabrique, and he turned, leaned against the window ledge of a restaurant, and tapped his shiny left shoe in time to the singers' rhythm. The old man with the cane had caught up with me now and his gimpy leg didn't seem to be dragging quite as heavily.

"C'est beau, hein?" he chuckled with a great grin as he shuffled past. I continued to the corner by the brasserie to which the group was heading.

A few doors down the street a grey-haired businessman dragged himself and a heavy attaché case out of a doorway and started down the street. His face was a grey raisin, wrinkled with worry creases and the cares of his world seemed equally distributed between his sagging shoulders and the bulging briefcase.

He noticed the singing after a few steps and slowed his pace to catch the lyrics. The frowns and scowls dissolved into a wide, happy smile and his eyes came alive behind the heavy spectacle lenses. He watched the youngsters sing their way into the brasserie before starting down the street with a discernible bounce in his step.

Later at the hotel I mentioned the incident to genial bartender Johnny Boîteau. I told him how such goings-on were foreign to Ontarians, even those in university towns filled with young people.

"How sad for you English," he observed. "Here it is our way of life to be happy whatever, and to not be ashamed of being in love with life, and showing it to everybody.

"It's just another little part of what we call our culture."

Travel Tip: *Universal driving tip*

If a large or slow-moving vehicle is approaching on a two-lane roadway, assume that a faster vehicle is going to suddenly pull out into your lane to pass that vehicle.

The best of intentions

Erawan Falls
Thailand

The government of Thailand was taking no chances that an incident might disrupt the visit of any guest. Each group of foreign travel writers was assigned police and military guards who brought along their rifles, machine guns and pistols and rarely let any member of the group out of their sight. On some excursions security men outnumbered the writers and photographers.

The security blanket was not without its light moments.

One day the group I was with picnicked on box lunches beside the Ta-Mong-Lai stream which cascades down Slob Mountain forming the seven lovely Erawan Falls. Our guide had suggested that after lunch we hike up the mountain to see the falls and he had apparently instructed the police and soldiers to show us the way.

An elderly editor left our picnic table and started down the path. A soldier promptly stepped onto the path and indicated with the barrel of his machine gun that the editor should go up the path. The editor shrugged and made an about turn.

He plodded up the pathway to the first waterfall. When he tried to return the way he had come, another smiling soldier waved him up the hill with his machine gun.

You don't argue with a man holding a machine gun, even when he's smiling, and the editor trudged slowly up the steep path. I followed, snickering to myself, having guessed the editor wanted to go either to a washroom down the hill, or for a nap in the air conditioned bus. When the pathway made its first bend, I saw the editor look quickly around him and then dart off into the jungle.

Later in the bus I kidded the editor about having to march up the mountain when all he wanted to do was find a washroom.

"You think that's funny?" he snorted. "When I got back to the pathway from relieving myself in the bushes there was another soldier waiting where I had left the path. He had his back to me and was making sure nobody wandered into the jungle to disturb me. He made me go up to the second falls and then a policeman made me climb up to the third falls.

"Thank God the bridge was washed out up there or I'd have had to spend the whole afternoon climbing that mountain. All I wanted to do was go to the washroom and then have a nap on the bus. The soldiers were only trying to be helpful. They thought everybody was going to climb the mountain and they were just trying to show me the way."

Airline tips: ***Things that go bump . . .***

▸ There's a variety of strange noises that are routine on most flights and nothing to get alarmed about. Shortly after takeoff you'll hear a thump and bang under the aircraft. It isn't one of the engines falling off. It's the landing gear retracting and the cover closing over the wheel well. There may also be a sudden cutback of power as though the engines had quit just when you've reached a height from which a fall would be very painful. This is often done over sound-sensitive areas.

▸ The wings are supposed to be flexible. That's what prevents them from breaking off when they're exposed to severe strain. And it's not uncommon for sheets of flame to spew out of an engine. In turbulence you might notice all sorts of other things moving, too, like the bulkheads (cabin walls and dividers). They're supposed to, so jiggling bulkheads aren't an indication that the great silver bird you're in is about to come apart at the seams.

▸ Landing gets most people – even the veterans. There's the initial bump and sometimes you can hear the tires scream on the runway. Then the moment the wheels are on the ground the engines roar like banshees as reverse thrust is used to help the brakes slow the aircraft. One type of aircraft has a housing over the back of the engine which flips off as though the engine has exploded, so the jet thrust can be reversed. It always seems to me the pilot ought to warn passengers who might see this happen that it's a normal procedure. I've still got scars on one hand from a jittery lady companion who drew blood with her fingernails the first time she saw that happen.

▸ Enjoy your flight. Statistics prove conclusively that flying is far safer than driving in a car!

Car rental company had class

Helen
Georgia, U.S.A.

When police had carted off the drunk driver and the wreckage of my demolished rental car was towed away they drove me to their office so I could phone the auto rental company.

"My name is Scott," I told the lady from National Auto Rental's Atlanta airport office "I rented a car from you yesterday afternoon and it's just been wrecked."

"Oh," she replied with no hesitation or emotion. "Do y'all want another car?"

"Yes, please."

"Do you have your rental contract number?"

"I'm sorry. The police still have all the papers."

"That's OK. I can look it up. I'll put Ron on the phone and you can tell him where you're at."

A moment later Ron Carter introduced himself on the phone. He hadn't heard of Helen, a dot on the map 150 km north of Atlanta, but said he'd bring another car to the police station right away.

"I'll be go-to-hell," muttered the policeman I'd been chatting with while waiting for the car. "That must be some classy company you rented from!" He gestured out the window.

A man was lowering a car from a tow truck. Reflected in the flashing amber roof lights of the truck was the identical make, model and colour of car I had been driving four hours earlier when the drunk missed a curve and hit me head-on.

Ron Carter, the tow truck driver, asked me to sign a paper stating that the car I had received was in good shape and he turned over the keys. "Hope you have better luck with this one," he chuckled as he drove off to retrieve the wrecked car.

I drove back to Atlanta chuckling over the hassle I'd had a few years earlier while returning a rental car in England with a scrape down the side that had been there when I rented it in Scotland. I concluded I had indeed rented from a "classy company" this time.

You'd better be right - - *or left ?*

Moorea
Society Islands, French Polynesia

The big truck was well over the 50 kilometres per hour speed limit when it hurtled around the curve on my side of the road. We were seconds away from a head-on crash when I realized I was on the wrong side of the road.

There wasn't time to switch to the lane where I should have been and the thought flashed through my mind that if I tried for it the truck driver might swerve that way too. I yanked the wheel hard left and the little rental car bounced onto the rough grass verge.

The truck roared past down the middle of the two-lane highway, horn blaring. "That bloke nearly killed us!" stormed my companion Jeff Newman, an Australian I'd invited to join me on a tour of the island. "That idiot was on the wrong side of the road. That was just too close! Good work thinking so fast."

We were less than a kilometre from the little shack where I had rented the car and beside the coast road I'd spotted a tramp steamer with attractive lines being loaded against a backdrop of those improbable-looking volcanic outcrops which formed this archipelago.

To go back for the photo I had turned into a driveway wide enough to allow a U-turn that brought us back to the highway's left-hand lane. It seemed natural to stay in that lane because I'd been driving on the left for three weeks in New Zealand and Australia. Jeff hadn't said anything because driving on the left seemed perfectly natural to him.

The nearly-fatal gaffe rankled me until I figured out why it had happened: I'd been distracted by the photo opportunity and acted too quickly, making moves before thinking them all the way through.

About the only other precaution you can take when moving frequently between left- and right-hand drive countries is to try to rent a car with manual gearshift when in a left-hand-drive country. This will mean your left hand will be on the shift lever most of the time, which is an unnatural position for North American motorists.

Guatemala's Mexican stand-off

Melchor de Mencos
Guatemala

A state of war exists between Guatemala and neighbouring Belize, but that doesn't interrupt *siesta* in this border town or for that matter anything else.

"Si, senor," acknowledges the *cantina* proprietor. "I have cold beer and I accept Belize dollars." A cold beer is produced from the clattering refrigerator and the Belize note disappears into a pocket of the baggy, dirty trousers. No change is offered: triple the going price for a beer in Central America appears to be the exchange rate.

The beer is delicious in the steaming jungle heat. The *cantina jefe* doesn't care to discuss Belize. Some villagers fled last summer when British troops appeared at the border in a dramatic show of strength, he finally tells me, but most have now returned.

"It's just politics," offers a travel poster native character who looks as though he has spent 50 of his 60 years on the same chrome-legged bar stool. He won't qualify the remark and his companion, the only other customer in the place, becomes deaf as other questions follow.

The only thing moving on the dirt-packed main street is a scrawny mongrel scuttling to a patch of shade after being kicked out of the only store open during *siesta*. The store is heaped with untidy stacks of clothing, grocery items and, incongruously, farming and hardware items. The two teenaged girl clerks manage "hello" for the *gringo*, but have only giggles for his questions asked in Spanish.

A tour of the village's side streets turns up no sign of the Guatemalan troops reported to number in the thousands along the eastern frontier facing Belize although this is one of the very few border points connected by road.

The troops could perhaps be deployed in the jungle which closes in on the village; that jungle could swallow a large city. But there's no sign of jeeps or Land Rovers and no telltale marks of tracked vehicles on the dusty tracks that pass for streets.

Leaving Guatemala is easier than entering. The polite, English-speaking immigration officer doesn't have to search the Canadian passport for visas to Communist countries again. The car trunk gets another check for weapons and the passport collects another rubber stamp. There is no passport stamp showing entry to Guatemala. That stamp went on a loose piece of paper stuck in the passport that has been thrown away in Guatemala.

A mile into Belize and the British presence makes itself felt. The machine gun emplacement is ill-concealed and the fresh track punched up a jungle hillside by tanks and Land Rovers is conspicuous. So are the half dozen rifle-toting members of the Staffordshire Regiment who were among the 500 troops rushed in to bolster the 200-member Belize garrison.

Travel tips: Make sure you wonder why

▸ Wonder why there's a special bargain rate to some exotic destination. If it's to the south, find out how hot and humid it will be and whether it's the rainy or hurricane season. You'd have more fun in your own back yard in September than you would sitting out a Caribbean hurricane! And it's depressing -- even if the weather is good -- to be knocking around a huge resort that only has a ten per cent occupancy rate. Moreover, a lot of popular attractions close during the off season.

▸ Wonder about the wording in the holiday brochure you're considering. Some of the word games may be fraudulent but most are likely honest oversights or the result of unclear writing. If the itinerary describing an excursion says "we'll stop for lunch" and doesn't specify who's paying, safely assume you will. Similarly if some other service is "available," the odds are good you'll enjoy that service only if you pay for it. "Optional" means you'll pay and if your hotel is "a scenic 10-minute drive from . . . " find out who provides the transportation. If you have to pay each time you want to go to the town nearest your hideaway resort, find out how much taxis cost (most have fixed, policed tariffs) or how frequently and until how late in the evening, the local bus service operates.

▸ Wonder about the length of stay of your package. A lot of operators seem to think a week contains only six nights. On that basis, three weeks would contain only 18 nights!

You'll wonder where they went when you get to where they were

The new package holiday brochures are out for the coming season . . . so I started browsing them to get an idea of price structures for this year. But it was other structures that kept arresting my eyes.

One was a full-colour photo of Paris where the old Eiffel Tower ran a dismal fourth to the trio of young ladies disporting themselves in front of it. The girls – in their shorts and tight T-shirts put the Spice Girls to shame.

It isn't a scene I remember from my last visit to the Eiffel Tower. That recollection is of a sweaty, unshaven taxi driver pelting me with coins I had given him as a tip while he loudly ranted that my parents hadn't spent enough time together to even swap first names.

And that golden-skinned lovely in another brochure wasn't in Antigua when I was there, either. Her grandmother was. She followed me for three blocks one evening insisting that for only $50 U.S. she could cure the attack of loneliness she was convinced I was suffering.

In yet another catalogue there's a photo of a beautiful young lady tossing coins into Rome's Trevi Fountain. This beauty could meet the physical requirements of any Playboy bunny club. The last time I was in Rome I couldn't find a place to park my car, let alone look for fountains.

I haven't been to Florida for a couple of years so perhaps the changes there as depicted in the new brochures may be correct. The catalogues suggest the Sunshine State may have banned anyone over the age of 30 from its beaches. On previous visits I recalled seeing acres of sagging and wrinkled flesh broiling in the occasional snatches of sunshine. A bartender told me that resort was known to the locals as Wrinkle City. *Siestas* were out of the question at my hotel because of the heavy wheelchair traffic along the walkway under my window.

The reality is that those bronzed Adonises and spectacularly beautiful ladies in bikinis never seem to be where they're advertised by the time we ordinary mortals get there.

False advertising? Hardly. Who'd want to visit those places if you and I were used as models in the advertising brochures?

Short trips that took too long

Kralendijk
Bonaire, Netherlands Antilles

"Eastern Airlines doesn't have an office here, sir, but I have also reconfirmed your flight from Curacao to Miami, Philadelphia and Toronto on Tuesday. It's at 7:54 a.m. and you should be at the airport by 6:54 a.m."

I thanked the lady at the Antilliaanse Luchtvaart Maatschappij Airlines booth for reconfirming all the remaining flights and resumed my tour of this delightful speck on the world map about 80 kilometres off the north coast of Venezuela.

I had interrupted that tour to pick up my suitcase which somehow hadn't arrived with me the night before. Nobody could explain why it hadn't come since I had sat through half a dozen over-booked flights the previous day.

In fact, it had taken 11 hours to make a 30-minute flight from Aruba to Curacao to here. On the first Curacao-Bonaire flight there was one no-show and my spirits rose because I had been assured the first available seat.

But another standby passenger was considerably more attractive than I and the male airline attendant offered her my seat and was rewarded with a warm smile. Confirmed flights in this part of the world don't mean a heck of a lot.

The ALM clerk sold me the ticket for the 10:20 flight from Aruba to Curacao that had been booked for several weeks. At 10 a.m. I signed the credit card slip, she handed me the new ticket and a standby boarding pass for the 10:20 flight.

The 10:20 flight is full," she said, "and so is the 1:30 flight, but on both of them you're confirmed from Curacao to Bonaire."

What had happened to the two-week-old reservation? "Honey, dat's not my problem. You stan' in line like all de udders on stan' by."

I had a guide laid on in Bonaire and a great one-time photo opportunity at 7 p.m. that night. Where was the airline supervisor? Forget it, fellah, they don't work on weekends which is when the screw-ups always seem to happen.

To make a long, perspiration-soaked story shorter, I landed in

Bonaire after 9 p.m. Since I had been expected before noon the hotel manager who had been meeting flights all day, concluded I wasn't coming and had rented my room. I didn't blame him a bit; a bird in the hand, and all that . . .

There's usually no problem with accommodation in the Caribbean in October, except that the Caribbean Police Association was holding its summer games here and the other hotel was full up with Americans attending the poolside wedding I was to have photographed at 7 p.m.

I had a pleasant night in a beautiful room at the local dive club out on Barcadera Beach a few kilometres from town. Just me and some lizards who resented the extra lights because that spread out the flies and made their evening smorgasbord more work to round up.

When I got to Curacao Monday morning it seemed like a good idea to reconfirm Tuesday's reconfirmed flight to Miami. That required a hike to an upstairs office where an obliging chap punched some computer keys, shook his head sadly and asked to see my ticket.

"You're not in the computer," he said, "but I think I can get you back in." He tapped some keys and announced with pride I'd leave Curacao the next morning at 6:54 a.m.

I thanked him and added, "those flights were reconfirmed yesterday in Bonaire. How can three flights fall out of your computer overnight?"

"I don't doubt you did reconfirm those flights, Mr. Scott," he smiled. "But even though you did reconfirm them yesterday, you took the time to come up here and reconfirm them today. That means you've been in these parts before . . . and you can answer your own question."

Travel tip: *Don't!*

Forget that Canadians are subject to the laws of whatever country they are in. Many countries have substantially different local customs, legal systems and judicial processes. Foreigners are not exempt from local laws and rarely receive preferential treatment when they are in violation. As in Canada, ignorance of any law is not an acceptable excuse for violating that law.

Con artists never short of ingenuity

Giza
Egypt

The Egyptian con artists who part the unwary from their money have some new wrinkles. Egypt's most impressive ancient ruins, including the Sphinx, are at Giza. It's close enough to both Cairo and Port Said that even cruise ship passengers can visit on a short port excursion, so the swindling techniques are highly refined.

There's no need to have a guide to climb up the inside of the Pyramid of Khufu, the tallest of the 4,500-year-old pyramids. The narrow set of steps goes either up, or down. And nowhere else.

But the smooth-talking man near the entranceway persuaded the young woman she would be safer with a guide. After all, it's a long, hard hike up the 170 stone steps. It's hell on claustrophobics, too, or people who need a lot of oxygen.

So she paid the man and he accompanied her to the small, poorly lit room at the top of the long stairs. There, both "guide" and tourist were confronted by a large, stern-looking man in a baseball cap who advised them he was a government warden and each would have to pay him a fee which, coincidentally, was the precise amount the woman had paid her "guide" before they started the climb.

The "guide" and the woman forked over the requisite amount.

When they ultimately reached the ground, the guide suggested in no uncertain terms it would be only fair and just for the woman to pay him the amount of the money he had been required to forfeit to the government warden. After all, he reasoned, he had only been trying to help her have a safe and pleasant tour of the pyramid.

You guessed it! The woman dug into her purse and paid yet a third "guiding" fee for the "tour" for which you don't need a guide or have to pay a government fee.

Within the hour she watched the "guide" and the "warden" divide up her money at a nearby refreshment stand. She consoled herself by rationalizing her losses would have been greater had either man just grabbed her purse and run off with it.

Dat's meaning cen-ter h'ice

Montreal
Quebec, Canada

Mimicking accents is a game enjoyed by the English in Quebec who can speak French. The game is also played by French people who mimic the accents of English people speaking French.

It is a gentle game and one without malice; the anglophones play it amongst themselves and would be dismayed if a bilingual French Canadian ever overheard and felt he was being mocked. A francophone would be similarly embarrassed if he believed his little linguistics game had upset an English-speaking person.

Each of the game players has mastered -- with varying degrees of expertise -- a second language. All but the most polished has some trace of an accent in the second tongue. And each has acquired both a respect and affection for the second language and its people, because he has come to know both during his language-learning efforts.

The late poet Dr. William Henry Drummond was a master at the game and published five classic volumes of Quebec habitant dialect poetry.

The three of us alternated in French and English during dinner that night, switching back and forth as waiters served in either language. The honest slips of pronunciation had brought a lot of laughter as the meal progressed and by the time we left the table we were swapping one-liners in "Franglais," a name some use to describe a cross between "joual" -- a slang French -- and English spoken as it might be by a French person learning English.

Quips like "j'ai fait un flat de mon tire," (I have made a flat to my tire) had been chuckled at and friend Jean-Paul, whose first language is French, had just cracked up our lady companion -- whose first tongue is Italian -- by explaining that the huge letters CH under the ice in the middle of the Montreal Forum stand for "cent-er h'ice."

The hotel elevator was full of conventioneering Americans from the mid-west when we got on at the 28th floor to ride to the lobby, known as the Grand Hall. The elevator button for that floor is marked GH.

Jean-Paul brought his Franglais with him into the elevator and enquired of the Americans -- with all the accents in the wrong places -- "did h'any of you guy push dat butt-on, g-h'aitch?"

The sneer on the face of one matron was almost audible as she examined the diminutive and cretinous native whose English was so heavily accented. Nobody in the elevator answered Jean-Paul's question so he pushed the GH button with a flourish.

"Hey, Jean-Paul, what's dat meaning, g-h'aitch?" asked our lady companion, picking up the language game.

"Dat's meaning gran' h'exit," he cracked loudly, looking earnest and somehow managing to keep a very straight face.

The chatter in the car stopped like a severed telephone line. You could almost hear the Americans trying to restrain their laughter. It would have to wait until the "natives" were out of earshot and then it would explode. Some would recount the vignette to their graves.

"H'I din't never know dat." said our lady friend, by way of driving the point home to the suffering audience, "but 'ere is de gran' h'exit!" She smiled sweetly at the other passengers as the elevator stopped at the lobby.

We fled. The Americans fled.

We could hear them hooting at the far end of the lobby.

It's a fun and harmless game to play -- if you've worked to learn the other language and made your own fair share of pronunciation goofs along the way.

Travel tip: *Jet lag*

Jet lag is the phrase applied to the results of jetting across a number of time zones. Your flight may leave Toronto at 8 p.m. and when it lands in Dublin the time there may be 7 a.m. If you check your watch, you'll discover it's only 3 a.m. Toronto time. Your brain will know it's daybreak in Ireland, but your body will want a few more hours sleep – even if you managed to sleep through most of the flight. Jet lag can be hard on you. If you're too excited upon arrival to hop into bed for a few hours, at least plan a very early evening so your next few days won't be loused up by feeling all dragged out. You'll make up for that lost time on your return trip to Canada . . . but not for the physical effects.

Everything's for sale in Haiti

Port-au-Prince
Haiti

This is another of those cities of the world where everybody has something to sell . . . and there aren't enough buyers. The vendors have to make sales to feed themselves so the obvious pressure point is the white-skinned tourist who stands out here like a man in a three-piece suit at a nude beach.

The pursuits are interminable; the sales pitches could bring tears to the eyes of a dedicated child beater and most of the hawkers will not accept "no" as a final answer.

Haiti occupies the western third of the Caribbean's largest island which Columbus named Hispaniola and the Dominican Republic occupies the other two thirds. Haiti gets its name from the native Arawak Indians who called it Hayti, meaning mountainous country -- which is an apt name since four-fifths of the island is covered with mountains which rear to 3,000 metres.

Of all the Caribbean countries, Haiti has the most exotic mix. Its people are from the Sudan, Senegal, Dahomey, the Gold Coast and France. Voodoo is part of the Haitian's life today and violence fills many chapters of its past and present. It was here in 1804 that kidnapped Quimas, Bambaras, Mandingues and Ibos broke the chains of slavery and rebelled against their masters, forming the first and only Black Republic in the New World.

The official language here is French and the most popular tongue is Creole, but it seems everybody knows the English for: "hey, meester, look me paintings . . . wood carvings . . . pottery . . . wicker baskets . . . wooden toys."

One gamin-faced girl of 12 or 13 staked out my taxi where the driver had parked it in the middle of the intersection of two four-lane roadways while we had a quick meal.

The girl had four or five woven leather purses and was determined her patience would be rewarded with a sale. Light and dark strips of thick, supple leather had been skilfully woven to form the bag part and the strips were tapered so they could be woven into the shoulder straps. The workmanship was superb.

The girl started at $16 U.S. and rapidly dropped to $10 as I climbed into the cab. "I have to have money to eat," she told me in French, impaling me with her enormous brown eyes. "If you don't buy a lovely purse for only $8 I will have to walk the streets and go with a man so I can eat."

When the taxi started to move the price dropped to $6. The last cry I heard was $5. "Would she sell for $4?" I asked the driver.

"You want one for $4?" he said hitting the brakes. "We will get one for $4." The purses weighed about a kilo each and with two weeks of travel still ahead I wouldn't have hauled one along if the girl had offered it as a gift.

The most common offering of street hawkers is a pair of carvings -- a stylized Haitian man and woman six to eight inches high. The asking price starts around $16 U.S. and rapidly drops to $4 for the pair. Equally popular is a carved wooden man whose grotesquely oversize genitalia springs from rubber bands into the tourist's face each time the hawker pulls down the man's shorts.

Guide books and guides insist that a visit to the old Iron Market here is "practically obligatory." The Iron Market is in two iron warehouses linked by a gate with North Africanesque minarets and is one of the landmarks of Port-au-Prince. If you've been to any other native market anywhere give this one a miss unless you're really eager to acquire a lot of junk of questionable real value.

You can get a feeling for the Iron Market by going to one of its edges. If after seeing the heaving, squalling mass of humanity and getting a whiff of the odours leaking out of the area, you want to have a closer look-see, there are a few don'ts worth considering: Do not take any valuables with you -- wallets, purses, flight bags, cameras, expansion bracelet wrist watches. If you're taking cash to make purchases carry it in your hand in your pocket -- and don't bring much. Never pay any asking price. If you really want something, figure on paying about 30 per cent of the asking price.

Your driver may get you a guide to take you through the market. It's a good investment if only because you will need the guide to find your way back to the cab, or the point at which you entered the market. And he'll run some interference for you -- at least against those vendors with whom he does not have a prearranged kickback agreement. Do not give the guide a penny until he returns you to your starting point.

"I've known this guide for years," my driver said when he introduced Jackson, a tall, under-nourished black man with darting eyes. "He'll see that you have no problems." A half hour later I got Jackson to admit he had never before laid eyes on my driver.

If nothing else, a tour of the Iron Market will banish forever any snide remarks you might ever be tempted to make in the crush of a department store sale or while queued at the understaffed checkout counters of a supermarket on Friday night. Jackson cut a path for me through the mass of humanity selling junk outside the market. The mass closed behind us like black stalks in a corn field.

Pathetic creatures with various deformities offered wares like one cigarette, a single comb with some teeth missing, a packet of two Chicklets or a single bottle of warm beer. There were vegetables, T-shirts, tooth paste, baubles, trinkets, soap, rusted cans of hair spray.

And then we were inside the Iron Market, a place where every square inch of floor space is accounted for. I had told Jackson I wanted to take away nothing from the market -- even if it was a gift. But that didn't deter him from leading me down interminable warrens of heaped up merchandise past the stalls of merchants he knew would kick back some of any money they were able to extract from me.

Hands grabbed at my wrists, ankles, shirt tail. Wares were pushed into my face, vendors closed in behind as though following a pied piper. A claustrophobic would have gone bananas. At a few stalls even Jackson wouldn't take my no for an answer, giving me more gears than I was getting from the vendors.

They really did have just about anything for sale, none of which I regret leaving without. There were chairs, tapestries, tables, leather belts, straw, rattan and wicker work, brass work, wood carvings and tiny stalls and cubby holes jammed with thousands of pieces of awful "art" which must be mass produced by paint sprayers because many widely separated booths offered identical pieces.

It was never ascertained what sort of payment would be considered fair for Jackson's services. Perhaps if I had bought some things he might have been satisfied with his kickbacks. But after 20 minutes of the pull-shove-grab-things-thrust-in-the-face routine, I told Jackson I wouldn't pay him anything if he didn't take me directly back to the taxi. Fortunately he didn't call my bluff or I'd probably still be trying to battle my way out of that fearful, filthy maze. I was so happy to escape the market that Jackson was delighted with the fee I paid him.

Refreshing approaches to tourism

Belize City
Belize

The large black man leaned back at an alarming angle in his creaking swivel chair and laughed uproariously. "That's it, you see," he said, still laughing. "You can't find it. That's why it's called Hidden Waterfall."

The man was Aloysius B. Palario, executive secretary of the tourist board of this former British colony in Central America, south of Mexico's Quintana Roo State and east of Guatemala. Palario had been telling me what there was to see and do here and I had asked for directions to the 1,500-foot waterfall.

Travel writers aren't used to tourist board people telling them they can't go and see local attractions. That's not how tourist boards work. The idea is to get travel writers to the places so they write about them. Interested readers follow their footsteps spending money as they go . . . which is what it's all about.

But Palario just lay back in his chair and laughed about Hidden Waterfall. The last person who went there, he chuckled, was lost for two days.

Palario was kind and helpful in a general way but his position on Hidden Waterfall pretty well summed up his country's attitude to tourism: We're here and we like to have visitors, but just take us as you find us because we're not going to push anything down your throat. We like it here and we like our pace of life. We're not going to change that for anyone or for any amount of dollars.

As if to underscore the informality of the country, Mrs. Palario poked her head through her husband's open office window partway through our interview. She was shopping for supper and wanted to make sure her husband would enjoy chicken that evening before she went to the store. We were introduced through the window.

Getting nowhere on my quest for Hidden Waterfall, I decided to rent a car and drive to the Mayan ruins of Xunantunich near Benque Viejo on the Guatemalan border, about 130 kilometres southwest of Belize City. The route would also include the country's new capital city, Belmopan, recently carved out of the jungle in the approximate centre of the small country.

That would be interesting, Palario agreed. I could probably rent a car from a Mr. Smith, whose address he provided, and if I needed anything else during my stay, "why you just drop in again and we'll see what we can do."

The rest of the day was spent trying to locate Mr. Smith and by 10 p.m. there was a firm promise he'd be at the hotel's front door the next morning "early" with an automobile. He was there at 8 a.m. with a 12-year-old Ford that would have been the despair of Hertz, but which appeared to be in good repair. Mr. Smith asked for $200 Belize for the day's rental, in advance.

It's an hour's drive over a good, black-topped two-lane highway to Belmopan, a town of 4,000 built by the British in 1970 on jungle-cleared land and which has the appearance of a planned Canadian mining or lumber company town. In the middle of the town site sits the new capital building and to one side a spanking new Bank of Montreal building.

The Canadian influence is everywhere here. The Canadian government built the new bridge in Belize City and also the airport control tower. The Canadian government built the $10 million water and sewage treatment plant and will install a Canadian-made toilet in every home in 40,000-population Belize City, whether folks want one, or not. (The project was then on hold until a toilet could be designed that householders could not easily rip out of their bathrooms).

The roadway to Xunantunich is another 48 kilometres south-west. A small, man-powered ferry crosses the crystal-clear waters of the Macal River, a main tributary of the Belize River which almost exactly divides Belize into northern and southern halves. The ferry holds one car and operates whenever one shows up -- except during the mid-afternoon *siesta* period. It's free, but the operator, sweating copiously in the high-humidity jungle heat, happily accepts a cold drink at the nearby *cantina* on the return trip.

A narrow track has been hacked for about four kilometres through jungle to the ruins, discovered only recently and reclaimed from the encroaching forest. This Mayan site goes back 1,400 years and recent field work has revealed the city was far more extensive than originally thought. The most striking edifice in the complex is a pyramid 127 feet above the plaza on which the community was built and believed to have been topped by a towering roof comb ten feet higher. A free translation of Xunantunich is Maiden of the Rock. There are good examples of Mayan vaulted masonry, elaboratelycarved stone and stucco friezes.

This day the only thing moving on the site is a custodian cutting the grass of the main plaza. When his power mower is shut down for a refill, the only sounds are of the 450 species of birds found in Belize, whistling, chattering and singing in the jungle that closes in steamingly on all sides of the site.

There are three other major Mayan ruins in Belize. Altun Ha, extensively excavated by Dr. David Prendergast of the Royal Ontario Museum is about 50 kilometres north of Belize City and was an important ceremonial centre of the Mayans.

The site, discovered in 1963, has produced some spectacular discoveries including the ornately-carved head of Kinich Ahau, the Mayan sun god. This idol weighs 9¾ pounds, measures six inches from base to crown and is believed to be the largest carved jade in existence.

Of lesser archaeological importance are the Mayan ruins of Lubantun near Punta Gorda in the south of the country and Caracol in the Pine Ridge Mountains at the country's central west border.

It was about 10 p.m. when I returned to my hotel in Belize City. As I opened the car door Mr. Smith materialized beside me as though he had just popped up through the pavement.

"Hello," he greeted warmly. "Did you have a nice day?"

I told him the car had performed well, that I had just topped up the gas tank and thanked him for the use of the car. I shook his hand and turned to go for a much-needed shower and meal.

"No, wait!" Mr. Smith commanded.

He slowly walked around the car and came back to me, digging in his pocket. He extracted a large roll of bills and began counting them out.

"Here," he said, when he had counted out $100, and extended a wad of bills.

"What's this?"

"You have taken good care of my car and you were thoughtful enough to replace the gas." (He hadn't checked the gauge). "This is for you," he insisted. "$200 is far too much to charge somebody to use a car for one day. Particularly someone kind enough to replace the gas."

Best of France on Canada's doorstep

St. Pierre
St. Pierre et Miquelon, France

"Are you a tourist from Canada or the United States?" asked my benefactor as he threaded his Peugeot up steep, pedestrian-cluttered streets in a cold, damp fog. The question took me by surprise because although a French government official had stamped my passport only a half hour earlier, I hadn't thought of myself as a tourist. After all, I had only travelled about 19 kilometres from Canada.

But during that two-hour boat ride from Fortune, Newfoundland to this fog-shrouded political anachronism off the toe of Newfoundland's Burin Peninsula, I had travelled from Canada to France. What likely disoriented me from fully appreciating the transition was that the man driving the Peugeot was the fifth stranger within that half an hour to go out of his way to be friendly and helpful.

That happens in Quebec, but rarely in France. And although I'd seen a policeman wearing the traditional képi pillbox cap of the French gendarmerie, French-manufactured cars with the long and narrow licence plates and most conversations had been in French, it still hadn't sunk in that I was actually in France.

St. Pierre is one of a group of islands whose land area totals 242 square kilometres and is home to less than 6,000 French citizens whose ancestors settled here early in the 17th century. Ownership of the islands changed several times between Britain and France but was restored permanently to France in 1816 under the Treaty of Paris.

The islanders speak French, have held to French customs and traditions and have one representative in each of the French National Assembly and Senate. A governor presides over the islands assisted by a privy council and an elected general council.

With the exception of a short-lived boom during the prohibition era of North America in the 1920s, when the island was a major trans-shipment port of rum-runners' booze, the main occupation of the islanders is cod fishing. That's a marginally sustaining occupation as is some fox and mink ranching and a trickle of adventurous tourists. But because St. Pierre is her last foothold in North America, the archipelago is subsidized by France.

The man driving the Peugeot had been buying gas when I enquired of him which of several streets I should follow to find a store that sold wine. He said the directions were a bit tricky to explain, "but jump in my car and I'll take you there as soon as I have my gas."

Later I mentioned the incident to Jean-Pierre Andrieux, owner of the 40-room Hotel Robert, the island's largest hotel.

"It's amazing, isn't it, this little bit of France so close to Canada," said Andrieux in the flawless English he learned while being brought up in nearby Prince Edward Island. "But we're different than France here. Here we smile and we're friendly."

The hotelier obviously has a vested interest in the island's friendliness but his appears genuine. When we checked in, wet and shivering after the short walk from the ferry dock, he tried to take us straight into the bar for coffee or tea. When we said we wanted to change into dry clothing he climbed the two flights of stairs with us to make certain the harbour view room would be warm enough.

Andrieux's dining room was closed that evening so he recommended an excellent restaurant where we dawdled late sipping superb French wine. When we returned to the hotel, Andrieux bounded out of his bar and insisted we "come and have a welcome drink."

His bonhomie hadn't come from his bar; he sipped straight fruit juice while rhyming off all the things we should see and do and telling of the rum-running activities during prohibition.

Andrieux punctuated some of the rum-running yarns with visits to a small museum off his bar where artifacts from the era are kept. St. Pierre's history is his passion and he's written four books about the St. Pierre et Miquelon archipelago.

A prized exhibit in his museum is a panama hat worn to St. Pierre by Chicago gangster Al Capone who was fascinated with the proximity of the French islands to North America. Capone arrived unannounced one day flanked by three body guards and checked into Hotel Robert.

Next day, while strolling around St. Pierre, Capone dropped into one of the larger waterfront stores. The quaking store manager, terrified that whatever he said might be taken the wrong way, complimented Capone on his rakish hat.

"Have it -- a souvenir from Al Capone," the gangster responded, handing the astonished man his skimmer.

About the author

David E. Scott was living in foreign countries and travelling through others long before he was offered the opportunity to do so on a newspaper's expense account. But fifteen years at that job certainly piled up the miles, scars, adventures, memories and passport stamps.

He was born in Quebec, and absorbed random doses of formal education there at Bishop's College School, in New Brunswick at Rothesay Collegiate Institute and in Ontario at Forest Hill Collegiate.

Scott seldom passed a history or geography exam, but has written a best-selling history book and happily lived in Andorra, Kentucky, Mexico, Spain and Indiana. His writing and photography have earned him more than 70 provincial, national and international awards.

Most of his spare time has been spent playing croquet, training turtles to race faster, fishing, canoeing and being one of the last guests at any cocktail party or convivial bar. He enjoyed a blessed reprieve from journalism in the '70s as the hands-on owner-operator of a bar-restaurant-discothèque in the European Co-Principality of Andorra.

He now lives in the tranquil hamlet of Allanburg on the Welland Ship Canal, equidistant from Welland, St. Catharines and Niagara Falls. He writes and publishes "fun Canadian books"-- his own and those of other Canadian authors, for DESPUB.

AGMV Marquis
MEMBER OF SCABRINI MEDIA
Quebec, Canada
2004